10647953

Currents in
Contemporary
Drama

Currents in Contemporary Drama

BY RUBY COHN

Indiana University Press
Bloomington and London

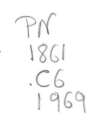

PN
1861
.C6
1969

COPYRIGHT © 1969 BY INDIANA UNIVERSITY PRESS
ALL RIGHTS RESERVED
No part of this book may be reproduced or utilized in any
form or by any means, electronic or mechanical, including
photocopying and recording, or by any information storage
and retrieval system, without permission in writing from
the publisher. The Association of American University
Presses' Resolution on Permissions constitutes the only
exception to this prohibition.
Published in Canada by Fitzhenry & Whiteside Limited,
Don Mills, Ontario
Library of Congress catalog card number: 70–85084
Standard Book Number: 253–11525–6
Manufactured in the United States of America

This book is dedicated to

JEAN-LOUIS BARRAULT

HERBERT BLAU

ROGER BLIN

PETER BROOK

ALAN SCHNEIDER

JEAN VILAR

who played these plays

Contents

Acknowledgments

This book has grown over the years, and I am grateful to those who nourished it. My deepest debt is expressed in the dedication. To the John Simon Guggenheim Memorial Foundation I owe thanks for free time in which I wrote a rough draft. Earlier versions of several parts were published in *Comparative Drama, Drama Survey, Educational Theater Journal, Modern Drama, Southern Review,* and *Yale French Studies*; I thank the respective editors for permission to revise and reprint. I wish to express appreciation for individual kinds of help to Arlin and George Armstrong, Valerie Caires, Sue Case, Dorrit Cohn, Bernard Dukore, Mickey Galbraith, George Griffin, Allen Mandelbaum, Michel Oriano, Leonard Pronko, Tom Rosenmeyer, Sue Severin, Erich Sommer, Richard Trapp, Daniel Weiss, and Elly Wilbert-Collins. With grace and despatch, Robert Berg and Sheila Knights of the San Francisco State College Library garnered books that that library lacked. My friends and Department Chairmen, Daniel Gerould of Comparative Literature and Caroline Shrodes of English, consistently encouraged my work, though the Administration of the College, and of the California State College system, tends to regard research as otiose. Last and lastingly, I am grateful to my students, particularly at San Francisco State College, where imagination and invention may no longer be borne.

San Francisco   RUBY COHN

February, 1969

Currents in Contemporary Drama

ONE: Contemporary Drama

ENGLISH, FRENCH, GERMAN

Like most significant playwrights, our contemporaries
immerse us in human experience, in manners and
morality and the disjunction between them. Today such experience is dramatized in an amazing variety of ways. More than
those of other ages, our playwrights have ingenuities of equipment at their disposal. More than those of other ages, our playwrights have centuries of culture at their disposal. More than
those of other ages, our playwrights are aware of working in a
minority art.

Today, as opposed to the first half of the twentieth century,
dramatists know that they cannot vie with photograph and
phonograph in surface fidelity to a familiar world. And yet surface realism continues to dominate the commercial theater.
Since World War II, however, exciting dramatists have turned
their backs on problems of realism as well as frivolities of entertainment. During the last quarter century, most serious playwrights have abandoned surface realism in the urgency of probing into deeper levels of reality.

Despite its variety, contemporary Western drama descends
from its predecessor, late nineteenth-century Western drama,
which erupted in languages far from the cosmopolitan centers

1

of Europe—the Norwegian of Ibsen, the Swedish of Strindberg, the Russian of Chekhov. These dramas were soon translated and presented in experimental theaters of those capital cities— London, Paris, Berlin—and after each world war, an important native drama emerged from these centers. Today, English, French, and German continue to be the main languages of drama, or at least of that drama that makes its way to the United States. Only very recently has there been any coherent effort to translate the drama of other languages.

Most obviously, a dramatic language points to a nationality, but languages are larger than nations. In the twentieth century, American drama declared its independence from English traditions, though both use the English language. And there is the half-truth that English comedy has been written by Irishmen. The twentieth century saw significant English language drama in Ireland, centered in the Abbey Theatre. Over several seas, a new English language drama is developing in Australia. Within tighter geographic limits, German language drama has been written by Swiss and Austrian playwrights. French language drama has been enriched by Armenian Adamov, Spanish Arrabal, Irish Beckett, African Césaire, Belgian Ghelderode, Lebanese Schéhadé, Swiss Tardieu and Pinget, Algerian Yacine. Translation is often immediate, and impact may be far-flung and far-reaching.

But impact may be skew. When Bertolt Brecht's plays were produced in English, and the dramas of Samuel Beckett and Eugene Ionesco became staples of American university theater, the words *Epic, Absurd,* and *Angry* were loosely used as synonyms for contemporary German, French, and English drama, respectively. More recently, Antonin Artaud's word *Cruelty* has been forced to embrace all kinds of contemporary experimental theater. Though the simplistic catchword always catches something, it is inaccurate and inadequate. Paradoxically, jargon shows that theater as news is infiltrating the very mass media that help drive drama into its minority corner.

Contemporary drama that is still being created tends to stimulate journalism rather than criticism. And if we are not beguiled by our own astigmatisms, it is difficult to attain a perspective on today's dramatic profusion. Most of it does not merit serious review, but attention has been earned by a minority of the practitioners of this minority art. Even that minority reveals no overall principle of order in a time of disorder. Navigation through variety may be facilitated by the mapping of cross-national currents, through empirical observation of recurrence of tone, theme, or technique. The bulk of this book traces such currents, which may be more clearly charted against the larger background of significant dramatists who have produced a corpus of plays in English, French, or German.

ENGLISH LANGUAGE DRAMA

Between two World Wars, English language drama was dominated by a giant on each side of the Atlantic—Bernard Shaw and Eugene O'Neill. Separated by a generation, each was locked in his own idiom—Shaw in his aphoristic shafts and O'Neill in his ponderous plaints. Shaw's drama was firmly rooted in the nineteenth century, whereas O'Neill experimented with several twentieth-century ideas—Freudianism, Expressionism, Jungianism. Except for *Saint Joan*, Shaw's best-known plays were completed by the end of World War I, and he wrote almost nothing after World War II. O'Neill, on the other hand, was famous for two decades before World War II, yet production of his greatest plays was delayed until after the war. Beneath their surface realism, these plays contain the prototypical Existential confrontation—man vs. his own mortality. Using stage whiskey somewhat like the tom-tom rhythms of *Emperor Jones*, O'Neill in his last plays strips away his own pretensions to reveal naked, unaccommodated man. A *Touch of the Poet* and *Moon for the Misbegotten* still suffuse his figures in soft light, but *The Iceman Cometh, Hughie,* and *Long Day's Journey Into Night* thrive on the dramatic rigor with which they expose the human pre-dicament.

Well behind the works of O'Neill and Shaw, English drama between two wars preserved its drawing-room manners, whereas American drama stridently attacked social problems. Even before O'Neill's death in 1953, he had been consigned to the past, while Arthur Miller and Tennessee Williams shared his mantle during the 1950's. Sociology and psychology peer from their plays, Miller tending toward social welfare cases and Williams toward case histories. More recently, this dual regency is giving way to Edward Albee, who is generally misinterpreted as a realist, in spite of his affinities with latter-day O'Neill and with the French Absurdists. During the late 1950's and the 1960's, in direct defi-ance of Broadway, American drama broke out in cafes and churches, cellars and attics. Loud and free, none of the brave new playwrights has as yet imposed a style upon a coherent body of works.

Less vulnerable to the necessity for box-office success, English drama has been more sustained in the postwar period. From 1945 to 1948 E. Martin Browne directed verse plays at the Mercury Theatre in London, mainly of dramatists whose first works were written for Canterbury Cathedral festivals. Only T. S. Eliot and Christopher Fry, however, reached large West End audiences. From *Murder in the Cathedral* (1935) to *The Elder Statesman* (1959) Eliot pared down his imagery and sim-plified his syntax in an effort to mould his verse into conven-tional dramatic dialogue. But no other verse playwright could survive on such lean lines, and Christopher Fry, the last of Eliot's Canterbury succession, swelled his pentameters with profuse, eclectic imagery that evoked the Elizabethans for those who were unfamiliar with them. Despite a corpus of nine verse plays, and an occasional nostalgic salute form Laurence Olivier, Fry's work has faded with that of Maxwell Anderson, America's blank verse playwright. But the influence of poetic drama is evident in the convoluted sentences of John Whiting's first play, *Saint's*

Day (1947). Despite Whiting's imagery, however, which reflected the poetic drama of the 1940's, he imbedded his inner struggles in a socially resonant content. Later, caught up in the antirhetorical trend of the 1950's, he continued to use imaged prose with more stripped dialogue. The English antirhetorical drama of the 1950's was in part a reaction against poetic drama and in part a rejection of drawing-room wit. And the Angry 1950's gained attention through a vigorous, vulgar idiom.

In the 1950's England seemed to erupt into a fever of experimentation. Antiestablishmentarianism exploded simultaneously in the drama (John Osborne's *Look Back in Anger*), the novel (Kingsley Amis' *Lucky Jim*), and nonfiction (Colin Wilson's *Outsider*). Joan Littlewood's Theatre Workshop and George Devine's English Stage Company welcomed this explosion and its dramatic manifestations. Recalling the Shaw-Barker revolution in drama a half-century earlier, George Devine said of his theater, "Twice in our century the bricks of the Royal Court have contained the dynamic, if not the dynamite, that effects essential change."[1] Part of the dynamic lay in the fresh approach of playwrights who had rarely seen a play; the Royal Court issued free passes to promising young writers so that they might gain some familiarity with the stage medium. But familiarity diminished anger. By 1962, John Russell Taylor called his survey of contemporary English drama *Anger and* AFTER (my emphasis). In that book, Taylor described the affinities of Harold Pinter as French Absurdist, rather than Angry. John Osborne, for all his preserved anger, also looked abroad—mainly to Brecht's epic theater. John Whiting and John Arden followed their individual paths, each treating the difficulty of moral action in an age of atomized anxieties. But Whiting died before he fulfilled his dramatic potential, and Arden is still feeling his dramatic way. Robert Bolt, Peter Schaffer, and, more recently, Tom Stoppard have tempered anger and domesticated alienation to middle-class taste.

Looking back over English language drama since World War

II, one can see a dominant trio on each side of the Atlantic—
T. S. Eliot, John Osborne, and Harold Pinter in England; Arthur
Miller, Tennessee Williams, and Edward Albee in the United
States. Each of them has completed a corpus of serious work,
and each has developed his own voice: Eliot preaches salvation
through comedies of adultery; Osborne wrenches love triangles
to individual corners; Pinter stammers clichés that mount up to
disaster. In America, Miller's early social interests are being dis-
placed by psychological studies à la Williams, while Williams
himself weaves in and around Kraft-Ebbing aberrations. Albee
builds symbolic structures on psychological foundations. In Australia, English language drama has barely reached export status.
In Ireland, after the loss of Brendan Behan, sentimentality has
often replaced originality, while plays and playwrights seek fortune abroad. In spite of commercial success, however, the trios
of the London and of the New York stage merit closer examination.

Condemning American commercial theater, Arthur Miller and
Tennessee Williams have both profited hugely from that theater.
But success has not changed their common predilection for hero-
victims who are rarely aware of the forces that destroy them. In
the plays of Miller, as in those of his mentor Ibsen, the guilt of
the past makes the prosperous present unlivable. In the plays of
Williams, on the other hand, the memories of the past make
the sordid present unlivable. Miller's characters are usually
broken by social pressure, whereas those of Williams break
within a society that stifles their best impulses. Together, Miller
and Williams combine to indict contemporary American life,
and yet Broadway audiences paid cheerfully to see that indict-
ment staged under the hard-hitting direction of Elia Kazan.

Influenced by Kazan's direction, both Miller and Williams are
sometimes called scenewrights rather than playwrights, and their
works are certainly uneven in quality; *Death of a Salesman*
(1949) is usually singled out as Miller's best play, but for

Williams the laurel wavers between *The Glass Menagerie* (1944) and *A Streetcar Named Desire* (1947). Since their work has been an economic commodity on Broadway and in Hollywood, they have had to struggle for artistic independence.

The differences between Miller and Williams are more obvious than their similarities. Miller derives from the proletarian literature of the thirties, and Williams from the Southern Gothic tradition. Miller's master is Ibsen, seen through social and humorless glasses; Williams' teacher is Strindberg, whose infernos he approaches by way of Lawrence. Miller's interests are rational and moral; those of Williams are associational and lyric. Miller's dialogue is commonplace, hammered out in clichés; that of Williams is cadenced, laced with images. It has been usual to suggest that Miller focuses on man's relation to his society, and Williams on man's inner life. For Williams, man's inner life is centered in the genital region, but Miller's plays show a similar tendency—the whore scene of *Death of a Salesman*, the adultery of *The Crucible*, the sexually motivated betrayal of *View from the Bridge*, and the three wives of a minimally Oedipal Quentin in *After the Fall*. Williams, however, continue to outdo Miller in violence—rape, castration, dismemberment and cannibalism. It would be misleading to reduce either playwright to their shock effects, but it is equally misleading to ignore them, for their concerns have shaped the subject matter of American drama—both broadening and limiting it.

Though Miller's plays are grounded in contemporary American society, and Williams is obsessed with sexual obsession, both dramatists have reached for wider meaning—toward what are sometimes called human universals. Thus, Williams has written an essay on "The *Timeless* World of a Play" (my italics), and Miller closes his "Shadows of the Gods" in uplifting abstraction that faintly echoes Shakespeare.[2] In the dramas themselves, Miller also confuses abstractions with universals. His common man heroes reflect their society, and increasingly they reflect upon it—John Proctor speaks of goodness, Quentin of innocence, Prince Von Berg of the seduction of death. Williams, on the other hand, seeks human breadth through the ubiquity of sexual motivation and the symbolism of imagery, the latter often summarized in the titles—a glass menagerie that serves as sexual sublimation, a streetcar named desire that all classes board, a rose tattoo that blossoms into passion, a highway that can be either royal or real.

The sex-oriented souls of Williams and the common man heroes of Miller are driven to scenes of violence. Through Hemingway and Faulkner especially, violence is often regarded as endemic to American literary tradition, and it is of course part of Western tragic tradition since the Greeks. But despite their yearning for universals, neither Miller nor Williams integrates violence into the breadth of tragedy, as did the Greeks. Rather, both playwrights are haunted by the middle-class, savage-civilized nightmares which their audiences share—the collective problems we fail to solve, the individual cruelties we fail to stop. The characters of both Williams and Miller are commensurate with our failure, so that their dramas become culturally emblematic. Miller's plays postulate an ideal of the good society—vaguely cooperative if not socialistic. Williams' plays postulate the ideal of uninhibited sexual expression, whatever form it may take. Often prey to illusion, their characters sin against these ideals, and therefore succumb to stage defeat.

More than in any other country, perhaps, America's significant plays turn on the conflict between illusion and truth—the multiple illusions of *The Iceman Cometh*, the socio-economic illusion of *Death of a Salesman*, the romantic illusion of *The Glass Menagerie* and the plays of Edward Albee. However, though this theme is prevalent in American drama, Albee's form is often European in inspiration—a combination of Beckett and Genet in *Zoo Story* (1958), Ionesco in *The American Dream* (1960), Strindberg in *Who's Afraid of Virginia Woolf?* (1962). *Tiny Alice* (1964) seems to move from an Anouilh comic quarrel in the first act to an erotically mystic Claudel in the third, by way of Eliot's *Cocktail Party*, Genet's *Balcony*, and Dürrenmatt's *Visit*. Albee is today's most controversial American playwright; his fervent admirers (such as director Alan Schneider) stress his "emotional wallop," and his sharpest critics (such as Tom Driver) grant him theatrical intuition. Other writers have admired the crispness of Albee's American idiom. Jerry, Nurse and Interne, George and Martha, Cardinal, Lawyer and Butler, speak in a crackling dialogue that has never before been heard on the American stage.

So adept is Albee at inventing dialogue that he has been accused of indulging in this pastime for its own sake, but he has explicitly stated the seriousness with which he takes his profession: "A playwright . . . has two obligations: first, to make some statement about the condition of 'man' (as it is put) and, second, to make some statement about the nature of the art form with which he is working."[3] Albee makes his statements about man *through* the changing nature of his art. From *Zoo Story* (1958) to *Box-Mao-Box* (1968), Albee has dramatized different facets of the human condition, and almost all his plays bend dialogue musically to do so.

Under a veneer of realism, Albee has been shifting his emphasis from America's social illusion to man's metaphysical illusion. Thus, the greedy, conformist American family of *The American Dream* evolves into the greedy, love-bound family of *A Delicate Balance*. A rebellious and apocalyptic Jerry of *The Zoo Story* evolves into an obedient and apocalyptic Julian of *Tiny Alice*. In an interview Albee stated, "The last thing I want to do is to try writing like me."[4] Most remarkable in his consistent development is what has aroused adverse criticism—that he has succeeded in not imitating himself, even while his idiom remains distinctively his.

No other American playwright of Albee's generation has produced a comparable corpus of plays, or perhaps it would be more precise to say that there has been no theatrical production of a comparable corpus of plays by anyone else of Albee's generation. Blame for this sad fact has been and must be laid on the economic organization (or disorganization) of the American theater. Very little has changed since Eric Bentley wrote in 1954: "No American play shall be performed unless a small group of wealthy men will bet on its having a long run"[5]—though "on Broadway" should be added. More and more, these bets are made on musical comedies rather than on legitimate dramas. Though subsidized theaters are appearing on the American scene in Minneapolis, Seattle, Washington, Los Angeles, Philadelphia, and even New York, to choose at random, the subsidies are too often tied to the cowardly conservatism of the donors. Significant American drama has a short past; if it is to have any future at all, it must be freed from commodity handling. One would like not to condemn businessmen who are interested in the arts; one would like even more not to have to condemn an interest that demands control. Most obstreperous in America, such control has also marred the European theatrical scene.

England, the ancestor of our own Puritan prurience, has suffered less interference from censors. The Government grants subsidies to little theaters. Avant-garde drama and adventurous production of classics dazzle audiences at the Royal Shakespeare Company, reorganized in 1960, and the National Theatre, founded in 1963. In and around London, independent theaters continue to live and die, while Shaftesbury Avenue cannot be distinguished from Broadway.

And yet, the poetic dramas of T. S. Eliot wooed audiences on that very avenue during the 1940's and 1950's. His uncompleted *Fragments of an Aristophanic Melodrama* (1926–1932) and his modern mystery, *Murder in the Cathedral* (1935) share the theme of his subsequent "modern" plays—the conduct of the Christian in a time of disbelief. Through a "double action," Eliot seeks to reconcile a deliberately trivial surface with Christian depth. Drawing very freely upon the plots of the three Greek tragic playwrights, Eliot adopts a conventional three-act structure; the dialogue may be very loosely scanned in a line containing three stresses and a caesura, with any number of syllables. Like *Murder in the Cathedral, The Family Reunion* (1939) and *The Cocktail Party* (1950) center on the spiritual conflict within the saintly soul—Harry and Celia. But whereas Eliot shows no interest in the souls of the rest of the family in his *Reunion,* he does dramatize the souls of the Chamberlaynes and Peter Quilpe in *The Cocktail Party.* Like Eliot's Prufrock, these characters are neither Prince Hamlet nor Saint Thomas à Becket; they nevertheless merit the injunction of Sir Henry Harcourt-Reilly to "Work out [their] salvation with diligence."

Though Eliot designated *The Cocktail Party* as a "comedy" and *The Confidential Clerk* (1954) as a "play," the surface of the latter is more comic, and the intrusion of the supernatural less evident. Moreover, Eliot continues to center his drama on a special soul—that of Colby Simpkins—who, however, does not choose the way of a martyr but of "an organist in a parish church." And like the more ordinary mortals of the play, Colby is in quest of his spiritual identity. After a series of reversals and recognitions, as in Victorian melodrama, all the characters become reconciled to their roles. It is the problem of reconciliation to the roles of this life that distinguishes Eliot's final drama *The Elder Statesman* (1958), the only one to contain no character who is of the spiritually elect.

Collectively, then, Eliot's plays dramatize the lives of saints, and those of more common mortals whose lives derive meaning from the martyrdom of the saints. As his characters grow less saintly in each successive play, so his lyricism is stripped down to the patently prosaic. Eliot expressed a wish for an illiterate audience, but his audiences have in fact been the very middle class whose language is attenuated in his plays. In a lecture on Yeats, Eliot provided a standard by which his own plays may be judged:

"What is necessary is a beauty which shall not be in the line or in the isolable passage but woven into the dramatic texture itself; so that you can hardly say whether the lines give grandeur to the drama or whether it is the drama which turns the words into poetry."[6] He has himself been so concerned about the dramatic texture of his plays that dramatic structure becomes secondary, and poetry approaches a vanishing-point. Hugh Kenner has claimed that Eliot's verse "is coolly adequate to anything that requires saying."[7] But it remains too cool for drama, a form that demands exceptionally adequate saying.

At one level, Eliot blended Greek tragic plots with English drawing-room banalities so as to produce, at a deeper level, modern Morality conflicts. In Eliot's "doubleness of action" virtue inevitably triumphs, since vice consists of a series of variations upon the biblical verse: "What is a man profited, if he shall gain the whole world, and lose his own soul?" (*Matthew* 16:26) But the worldly gains of Eliot's characters tempt them so little—an English country estate, a tired adultery, a promising business, and a faded celebrity—that their souls run no great risk. In Eliot's poetic drama, as in that of John Marston, "an under-pattern [is] less manifest than the theatrical one," but the theatrical is insufficiently manifest in the theater.[8] The theatrical pattern (based on Greek tragic pattern) is conveyed through a thin, flat texture that only rarely suggests hidden riches. Somewhat like the martyrs he admired, Eliot sacrificed his lyric gift so as to join worldly surface to Christian depth in drama, but the way of the martyr is not the way of the theater.

In sharp contrast to Eliot, who was a celebrated poet when he turned to drama, John Osborne began to write as an unknown actor in his early twenties. Unable to achieve production, he sent a manuscript to George Devine at the Royal Court Theatre, who had advertised for new plays. Devine later claimed that *Look Back in Anger* leaped at him from the page. Immediately put into rehearsal, the play opened to mixed reviews on May 8,

1956. But on the credit side of the mixture was the influential critic, Kenneth Tynan of the London *Observer,* who closed his review: "I agree that *Look Back in Anger* is likely to remain a minority taste. What matters, however, is the size of the minority. I estimate it at roughly 6,733,000, which is the number of people in this country between the ages of twenty and thirty. And this figure will doubtless be swelled by refugees from other age-groups who are curious to know precisely what the contemporary young pup is thinking and feeling. I doubt if I could love anyone who did not wish to see *Look Back in Anger.* It is the best young play of its decade."[9] And it gave that decade its name.

The fear of losing Tynan's love must have been considerable, for Osborne's *Anger* became the passion of the late 1950's, when graduates of red brick universities beat at the old oak doors of the English Establishment. Yet, before and after *Anger,* Osborne pursued a personal path of dramatic exploration. Had he been lured by success, he could have written his own artistic epitaph in *Epitaph for George Dillon,* who does succumb to the bitch-goddess. But Osborne persisted in dramatizing his subjects of scandal or concern through sometimes shaky structures.

Formally, *Look Back in Anger* is the least interesting of his plays. Even Tynan took exception to the sentimental ending, and John Russell Taylor pointed out its conventional, realistic mode: "It is a well-made play, with all its climaxes, its tightenings and slackenings of tension in the right places."[10] However, its topical mood wooed a wide audience, and its angry invective wooed the actors.

Immediately after his first success, Osborne turned to a different dramatic form in *The Entertainer* (1957), also produced by the Royal Court, with a bravura performance by Laurence Olivier as Archie Rice. In *The Entertainer* Osborne used an open structure of a Brechtian succession of scenes, and like Brecht he was inspired by a popular art-form, the music-hall. Though Osborne claimed in his preface that music-hall techniques "cut right across the restrictions of the so-called naturalistic stage," he naturalistically "justified" his use of the music-hall because the play is a story of a music-hall family. Or, to be more explicit, it is the story of the degeneration of a music-hall family, from the talent of Billy to the cheapness of Archie to Frank's death at Suez. The degeneration of the Rice family has generally been taken to symbolize that of the British Empire, emphasized by the Brechtian songs.

Into *The World of Paul Slickey* (1959), a realistic drawing-room world, Osborne continued to introduced Brechtian songs. Brecht, however, attempts to preclude audience sympathy through such songs, whereas Osborne's Paul Slickey is already beyond the pale of sympathy, and the songs serve to thin one's interest. For his next two plays Osborne abandoned interpolated song, but resorted to the chronicle history—as revived by Brecht. Though *Luther* (1961) was a resounding success and *A Subject of Scandal and Concern* (a television play) a stuttering failure, both dramas are energized by the rhetoric of the actual utterances of the German protestant, Martin Luther, and the English atheist, George Holyoake. Both plays feature rebellious and unlikable protagonists. Despite structural slackness, the two plays are, like most of Osborne's dramas, splendid actor's vehicles.

It is also the acting potential that distinguishes Osborne's *Inadmissible Evidence* (1964) and *A Patriot for Me* (1965), which mark a stronger concentration on the sexually frustrated individual. The very name of the protagonist of *Inadmissible Evidence* —Bill Maitland (mate-land)—puns on his problem, to grasp desperately after mates in order to affirm an identity. The frame of a hero-on-trial recalls scenes of Brecht; Bill's long, legalistic monologues recall the speech of Lucky in Beckett's *Waiting for Godot*; the incommunicative London repartee recalls Pinter's dialogue; the fading of events into memory recalls Miller's *Death of a Salesman*; Bill Maitland looks back on his life in despair more than anger. The play on stage is unified by his suffering, as a lawyer damns himself with evidence that would not be admitted in court.

Similarly, the crowded canvas of A *Patriot for Me* is unified by the gradually revealed homosexuality of an Austrian army officer, who is thereby compelled to be a patriot for himself rather than his country. Suicide is mandatory when his espionage is discovered. Since England's Lord Chamberlain banned the play, its public notoriety obscured Osborne's adroit combination of lavish staging with the chronicle form.

In 1968, Osborne produced two plays in London, *Time Present* and *The Hotel in Amsterdam,* both set in the contemporary world of the theater, and both adhering to more conventional dramatic forms than he had attempted since *Look Back in Anger.* All his plays—some dozen in that many years—focus on a single memorable character, who moves us by the vigor of his idiom.

Harold Pinter, like Osborne, began to write as an unknown actor in his twenties. He was first viewed as another angry young dramatist, protesting the drabness of lower-class life. But Pinter objects to labels, and he insists that his playwriting is personal and natural: "I went into a room one day and I felt that the only way that I could give it expression and get it off my mind was dramatically. I started off with this picture of the two people and let them carry on from there. It wasn't a deliberate switch from one kind of writing to another. It was quite a natural movement. . . . I was always surprised that anyone initially came in to see my plays at all, because writing them was a very personal thing."[11]

But people *have* come to see his plays, and reviewers have fastened labels on him. Particularly apt has been the phrase "comedy of menace" for his work, indicating how Pinter joins the comic to the threatening. Both his comedy and his menace rely on an extraordinary ear for seizing, and gift for stylizing, contemporary London speech. By the fragmentation of his speech shall ye know a Pinter victim in his comedies of menace. His protagonists are never, like Eliot's, destined for sainthood.

Never, like those of Osborne, do they enthrall us by the volubility of their suffering. Rather, they haunt us through their verbal disintegration while skirmishing for a minimal position.

In Pinter's early plays, comedy arises from the inarticulateness and incoherence of his characters. They pelt us with clichés, repetitions, fragments, contradictions, and spurious logic. The staccato rhythm probes more deeply into reality than does the everyday speech they only *seem* to echo, for Pinter implies that there can be no articulate certainty about the world. Thus, the impossibility of verification becomes the only verity, whose theatricalization is skillful and resonant. To quote Pinter, "I'd say that what goes on in my plays is realistic, but what I'm doing is not realism."[12]

Realistic or not, Pinter's early drama tends to be climaxed in violence. Thus, Bert Hudd suddenly attacks a blind Negro in *The Room* (1957); Goldberg and McCann take Stanley Webber for "special treatment" in *The Birthday Party* (1957); Ben is about to shoot Gus as the final curtain falls in *The Dumb Waiter* (1957); a half-crazed Len is tortured by the titular dwarfs of *The Dwarfs* (1960). But these murderous villains are mere surrogates for mysterious, malevolent forces. The totality of Pinter's early plays indicts an Establishment of mechanical comfort, vulgar brand names, and vestigial religion. Pinter's victims finally splutter helplessly, stricken by a brutal stylization of contemporary English cliché. As Pinter said in an interview: "The world *is* a pretty violent place . . . so any violence in the plays comes out quite naturally."[13] With *The Caretaker*, however, Pinter felt violence was no longer necessary, and in other Pinter plays sex is the prime force in the breakdown of the individual. Rarely do these plays erupt into violence; instead, they smoulder in menace. In none of these realistically set plays can the meaning be realistically explained, for explicit resolution is always rejected in favor of unanswered questions. In *A Slight Ache* (1959) one of the three characters never speaks, and we learn nothing about him; in *The*

Collection (1961) the suspected adultery remains uncertain; in *The Lover* (1963) husband and wife deliberately assume a series of roles to express their love-hate for each other; in *The Homecoming* (1965), Pinter's own favorite among his plays, several family members play changing and ambiguous roles for one another, as the males hover over their single female—huntress or prey. Through a decade of playwriting, Pinter has remained in superb control of London idiom, so that his plays are almost impossible to translate and many of his nuances do not survive transplantation to America despite the 1967 claim of a New York critic that America had arrived at "the moment of Pinter."

FRENCH LANGUAGE DRAMA

The French phrase *avant garde* has penetrated all cultures more effectively than its military ancestor. An art that separates itself from the main body of society is today expressed with a French flavor, and, despite its dense bourgeoisie, Paris has been the most hospitable of capitals to avant-garde movements. The dramatic avant-garde is sometimes pinpointed at Paris, December 10, 1896, when Alfred Jarry's *King Ubu* was given its first performance. Its opening word "Merdre" reeked and screeched at a bourgeois audience, exuberantly parodied in the farce about a *petit bourgeois* monster parading as king. Ubu's shock effect was instantaneous, but Jarry's spirited anticonformism might have died if, over two decades later, the Surrealists had not elevated him to a precursor. Jarry's intuitive effort at Total Theater (using masks, slapstick, and mime) was converted by Antonin Artaud into a mystical program announced in a series of manifestoes, which, however, were acted upon by playwrights and directors only after Artaud's death in 1948.

In 1917, an admirer of Jarry, Apollinaire, invented the word "surrealism," using it twice in prefaces to theatrical works—in May for the Cocteau-Satie-Picasso-Diaghilev ballet *Parade*; and in June for his own *Breasts of Tiresias*. The context of the latter is still worth quoting: "To attempt, if not a renovation of the theater, at least a personal effort, I thought it necessary to return to nature itself, but without imitating it in the manner of photographers. When man wanted to imitate walking, he created the wheel, which does not resemble a leg. He thus practiced Surrealism without knowing it."[14] Even for nonsurrealists, Apollinaire enunciated the implicit claim of all nonrealistic art—that it deals with a more profound order of reality than can be grasped by the camera.

After the abortive avant-garde dramatic efforts of Jarry and Apollinaire, and the largely unproduced plays of Yvan Goll and Roger Vitrac, two French playwrights graduated swiftly from the avant-garde to commercial success—Jean Cocteau and Jean Giraudoux, both reacting against the realistic problem play and the pseudo-realistic adultery drama of the Boulevard theaters. Cocteau emphasized the visual and spatial possibilities of the theater, whereas Giraudoux introduced a language of whimsy and imagery. But World War II virtually ended their hegemony.

Since Paris theaters were open throughout the war, a new generation of playwrights reached the stage—Anouilh, Montherlant, Sartre, Camus, and Claudel and Ghelderode, whose plays had been written earlier. These playwrights represented a more serious avant-garde than that of the effervescent twenties; the audience was challenged and shocked by the anguished faith of Claudel, the blasphemy of Ghelderode, the arrogance of Montherlant, the violence of Sartre and Camus. Though Camus alone was directly influenced by Artaud, these dramatists all brought to the theater a similar sense of mission which did not degenerate into didacticism. It remained for later playwrights, however, to concretize Artaud's mystique: "In our present state of degeneration it is through the skin that metaphysics must be made to re-enter our minds"[15] (Mary Richards translation).

For a decade after the war the theatrical variety of Paris exceeded that of any other city of Europe, with as many as fifty spectacles running concurrently, about half of them of serious interest. Even the most successful postwar dramatist, Jean Anouilh, has been awarded serious attention. Postwar French drama may be roughly divided into those plays rarely translated or exported, and those that inspired imitation throughout the world. The first group is poetically oriented, though only Supervielle, Claudel, and Pichette wrote in verse; other dramatists often labeled "poetic" are Tardieu, Vauthier, Audiberti, Schéhadé. With the exception of Claudel, their vision of the world is highly personal, sometimes fantastic; that vision is expressed in carefully wrought language whose translation is difficult. Overshadowed by the so-called Theater of the Absurd, with whom they occasionally share assumptions or verbal techniques, these playwrights (again with the exception of Claudel) have met with little commercial success, and they are little known outside of France (and in the case of Tardieu and Schéhadé, Germany).

The other group is philosophically oriented, and, especially since the publication of Martin Esslin's book, *The Theatre of the Absurd*, worldwide attention has been focused on Absurdists. The collective impact of Samuel Beckett, Jean Genet, and Eugène Ionesco has been an influential force upon Western theater, comparable only to that of Bertolt Brecht. However one may differ in detail with Martin Esslin, he was brilliant to recognize that the new drama derived conceptually from metaphysical Absurdity. Beckett, Ionesco, early Adamov, Pinget, Arrabal, and Tardieu implicitly accept the metaphysics of Absurdity. To explain such Absurdity, Esslin has used the words of Albert Camus in *The Myth of Sisyphus*: "This divorce between man and his life, the actor and his setting, truly constitutes the feeling of Absurdity."

Like Artaud, Camus relates the cosmos to the theater. Artaud seeks a metaphysical impact through his Theater of Cruelty, and Camus revives the old *theatrum mundi* metaphor to describe modern man deprived of supernatural guides. A sentence from Sartre's review of Camus' *The Stranger* further elucidates the axioms of Absurdist drama: "The absurd is neither in man nor in the world, if they are considered separately; but since the essential characteristic of man is being-in-the-world, the absurd is finally the same as the human condition." In the Existentialist theater of Sartre and Camus, man is free to make himself and to make an impact upon the world; conversely, in the Theater of the Absurd, man rarely possesses such freedom, and Absurdist dramas portray the dread and/or derision of being-in-the-world, which is to be human.

As Esslin points out, playwrights of the Absurd implicitly share the metaphysics of Sartre and Camus, but their form more faithfully reflects fragmentation and discontinuity. In dramatic practice this comes to mean a de-emphasis on plot and motivation of characters; instead, non sequitur is raised to a structural principle, and the action tends to evoke the question "What is happening?" rather than "How will it end?" If traditional drama is plot-centered, Expressionist and Epic drama theme-centered, perhaps one might say that Absurdist drama is tone-centered beneath a surface that seems to have no center at all. The tragedy in these dramas is that tragedy is no longer possible within man's awareness of metaphysical Absurdity; he can only enact the metaphysical farce. John Hurrell, editor of *Drama Survey*, has succinctly characterized Absurdist drama: "The elements of the theater of the absurd cannot be detached; it is defined neither by the idea of the world that it promulgates, nor by its forms, but by its absolutely organic presentation of the one through the other. Thus a play that shares either the ideas or the form of what we now call absurdist drama, without having both, is not really a play of the 'absurd.' "[16]

On the other hand, it would be foolish to view the Absurdist dramatists as a self-conscious avant-garde, who inhabit Paris cafés to celebrate their avant-gardism. Edward Albee, calling himself a playwright of the Absurd, presents us with an amusing example of what not to imagine about them:

> the majority of them [Absurdist playwrights] wouldn't be caught dead in a colloquy remotely resembling the following:
>
> IONESCO: *(At a Left Bank cafe table, spying Beckett and Genet strolling past in animated conversation)*: Hey! Sam! Jean!
> GENET: Hey, it's Eugene! Sam, it's Eugene!
> BECKETT: Well, I'll be damned. Hi there, Eugene boy.
> IONESCO: Sit down, kids.
> GENET: Sure thing.
> IONESCO: *(Rubbing his hands together)*: Well, what's new in The Theatre of the Absurd?
> BECKETT: Oh, less than a lot of people think. *(They all laugh)*[17]

Absurdity as a philosophic, even a dramatic, attitude has crossed language boundaries, claiming Hildesheimer in German, Pinter in English (who denies it), Albee in American, Mrozek in Polish, and Havel in Czech. But French language drama since World War II cannot be reduced to Absurdity. A few playwrights who are building a corpus in the 1960's—Armand Gatti, René de Obaldia, Romain Weingarten—are linked by neither method nor metaphysics.

Far from being atheist Absurdists, Paul Claudel and Michel de Ghelderode were practicing Catholics. Though most of their work was written before World War II, their plays were widely produced and published only after the war. Catholics who turn their dramatic vision back toward an age of monolithic faith, they are nevertheless modern in their theatrical impact and in the non-complacency of their faith. French Claudel and Belgian

Ghelderode wrote non-realistic dramas when surface realism dominated the theater; both combine a highly visual with a highly verbal imagination.

The plays of Claudel may be divided into three groups: 1) the sinning world in need of salvation: *Head of Gold, The City, The Seventh Day Rest, The Exchange, Break of Noon,* and *The Tidings Brought to Mary;* 2) the working out of Christian destiny in a vaguely historical situation: *The Hostage, Hard Bread,* and *The Father Humiliated;* 3) "total" dramas culminating in grace: *The Satin Slipper, The Book of Christopher Columbus, Joan at the Stake,* and *The Story of Tobias and Sara.* Written between 1884 and 1938, the plays make no concessions to commercialism. In 1909 Claudel wrote to the playwright-director Henri Lenormand: "Do you think that the public could consider my dramas as anything but boring extravagances?" Such stage extravagance, without boredom, had to await Jean-Louis Barrault's 1942 production of *The Satin Slipper,* with music by Honneger, set and costumes by Lucien Coutaud, mime and ballet, and a human sea that bound together the parts of the far-flung Spanish Catholic Empire in the play. Educated by Artaud, Barrault in turn educated a public for Claudel's "total theater," which combined farce and faith, technical diversity and monolithic belief. After the war, Barrault staged *Break of Noon, The Exchange,* and *The Book of Christopher Columbus,* exploiting theatrical resources to a greater extent than did Jouvet and Giraudoux before the war.

Though Ghelderode did not enjoy such sustained collaboration with a director, he too won an audience in the 1940's, for plays written between two wars. Working with the Flemish Theater, fascinated by the Flemish Middle Ages, Ghelderode drew directly upon Flemish painting, but used the French language for his drama. He composed over thirty plays: one-acters and longer pieces, farces and supernatural fantasies, puppet-plays and ghost-plays. His published drama may be conveniently but not rigidly grouped into plays of blasphemy and plays of buffoonery, though both are based on the religious conviction to which he has given expression in interviews, letters, and stories.

In the first group are *Barrabas, The Women at the Tomb,* and *Miss Jairus,* which present intensely personal views of the cruci-fixion and the resurrection; the blasphemous *Chronicles of Hell,* about a dying bishop and a poisoned host; *Red Magic* and *Hop Signor!,* based on Breughel paintings, about the visible evils of sin. In the fool-protagonist group we find Pirandello-like plays before Ghelderode had heard of the Italian playwright—the 1926 *Three Actors and Their Drama* and the 1930 *Exit the Actor; Pantagleize,* about a Chaplin-like clown-innocent, who is de-stroyed in a parody, which may not have been intended as parody, of revolution; *Escurial,* in which Folial the jester is killed while he mimics the king's role, and *School for Buffoons,* in which Folial plays a jester's role through his own tragedy; plays of legend and legendary history such as *Christopher Columbus, Don Juan,* and *The Death of Doctor Faust.* As Helen Hellman has ob-served, Ghelderode's religious plays and fool plays meet in "the Christ figure, symbol of compassion, faith and suffering, who was forced to play the buffoon."[18] Ghelderode expresses faith through blasphemy and suffering through farce, but the blas-phemy and farce are more dramatically convincing than the faith. In 1949 Barrault's production of *Chronicles of Hell* became a *succès de scandale scabreux.*

Roger Blin remarked of Claudel: "His plays, written in a mar-velous language, are the living incarnations of something that has long since disappeared—they are like goiters, like gothic fibro-mas."[19] Insofar as the description is apt, it fits the similarly gothic dramas of Ghelderode as well. But that is why these plays have meaning for our time, which is highly aware of its own festering diseases.

Very differently oriented dramatists, Jean-Paul Sartre and Albert Camus, also used the imagery of disease for moral commentary. Two decades after Sartre and Camus burst off-Broadway, it is difficult to reconstruct the shock effect of their first American productions. Shock vanishes swiftly, and with it vanished sustained interest in the two writers as playwrights, though their essays and fiction are still widely read in America. Yet, before his death, Camus wrote four original plays and six adaptations; Sartre has written eight original plays and three adaptations. After the initial impact, American comment has often been that Camus was too honest to be a successful dramatist, and that Sartre is, variously, too philosophical, too melodramatic, or too sympathetic to Communism. They have often been dismissed as forerunners, without whom the Theater of the Absurd could not have reached the stage.

Though Camus hated to be labeled an Existentialist, while Sartre was popularly considered a founding father of the school, the metaphysical assumptions of the two men are similar—that being-in-the-world is absurd, and that man must be aware of that Absurdity, then go on to carve his destiny. For both authors, man is defined by his acts—an axiom that is particularly susceptible to dramatization. Sartre's dramas usually include the coming to a consciousness of Absurdity, and both playwrights dramatize the actions performed, once that consciousness is acquired. Though philosophically based, therefore, their drama is filled with action, which often takes a violent form: in *No Exit* a lesbian, a nymphomaniac, and a sadist are locked together for all eternity; in *Caligula* a Roman Emperor is savagely bent on imitating the Absurdity of Destiny. In America, production of the plays was followed by publication of Sartre's generalizations about them, and, as is frequently true of Sartre's generalizations, he reached beyond specific dramas to what he hoped to create. Under the hubristic title "Forgers of Myth" he claimed: "Dramas which are short and violent, sometimes reduced to the dimensions of a single long act. . . , dramas entirely centered on one event—usually a conflict of rights, bearing on some very general situation—written in a sparse, extremely tense style, with a small cast not presented for their individual characters but thrust into a conjunction where they are forced to make a choice—in brief this is the theatre, austere, moral, mythic, and ceremonial in aspect, which has given birth to new plays in Paris during the occupation and especially since the end of the war" (Rosamund Gilder translation).[20]

In brief, this is a summary of what Sartre was trying to do in his first four plays, dramas of situation in four different settings —the Argos of *The Flies* (1943), an atheist hell in *No Exit* (1944), a horror story of the French Resistance in *Death Without Burial* (1946), and a melodrama about a French liberal's idea of the American South in *The Respectful Prostitute* (1946). But Sartre's essay did not accurately prophesy the increasing complexity—in both conception and cast—of his own plays; nor does it quite describe two of Camus' four plays—*Caligula* (1945) and *State of Siege* (1948)—the latter not yet written when Sartre's essay was published. In the essay, Sartre calls attention to a new emphasis on action and to the moral meaning of stage violence. Moreover, although Sartre further claims: "Our aim is to explore all the situations that are most common to human experience, those which occur at least once in the majority of lives," the plays of Sartre and Camus deal largely with *un*common experiences that occur in very *un*common lives. Among Sartre's characters are a Greek prince, a South American deserter, a Communist party leader, a general of the Peasant Wars, a prince of German industry; those of Camus are a Roman Emperor, a Russian poet-assassin, a Spanish hero. Both writers did attempt to "forge myths" with these towering figures—myths of rebels who seek clarity despite the Absurdity of being-in-the-world.

Though the myth is similar, however, the forging technique is quite different in the dramas of Sartre and Camus. Except for *No Exit* and a lost play written while he was a prisoner of war in Germany, Sartre's plays accept the dominant realistic form of drama, with rationally motivated characters, plots of obstacle and resolution, and purposeful colloquial dialogue. Within that form, he achieves variety—from the comedy of *Nekrassov* (1955) to the half-mad anguish of *The Condemned of Altona* (1959), from the suffocating compression of *Death Without Burial* (1946) to the free-swinging chronicle of *The Devil and the Good Lord* (1951). But for all their diversity, the dramas focus on characters who are faced with similar moral choices; for all the violence on Sartre's stage, he is interested in the moral action. He has admitted throwing laugh lines to the audience so that they will remain serious when he wishes them to be; similarly, he throws them violent shock effects, so that they will be less shocked by his ideas. For from the "common human experience" with which Sartre claims to deal, he plunges his audience into lurid adventures that are journalistically familiar; and if one is moved to draw existentialist conclusions from these adventures, one *may* generalize them into "common human experience."

In Camus' plays, on the other hand, though the settings are similarly various, a symbolic level is soon suggested. Despite his research into history, *Caligula* (1945) depicts an Absurdist Rome through its extravagance; despite his dependence upon Savinkov's *Memoirs of a Terrorist*, *The Just Assassins* (1949) depicts an Absurdist Russia through its moral concerns. In both plays, the heroes are artists, and in both plays the resonance is widely human rather than specifically realistic. Similarly, though Camus' *Misunderstanding* (1944) is based on a news incident, dialogue and setting emphasize its wider meaning. *The State of Siege* (1948), commissioned by Jean-Louis Barrault, shows the influence of Artaud on both author and director; despite its failure at the box office, it is a breathlessly integrated attempt to make metaphysics penetrate through our skins.

Germaine Brée has written, "Camus's plays all follow a basic common pattern; the 'natural' order of human life is dislocated; . . . life is drained of its substance, then comes a struggle and a final resolution in which, temporarily, the natural order reasserts itself."[21] But that natural order is like the calm after a tempest, or, to use the metaphor shared by Artaud and Camus, like health after the plague, when all the corpses have been cleared away.

In his plays, Camus supplies small exposition; he furnishes few thrills and no laughs. All his works are written with sparely imaged, elliptical elegance. Largely because of their style, they suggest the wider resonances of the concrete events on stage. Germaine Brée has also pointed out that Camus' adaptations resemble his plays; in all of them, the protagonist is the victim of some form of collective murder, and to that murder he gives assent, whether consciously or not.

In his book on the Theater of the Absurd, Martin Esslin claims that "the *theatre* of Sartre and Camus is less adequate as an expression of the *philosophy* of Sartre and Camus . . . than the Theatre of the Absurd."[22] Esslin may be right, and if he is, Sartre and Camus will be viewed as not quite adequate forerunners of Beckett and Ionesco, though as worthy of attention as Marlowe and Peele, forerunners of Shakespeare. On the other hand, one may ask whether theater is ever an *expression* of philosophy, and whether it is not time to see their plays as plays.

When Martin Esslin published his *Theatre of the Absurd* in 1961, his four major figures were Beckett, Adamov, Ionesco, Genet. Though all wrote in French, only Genet was native to France, but his life outside the law made him an alien in his own country. While Sartre and Camus wrote about alienation, the playwrights of the Absurd—many of them foreigners in France— accepted it as *given*. In their plays, such alienation took different forms, though all made use of techniques of disjunction—in plot, character coherence, flow of dialogue. Despite these devices, Beckett and Genet are controlled writers, using their nightmares architecturally. Adamov and Ionesco, on the other hand, have close affinities with the surrealists who revelled in dreams. Adamov has literally theatricalized his nightmare in *Professor*

Taranne. It is in part this reliance upon personal nightmare that explains why Adamov is a less significant playwright than Esslin's other major figures. Unlike poetry and painting, where personal intensity can have an immediate impact, drama seems to demand more gradual revelation. Influenced by Artaud's de-emphasis on dialogue in the theater, Adamov concentrates on the visual, which highlights his personal vision.

Born in Russia, Arthur Adamov settled in Paris during the Surrealist 1920's. Living largely by translation, he turned to drama under the influence of Strindberg's *Dream Play*, which seemed to provide a form for his private feelings. In spite of Esslin's claim of Adamov's metaphysical Absurdity, his plays are more redolent of personal paranoia, sometimes schizophrenically divided into two characters—the employee and N in *The Parody* (1947), Pierre and his mother in *The Invasion* (1948), the Mutilated and the Militant in *The Great and the Small Manoeuver* (1950). Protagonist-centered are *The Direction of the March* and *Professor Taranne*, both written in 1941, and, to a lesser extent, *Everyone Against Everyone* (1952)—demonstrating that whatever one does, one is crushed. As in the works of Kafka, whom he admires, the personal persecutions are so intense that one has the feeling of being in a totalitarian state. His next two plays, *As We Were* (1952) and *The Recoveries* (1953), as their titles suggest, dramatize the regression of adults to situations of childhood. As Adamov's astonishingly frank confession, *L'Aveu* (1946), seemed to free him to write drama, these plays seemed to free Adamov for more socially oriented drama. In this first group of plays, however, scenic action is virtually limited to expression of swiftly changing emotions, evoked by abrupt and irrational persecutions.

Ping Pong (1954) and *Paolo Paoli* (1955) still retain the nightmare qualities of Adamov's earlier plays, but the setting is more recognizably social. In the former play, two protagonists waste their lives, obsessed by pin-ball machines, a symbol for a

mechanical capitalist society. Less symbolic, *Paolo Paoli* dramatizes a whole social system based on commercialism, in which
the key-products are butterfly-wings and ostrich-feathers. Implicit in these commodities is a critique of the purely esthetic,
as well as of the profit motive which values such animals above
man. An avowed Marxist at the time he wrote this last play,
Adamov has since written only two other dramas, *Spring '71*
(1960), a chronicle of the Paris Commune, and *The Politics of
Leftovers* (1963) about racial injustice—directly influenced by
Brecht's "epic" style and "learning-play" style, respectively. But
linguist through he is, Adamov lacks Brecht's incisive and versatile dramatic dialogue. Since he himself turned his back on his
earlier plays, Adamov's durable contribution to drama may be his
translations of Chekhov, Strindberg, Kleist, and Gorki.

In his *Theatre of the Absurd*, Esslin devotes some thirty pages
to Adamov and a bare five to Fernando Arrabal, and yet by 1961
both had produced a body of plays deriving from personal nightmares. As Adamov oriented his thought more socially, he seemed
to find the dramatic form less congenial. Arrabal, in contrast,
continues to weave his private sado-masochistic visions into short
plays, long plays, mimes, and happenings.

Born in Spanish Morocco in 1932, Arrabal has lived in France
since 1954 and has done his creative writing in French. He
has published four volumes of plays in less than a decade, the
plays of the 1950's running to short, metaphoric structures, and
those of the 1960's to longer or very short "ceremonies," which
he describes as "panic theater" (a pun on the noun *panic* and the
adjective derived from *Pan*). Common to many of these plays
is a naïve, childish dialogue that reveals cruelty and tenderness
as twin aspects of each character.

Though he lives in Paris, Arrabal's works contain the high
color, flamboyant sensuality, erotic cruelty, and grotesque humor
of the countrymen he admires—Calderón, Goya, Valle-Inclán,
and Lorca. Brought up during the Spanish Civil War, witness at

the age of three to his father's arrest by the Falangists, Arrabal has written anti-war satires—*Picnic on the Battlefield, Guernica*. More of his plays focus on couples as he explores the horrors of the love relationship, in an idiom quite different from that of Strindberg—*Orison, Fando and Lys, Bicycle of the Condemned, The Coronation, The Great Ceremony*. Child-couples with invented nicknames exist in their private worlds, into which others occasionally intrude. Devoid of conventional morality, whose clichés they may voice mechanically, the couples resort to games and rituals. Like the paranoid victims of Adamov's early plays, the not-so-innocent children of Arrabal are crushed, whatever they do.

Though these plays syncopate disparate incidents in a dream-like way, Arrabal has denied that they are surrealistic: "My theater is not surrealistic but is not merely realistic; it is realistic in including nightmares. Nightmares are very important in my life. Why not put them in my books? In my theater, situations often change; characters and ideas are interchangeable; beauty is concealed in the monster, sainthood in the criminal, the executioner in the victim. . . . I am obsessed by the idea of confusion, and by confusion I mean everything that is contradictory, inexplicable, unexpected, everything that makes for *coups de théâtre*. . . . I am creating realistic theater which represents this confusion."[23]

Particularly in his longer plays, *The Coronation* (1964), *The Great Ceremony* (1964), and *The Architect and the Emperor of Assyria* (1967) it is evident that Arrabal creates this confusion through careful manipulation and articulation of theatrical techniques. Not only are characters and ideas interchangeable, but all human action is repetitive, so that, as in more recognizably Absurdist drama, the play ends where it began. In the interim, however, the few characters have played many roles, providing scope for the actors. In *The Architect and the Emperor of Assyria*, the two characters are designated by the title; yet each one plays half a dozen roles, and the implication is that each could have played the roles of the other. At the end of the play, the Architect, having eaten the Emperor, becomes the Emperor; then the Architect arrives, speaking the Emperor's opening lines.

But though the play ends as it began, its beginning plunges us immediately into a theatrical world. Eugène Ionesco described that sense of theatrical immediacy in Arrabal, which fits his own plays even better:

> From the very beginning we have an unexpected, surprising event; from the moment the curtain rises, it is as though we look at a world we didn't know and which we nevertheless recognize, a world in which only the important and the essential appear, in which actions and gestures happen swiftly, distinctly, surely, each event being surprising; from the beginning, the situation is tense, simple, the image violent, dynamic.
>
> This is what it is to have a dramatic vision of the world, and when the world appears to you in this way, you can only express it by theater.[24]

Ionesco and Arrabal both have this dramatic vision of the world, but Ionesco claims that he came to theater by accident. Studying English by a method called "English Without Toil," Ionesco was struck by the mindless clichés of the textbook, and he found that the phrases fell of themselves into a parody play. Ionesco's friends showed his dialogue to the young director Nicholas Bataille, who staged it, playing often to audiences that were smaller than the cast. Slowly, however, Ionesco's farces attracted appreciative audiences, and today he is the most widely produced dramatist of the avant-garde, if indeed he can still be considered avant-garde.

"English Without Toil" led Ionesco to the tradition of Flaubert and Jarry, who also committed petrified language to art. Flaubert's Bouvard and Pécuchet were so earnest about their erudition that most of us can laugh at them with comic detachment; on stage, King Ubu belches his clichés so farcically that most of us dissociate ourselves from them. But the seemingly senseless repartee of Ionesco's plays leaves few of us unscathed, however we may laugh. Particularly at first theatrical exposure, we are appallingly interchangeable with the Martins and/or Smiths; all too often, we attend gatherings of chairs. In these logorrheal farces, Ionesco's characters speak a thoughtless language, an automatized language. Ionesco's plays dramatize the inadequacy of language as a means of expression or of communication; he proves that inadequacy not with discursive but with mimetic dialogue, containing puns, inversions, sonic associations, neologisms, non sequiturs. Blow by blow, his words demolish names, nouns, time, place, memory, and people themselves; they demolish our precarious footholds on reality.

Though his manipulation of cliché and fragmentation of language remain Ionesco's major dramatic innovations, he has often pointed out his contribution to staging technique as well. Proliferation of matter parallels proliferation of language; in the theater, man is smothered by a pincer movement of words and things. The tragi-farcical impact of *The Chairs* lies in the organic interconnection between the multiplication of empty chairs and the multiplication of empty politenesses. Adroitly, Ionesco balances the outrageousness of language run wild with that of props run wild—be it chairs, furniture, eggs, mushrooms, or rhinoceroses. Almost under Bergson's aegis, Ionesco's farces show the displacement of the human by things and by reified words. Richard Schechner has emphasized the meaningfully farcical gap between Ionesco's realistic exteriors and his interior action; this farcical gap reflects ontological insecurity.[25]

In later Ionesco plays we find figures of non-farce—Choubert, Amédée, Jean, and especially Bérenger; unlike his glib marionettes, these hesitant heroes stutter and stammer; but Bérenger alone is aware of the meaninglessness that surrounds him and threatens to engulf him. Opposing Bérenger are malignant characters or forces—a killer, rhinocerositis, and the cold fact of death. Unprepossessing, Bérenger emerges as a comic Everyman who must face death, even as his medieval ancestor. Haunted by death, Ionesco rarely produces a play that is free of that obsession; in the earlier plays, farce explodes into death or nothingness, but the deaths themselves are not farcical (as is often the case with Dürrenmatt). In more recent Ionesco plays death becomes a natural terror, but terror nonetheless.

Though Ionesco has insisted that he is a disengaged writer, no playwright has engaged in more personal and virulent polemics on behalf of his art. He seems to view himself as the heir of the Surrealists and as the leader of French avant-gardists such as Vauthier, Weingarten, de Obaldia, Dubillard. He undertook a debate in print with the English critic Kenneth Tynan; in these free-swinging press-fights Tynan has rarely dealt directly with Ionesco's drama as opposed to his a-politics, and Ionesco in turn has rarely dealt with the drama of Brecht (Tynan's patron-saint) as opposed to *his* politics. The very name of the clown Brechtoll of *Thirst and Hunger* recalls the German dramatist. Ionesco writes his polemics too swiftly and too often, even collecting many of them in *Notes and Counternotes*. As dramatist, however, he has theatricalized a distinctive blend of farce and anguish. His character named Ionesco, in the *Impromptu of Alma*, states: "For me, the theater is the stage projection of my inner world."

Born of *his* inner world, the parables of Samuel Beckett also embrace multiple absurdities of being-in-the-world. As most of Beckett's fiction focuses on a man writing, so his drama focuses on a man acting. The drama that is an imitation of an action is reduced to the acting of an actor—sometimes without words, as in his mime-plays, sometimes without gestures, as in his radio plays and *Play*. Through Beckett's successive plays, the scope of the actor is crystallized to gesture or word. In *Waiting for Godot* everyone is differently mobile and verbal, in *Endgame* only Clov can move, in *Krapp's Last Tape* the tape is more verbal than Krapp, in *Happy Days* Winnie and Willie embody, respectively, speech and motion; in *Play* no one moves. Entrances and exits, those staples of drama, grow pointed and rare; dialogue, another staple, grows more curt and cryptic, from the refrains of *Godot*, to the ironic repetitions of *Endgame* and *Happy Days*, to the incantation and complete replaying of *Play*. *Come and Go* momentarily recaptures the capacity for entrance and exit, but the dialogue is almost pure echo, rendered possible only by exit-entrances.

Beckett was over forty when he turned from verse and fiction to the drama that we know (though he had earlier written a scene in English). Vast experience and erudition are reflected and ridiculed in the skeletal structures of his plays. "It's a game," he told me disparagingly of his drama. "You can't get away from actor and audience." In each succeeding play, Beckett tightens the rules of his game, placing sterner demands upon actor, audience, and himself. In an age of elaborate technology, Beckett strips the stage, subjecting it to excruciatingly minute examination. He dramatizes the process of playing, and at the same time he suggests that all of human civilization has been a process of playing, and that that is all it is, decked out in costumes of ethics, esthetics, history, or religion.

Beckett juxtaposes playing and waiting, folly and philosophy, scatology and eschatology. In contrast to the familiar settings of many Ionesco plays, those of Beckett are concretely symbolic—paradoxical as that sounds; in contrast to the proliferation in Ionesco's plays, those of Beckett are daringly bare. Though both playwrights dramatize the inadequacy of language, Ionesco pulverizes its commonplaces; Beckett dissects it with precision. Though both playwrights write parables, Beckett's characters have more presence that those of Ionesco; Beckett's details individualize his characters and simultaneously generalize their resonance. Thus, Pozzo-Lucky suggest an external, social relationship, and Didi-Gogo an internal need of dissimilar people for one another's tenderness. Nagg, Hamm, and Clov suggest three generations of civilization, art, or knowledge; Winnie and Willie a cultural center and its material peripheries. But these people are not reducible to allegory, for they are individuals under their various hats, above their different containers. And as individuals, they are not unaware of the absurdity of their condition, but they express such awareness only sporadically, seeking instead to kill time with stage busyness. Their alternatives to thought seize upon Godot, games, lines of verse, memory, coming and going.

Waiting for Godot (1952) sprang full-grown from Beckett's parabolic head. Roger Blin felt that his production took nearly four years of meditation and preparation. Both on stage and on the page the play demands interpretation: four characters with cross-national names, the road and tree that are traditional metaphors for life, the paradoxical opening that closes discussion: "Nothing to be done." The play is constructed of symmetries—two acts, two couples, hat and shoe, blind and mute, sheep and goat, but the symmetries lead to imbalance in the endless, repetitive wait for Godot. During the wait for Godot, the most frequent recurrence in the play is neither word nor gesture, but gap: *pause*, in French *un temps*. Time is endless, and time is now, splintered into pauses, as the waiters contrive to find something to give them the impression they exist. This something may be eating, drinking, excreting, dreaming; words about the Bible and the vegetation, about place as space, about time as doubt, which reflect skeptically upon history, psychology, religion, philosophy, and above all upon theater, itself a way of filling pauses while waiting.

In *Endgame* (1957) there is little time left, and less knowledge of what is awaited—except that the game is bound to end. "Finished, it's finished, nearly finished, it must be nearly finished"—Clov opens this play even more paradoxically than Gogo did his, but Clov's line, like Gogo's, is followed by the inevitable *pause*. As the action of *Godot* was an imitation of waiting, so that of *Endgame* is an imitation of finishing. And both processes involve acting, playing. In *Godot* there were still hints of journeys, religions, societies, cultures; in the dying world of *Endgame* there are remnants of a family, remnants of a chronicle, remnants of an idea of order; but everything is running out as the something, whatever it may be, entropically takes its course. Playing to the last, Hamm closes the play by curtaining his face and sitting motionless for a final tableau.

Similarly, in the final tableau that is announced by the title *Krapp's Last Tape* (1958), Krapp sits motionless as *"The Tape runs on in silence."* Like *Endgame, Krapp's Last Tape* is an imitation of ending; all the recorded events are of endings; Krapp's own words point toward an ending, and since the play is set in the future, today's tapes lead to a last tape; the flow of words leads to silence.

In *Happy Days* (1961) the Zenonian heap, the impossible, grain-upon-grain heap (literally, of sand; metaphorically, of words or memories) has nearly buried Winnie. The play is the imitation of the action of being buried. Or the passion. For in each successive Beckett play, action and passion are less distinguishable from one another, but nihilism is as difficult as complete annihilation. When only Winnie's head remains above ground, she still has spirit to recite memories of vanished verses, of possible events, of impossible stories. When the three characters of *Play* (1963) have only their ghostly heads above their funeral urns, they recite memories of days gone by, they indefatigably search events for meaning; oblivious of the others, each meditates a monologue. In *Come and Go*, conversely, the three characters play three separate two-and-one scenes, the two always conspiring to conceal from the one her mysterious catastrophe.

Günther Anders analyzes *Waiting for Godot* as a parable, in terms that are applicable to all Beckett's plays, and that also illuminate much of contemporary drama. He points out that classical parables work by inversion; wishing to say that men are like animals, they show animals behaving like men. Similarly, Brecht in *Threepenny Opera,* wishing to show that businessmen are like gangsters, shows gangsters behaving like businessmen. Beckett works similarly but more subtly: "In order to present a fable about a kind of existence, which has lost both form and principle and in which life no longer goes forward, he destroys both the form and the principle so far characteristic of fables; now the *destroyed* fable, the fable which does not go forward, becomes the adequate representation of stagnant life; this meaningless parable about man stands for the parable of meaningless man. . . .[26] And although the mere tone of humaneness which springs from this barren soil of meaninglessness may only be a tiny comfort; and although the voice which comforts us does not know why it is comforting and who the Godot is for whom it makes us hope—it shows that warmth means more than meaning; and that it is not the metaphysician who has the last word."[27]

Though Jean Genet was of enormous interest to Sartre the metaphysician, overt metaphysics do not intrude upon Genet's own drama. The titles of Genet's five published plays refer to an action (*Deathwatch*—1947), characters (*Maids*—1947 and *Blacks* —1960), setting (*Balcony*—1956), and props (*Screens*—1961). One might suspect that this dramatist is so steeped in his medium that his very titles announce the ingredients of drama. But in his dramas Genet sought to escape from the autobiography of his earlier poetry and fiction.

Why or how Genet ventured into drama is uncertain. In his careers of thief, prostitute, prisoner, he had been exposed to it neither as spectator nor as reader. But Genet's novels contain impassioned gesture and dialogue that would seem suitable for dramatization. When Louis Jouvet commissioned Genet to write *The Maids* in 1947, he had not read Genet's *Deathwatch,* a prison drama that was perhaps written in prison. Genet disagreed with various aspects of Jouvet's production of *The Maids* (although he has since come to prefer the "Jouvet version"), and in his preface to the 1954 edition, he wrote: "But what can I say about a play from which I felt detached even before it was finished? . . .I would rather say a few words about the theater in general. I don't like it" (Bernard Frechtman translation).

Disliking the theater, he nevertheless launched into a far more ambitious undertaking in the dramatic domain, *The Balcony* (1956). Nearly a decade elapsed between *The Maids* and *The Balcony*, but the latter repeats the ritualistic role-playing of the former. Genet astounds us by this shift from the constricted setting of *The Maids* and *Deathwatch* to the theatrical boldness and explosive comedy of *The Balcony*, which is a clown-play, even as *The Blacks*. In his 1954 comment on *The Maids* Genet mentions that already he had "tried to obtain a displacement which, permitting a declamatory tone, would set the theater on the theater. . .to contrive that the characters on the stage would be only metaphors of what they were supposed to represent." In *The Balcony* one of the characters enunciates this explicitly: "Our function will be to support, establish, and justify metaphors."

Genet's metaphors, like Eliot's doubleness of action or the different parables of Brecht and Beckett, reach out for a general meaning below, or beyond, or around the action on stage. As in classical drama, the compression of space and time in Genet's first two plays, *Deathwatch* and *The Maids*, suggests a stable, ordered background for an inner struggle. Moreover, the respective backgrounds themselves appear as metaphors for our world —the lace-flowery bedroom of *The Maids*, and the oneiric jail of *Deathwatch*. (The latter metaphor has been re-used in Kenneth Brown's *Brig*, Rick Cluchy's *Cage*, John Herbert's *Fortune and Men's Eyes*, and Megan Terry's *Keep Tightly Closed in a Cool Dry Place*.) With these small casts, as with the larger casts of Genet's last three plays, "every character must play the role of a character who plays a role."[28]

In Genet's first two plays, the role-playing is sketchy but intense: Green Eyes and Madame ruling the roost, LeFranc and Claire imitating and hating, Maurice and Solange enacting the degraded state. In Genet's last three plays, role-playing *is* the play. To the basic components of his drama, metaphoric meaning and ritual re-enactment, Genet adds the irony achieved by the characters' commentary on the roles they are playing. Genet's last three plays fulfill his own requirement for Western theater, which he enunciated in his 1954 post-script to *The Maids*: "[Western theater] can only refine the reflection of a play of a play, of a reflection of a reflection, which ceremonious performance might render exquisite and close to invisibility. If one has chosen to watch himself die voluptuously, he must rigorously pursue and order the funeral symbols." (My translation differs somewhat from that of Bernard Frechtman.)

The Balcony, The Blacks, and *The Screens* all deal ironically and voluptuously with death; balcony, blacks, and screens are aspects of death through and into illusion; they are funeral symbols by which Genet dramatizes decadence, and they embrace a social range beyond that of his earlier works. Death strikes not only individuals, but in *The Balcony* the ruling government, in *The Blacks* the ruling race, and in *The Screens* the ruling culture. Genet rigorously pursues and orders *their* funeral symbols, as well as his own. His plays of plays, his reflections of reflections, are tinged with irony upon irony upon irony, all with cutting edge.

Sartre has commented on Genet's "Whirligigs of being and appearance, of the imaginary and the real." But Genet constructs his playthings to shift their illuminations in the direction he intends, and not at the wind's caprice. Thus, the imaginary becomes the real, and the new reality will again turn toward the imaginary. The imaginary Establishment of the Balcony replaces the real one, but when the revolution falls prey to Establishment illusions, this new level of the imaginary is newly vulnerable to the real. In a more complex juxtaposition of the real and imaginary in *The Blacks*, real Negroes condemn mock-whites to death, but the mock-ritual is deliberately left at the level of entertainment while Black Power gathers force off stage.

After Genet had written only two plays, Sartre wrote, "It is

the element of fake, of sham, of artificiality, that attracts Genet
in the theatre. He has turned dramatist because the falsehood
of the stage is the most manifest and fascinating of all."[29] (Bernard Frechtman translation). After his first two plays, however,
the theater seems to have attracted Genet as the medium which
can best reflect the fake, sham, and artificiality of the Western
world. Through the inclusiveness of Genet's last three dramas,
he assaults his audience as Artaud would have wished, so that it
is "through the skin" that metaphysics, *and* history, *and* eco-
nomics, *and* legend are "made to re-enter our minds." Genet has
written a Theater of Cruelty in both the literal sense and the
sense of Artaud.

Genet's last play, *The Screens*, contains 94 characters, 17
scenes, and 9 screens, which he manipulates as funeral symbols
of our world. As Leonard Pronko has noticed: "The servants of
The Maids, the prostitutes of *The Balcony*, the prisoners of
Deathwatch, the decried race of *The Blacks*, themes of sacrilege,
obscenity, the inverted religion of evil, hatred, treason, all find
place in Genet's latest play."[30] Each of the drama's seven groups
has its myth and/or metaphor: the holy family, the brothel, the
Arab village, the Arab army, the European colonists, the French
Foreign Legionnaires, and the Dead. But myth and metaphor
are not abstractions for Genet, since they are concretely involved
in theatrical action. Myth and metaphor achieve stage definition
through the calculated quest of Saïd, the hero of *The Screens*.
Saïd subsumes and surpasses Genet's earlier criminal-saints, for
his determined degradation is an apotheosis. Because of his degradation, the Arab race can design flames that explode into a
revolution. Always in the background—of heroic odyssey and
social upheaval—are the screens, merging the real legends with
the legendary realities of our dying world.

Genet's last three plays were written in succession, after a
six-year silence—his traumatic reaction to Sartre's monumental
study *St. Genet, Actor and Martyr*. To some extent, these three

plays explore and unite the roles of actor and martyr, as earlier works had explored and united the roles of criminal and saint. The emphasis shifts to *roles*. What remains consistent, however, is adherence to a Satanic tradition, in which Evil is the desired Good. In this elevation of Evil to an absolute, the plays of Genet, France's most ostracized playwright, bear ironic analogy to the plays of Anouilh, France's most successful playwright during the same period. The bulk of Anouilh's plays condemn a relativistic, compromising world in which purity is the province of the saint alone. For Genet, pure dedication to Evil is the province of the martyr who rises above relativism, compromise, or traditional virtue that brings social reward. Though this comparison of Anouilh and Genet should not be pushed too far, it indicates that French drama since World War II presents a diminishing gap between the experimental and the successful. Beginning in small, makeshift theaters, Ionesco, Beckett, and Genet have now been consecrated in state-subsidized theaters—to the confusion of state officials.

GERMAN LANGUAGE DRAMA

Though Hitler's regime was not the cultural desert we like to suppose, it strangled free development of the drama. While the prewar Nazi government continued state subsidies to theater, and production maintained a high level, the dramatic repertory underwent changes: classics were presented with more patriotic fervor, historical plays took on a nationalist élan, and peasant dramas sang a blood-and-soil mystique. The most interesting drama in Europe—loosely called Expressionist—was buried in anathema.

Only after World War II—two decades afterward—is theatrical and critical attention being focused on Expressionist drama, which rebelled against conformity and common sense. Forerunners of the Absurdists, the Expressionists worked in distortion, non sequitur, and incongruity. Structured in scenes rather than acts, their dramas were influenced by the swift pacing of Büchner's plays, the dream quality of Strindberg's late plays.[31] Often, dramatic development was based upon quest rather than conflict, as in pre-Marxist plays of Brecht.

Before fleeing from Nazi Germany, and after his conversion to Marxism, Brecht wrote propaganda pieces that he candidly called "learning-plays." Less candid about *their* propaganda, the Nazis proclaimed a cultural rebirth for Germany, which often took the form of sacrifice plays for the fatherland. Even Nazi supporters such as Johst, Bronnen, and Moller found difficulty in dramatizing such chauvinism, and after World War II began, theaters gradually closed down; they were forbidden in 1944. The venerable Gerhart Hauptmann, who had begun his playwriting career in social protest, ended it in Greek myth. Carl Sternheim died exiled in Belgium, and Georg Kaiser in Switzerland; Paul Kornfeld was killed in a concentration camp, and Ernst Toller committed suicide; refugees both, Carl Zuckmeyer wrote *The Devil's General* about Nazi Germany, and Bertolt Brecht wrote his epic parables with exotic settings, which are more relevant to a world of democratic capitalism than to barbarous fascism.

Playwright, theoretician, and director, Brecht looms larger today than before his death in 1956. Strehler in Italy, Planchon in France, Littlewood in England, and Hancock in the United States show the wide reach of Brecht's staging concepts, and every serious director and playwright today is aware of Brecht, if only, as in the case of Ionesco, to react against him. After Brecht's return to East Berlin, in 1950, he limited his dramatic writing to adaptation, but both his plays and productions are part of the postwar theatrical scene.

Within a decade after World War II, the decentralized theaters of Germany and Austria were largely rebuilt, and state subsidies supported repertory companies that were nourished generously and eclectically on classics and translations. Berlin today offers the widest theatrical variety in Europe or America—classics and contemporary plays of all countries in West Berlin, classics and realistic plays of all countries in East Berlin—the totality available to everyone but Berliners, East or West.

German drama recovered more slowly than German theater. At the peripheries of Germany, in German-speaking Switzerland, German drama was kept alive by the Austrian refugee, Fritz Hochwalder, and by the native Swiss playwrights, Friedrich Dürrenmatt and Max Frisch. Until German-born, Swedish citizen Peter Weiss turned to drama, the two Swiss writers were Brecht's principal German language heirs.

So starved has German theater been for new drama that even isolated plays have aroused interest. Wolfgang Borchert's *The Man Outside* was written in 1947, the year of Borchert's death after extreme brutalization at Nazi hands. An Expressionistic dramatization of the fate of the returned German soldier, the play propounds metaphysical as well as social questions. And it offers no answers. Its force lies in swift scenes, imaginative staging, and a dialogue which ranges from the topical to the symbolic.

Günther Grass and Wolfgang Hildesheimer have produced dramas in experimental forms, and recently West German playwrights have turned to "documentary dramas," which incorporate documents into the dramatic dialogue. Unlike the old problem plays that occasionally did this, the contemporary plays focus on people as well as problems, and they only imply solutions. Rolf Hochhuth's *Deputy*, Heinar Kipphardt's *In the Matter of J. Robert Oppenheimer* and Peter Weiss' *Investigation* may be cited as examples. Though Weiss alone has insisted upon his debt to Brecht, documentary theater resembles Brecht's Epic Theater in presenting a series of episodes on a single subject. It was Erwin Piscator, and not Brecht, who originated Epic Theater, which is more readily associated with Brecht's name.

The earliest plays of Bertolt Brecht were written before Erwin Piscator founded the first Epic Proletarian Theater in 1923, and before Brecht's 1935 visit to Russia, where he heard the Russian equivalent of *Verfremdung* or estrangement.[32] Not until 1948 did Brecht gather his theoretical writings into the *Small Organon for the Theater*; many of them were written as manifestoes during the heat of political and esthetic battles—rarely separate for Brecht. Even during such strife, Brecht pointed out that his opposition of Epic Theater to Aristotelian Theater was a matter of emphasis rather than an absolute polarity. In his last years, Brecht came to prefer the term Dialectical Theater to Epic Theater. Moreover, as Reinhold Grimm indicates in his book on Brecht, estrangement operates in three realms: the writing of the plays, the production in the theater, the role-playing of the actor.[33] Most of Brecht's theory refers to the latter two domains. Epic staging devices include strong white lights, half-curtains, revolving stage—all intended to estrange the audience, to make us aware of being in a theater.

Brecht rejected the honorific German word *Dichter* (poet), and, leaning on the English word playwright, called himself a *Stückeschreiber*, which rings familiarly through German, punning on *play* and *piece*. Brecht wrote poems, aphorisms, stories, essays, polemics, novels—all pieces—while composing his forty-odd plays and adaptations. His playwriting career is usually divided into four periods: 1) early plays through his two operas, 2) learning plays, 3) plays of exile, 4) adaptations. Most of these are distinguished by the pithy language that marks Brecht as a *Dichter* in spite of himself.

Brecht's first play, *Baal*, written at the age of twenty-one, already exhibits a mastery of conception and construction, casting doubt on the anecdote that Brecht wrote it in four days on a bet that he could do better than Hanns Johst in his drama about Grabbe, *The Lonely One*. Brecht's monolithic hero, Baal, is an anti-hero, and the drama is the odyssey of his life, developed through a series of episodes. At once a Romantic drama and a parody of the Romantic ego, at once an Expressionist drama and a parody of the Expressionist pilgrimage, *Baal* foreshadows Brecht's lifelong admiration for the Phoenician deity of insatiability, condemned by Judaeo-Christian tradition. Brecht's *Baal* possesses the attractive vitality of his later protagonists, Mack the Knife, Mother Courage, Galileo, and Azdak.

Within five years, Brecht wrote *Drums in the Night* about a returned soldier after World War I, *In the Jungle of Cities* about a love-hate relationship inspired by Rimbaud and Verlaine, *Edward II* (with Lion Feuchtwanger), an adaptation of Marlowe, and his first parable or Everyman play, *Man Is Man*. Into the episodes of this last play Brecht inserts estrangement techniques that he was later to build into a theory—interpolated songs (called *songs* by Brecht in German), projections, direct address to the audience, and reference to himself as author.

At about the time of his conversion to Marxism, Brecht wrote his two operas, *The Threepenny Opera* and *Mahogonny*, then shifted sharply to the lean lines of his propaganda plays, which he called *Lehrstücke*—learning-plays. Intended for a worker audience and unprofessional actors, these short pieces are modeled on Jesuit plays of the Counter-Reformation, and they present similarly abstract problems, similarly discursive doctrine, and a similar concern with salvation; but the axiomatic basis is radically different, lying in class solidarity rather than divine grace. Though *St. Joan of the Stockyards* and *The Mother* may be grouped with the learning-plays in their agit-prop aspects (agitation and propaganda), the treatment is at once more concrete and more complex, pointing toward the dramas of exile—Brecht's condition from 1933 to 1948.

The best-known plays of these years are *Mother Courage, Galileo, The Good Woman of Szechwan,* and *The Caucasian Chalk Circle.* In these works estranged, respectively, to seventeenth century Germany, seventeenth century Italy, a never-never China, and a Golden Age Georgia, Brecht dramatizes not the problems but the life-style of our contemporary Western world.

A single prop may reflect this style—Mother Courage's wagon, Shen Te's shop, the dwindling bundle of Grusha—and human emotions, cramped by that style, emerge more powerfully than Brecht's ideological commitment.

In exile, Brecht wrote seven other plays. In the United States, where he spent about half his exile period, he was virtually unknown, though a few admirers early praised and translated him—Charles Laughton, Frank Jones, Mordecai Gorelik, and above all Eric Bentley. *Galileo* was the only play to receive professional production with Brecht's collaboration. After Brecht's Schweikian testimony before the House Un-American Activities Committee, he returned to Europe, and then to participation in a theater group which became the Berliner Ensemble. Back in Berlin, largely occupied with theory and production, Brecht adapted various plays, changing the class emphasis—Sophocles-Hölderlin's *Antigone*, Lenz's *Tutor*, Shakespeare's *Coriolanus*, Farquhar's *Recruiting Officer*, and Molière's *Don Juan*.

For a younger generation, East and West, Brecht is at once an old master and a living model. His production methods and dramatic structures are widely imitated, but what remains inimitable is the flavor of his language, the concreteness of his characters (Brecht's favorite saying was, "Die Wahrheit ist konkret"), and the subtle texture as opposed to the loose structure of his plays.

The journal of Max Frisch, written during 1945–1948, records his meetings with Brecht but does not record reactions to Brecht's plays that were first produced in Zurich—*Mother Courage* in 1941, *The Good Woman of Szechwan* and *Galileo* in 1943. Nor does it record the intimate details of Frisch's life; instead, it is a personal impression of public events, related in impersonal guise. Frisch shared the social anxieties of Brecht, but he did not share his political allegiance to Marxism. In journal and fiction, and even in drama, Frisch reveals an individual's concern about his world—a member of no political party, and a Swiss citizen who is highly critical of Swiss neutrality and prosperity. In his journal Frisch wrote, "The moral problem always has to be resolved." Through his work threads a question about the position of the intellectual today in a world of social clichés.

Frisch's first play, *Santa Cruz* (1944), called "a romance," is atypical because of its romantic, fantastic quality. It dramatizes the entrance into a tired bourgeois marriage of the romantic past of Santa Cruz, reactivating old romantic longings. The play is interesting chiefly for its free-wheeling locales, shifting from present to past, from Switzerland to Santa Cruz. In his next play *Now They Sing Again* (1945), called "Essay at a Requiem," Frisch again uses short scenes, shifts between past and present, and, influenced perhaps by *Our Town*, he has the dead enter the realm of the living. Tangentially appears the theme that haunts Frisch—the responsibility of the humanist intellectual for barbaric events.

The Chinese Wall (1946), "a Farce," is directly indebted to Brecht—estranged to China at the time of the building of the Great Wall. Like Brecht, Frisch borrows characters from history and literature; he uses masks and quotations. Unlike Brecht, however, Frisch introduces a contemporary intellectual who takes part in and comments on the action. As in Brecht's plays, there is no possible moral resolution within the existing social order, but Frisch has no hope for any other social order.

Frisch's next three plays, written between 1948 and 1952, focus more on individual than on social morality, but the individuals are always dramatized within a social context. *When the War Was Over* deals with the problem of German guilt under the surface of a love affair between a Russian captain and the German woman whose house he occupies. In *Graf Oderland* (*Count Wasteland*) an eminently respectable public prosecutor suddenly leaves his home for the untrammeled forest, killing all who stand in his way. Roaming and killing, the neophyte anarchist eventually finds himself in a position of authority that demands a new conformity. More circular than Brecht's epic parables, that of Frisch ends where it began, with the public prosecutor back in his bourgeois Swiss home; like Brecht, Frisch verbalizes the lesson of his rambling learning-play: "Whoever disturbs power in order to be free, takes over power, the opposite of freedom." Less clearly linked to our own society is *Don Juan or the Love of Geometry* (1952). The title indicates that Frisch sees the legendary lover as another troubled intellectual. Don Juan seeks to pursue his studies in geometry, trying to evade his legend by staging his own spurious death. Married to a courtesan-turned-duchess, he becomes bored by studies and domesticity. When the Tirso drama appears, its legend replaces the truth about Don Juan; while the seducer of Seville acquires world fame, the real man will become a father.

Frisch's next two plays center on social rather than individual clichés. *Biedermann and the Firebugs* (1958) presents a German Babbitt behaving with avaricious stupidity in the "learning play without a lesson." Because he is imprisoned by his property, because he cannot think in a larger socio-moral context, Biedermann first tolerates and then aids the firebugs to blow up his house.

In *Andorra* (1961) the cliché portrait is that of victim, as well as villain. Andri is thought to be Jewish, adopted by the village school-teacher, and tagged with ready-made characteristics by the inhabitants of Andorra. When an anti-semitic country invades Andorra, it proceeds to destroy the Jews. Though Andri is the illegitimate son of the school-teacher, and therefore not Jewish, he refuses to save himself from Andorran hostility and enemy execution. During the play's action, Frisch uses the estrangement technique of having several of the characters turn to the audience to explain their conduct; having learned nothing from Andri's tragedy, they rationalize their behavior. Though Frisch merely calls *Andorra* "a play," it is another learning-play without a lesson; "The moral problem always has to be resolved."

In Frisch's *Biography: A Play* (1967) it is not only the moral problem that has to be resolved, but all the personal problems that constitute a life. And the play suggests that no such resolution is possible in and by life. Using some of the techniques of his novels, Frisch reconstructs several possible biographies for his protagonist, Hannes Kürmann. Theater permits what reality does not: "to repeat, to try out, to change." In a note to the published version Frisch warns against viewing the play metaphysically, and concludes, "I meant it as comedy."

"Comedy alone is suitable for us," declares Friedrich Dürrenmatt in his theoretical writings. Almost all of his plays are designated as comedy, and all his work contains his distinctive mode of comedy—the grotesque—upon which he also comments: "The grotesque is only a way of expressing in a tangible manner, of making us perceive physically the paradoxical, the form of the unformed, the face of a world without face"[34] (Gerhard Nellhaus translation). Brecht, too, preferred comedy to tragedy, but he rarely showed death on stage, whereas Dürrenmatt litters his stage with corpses, reducing death to a macabre farce. As he himself is aware, Dürrenmatt's grotesque humor rests upon his parodic attitude towards the ideals of the past—ethical and aesthetic.

His first two plays *It Is Written* (1947) and *The Blind Man* (1948) reveal Dürrenmatt as a pastor's son, for both deal with man's search for God—the former during the time of the Anabaptists in Münster and the latter during the Thirty Years' War. The former play uses stage pyrotechnics, rhetorical flights, sharp shifts in mood, and rapid scenic pace, whereas the latter drama takes place on an almost bare stage, with a minimal cast of characters, within an illusionist framework. Apprentice works, both show Dürrenmatt in search of his own dramatic idiom.

In *Romulus* (1949) he finds it. The grotesque—comedy through horror—borders on farce—would-be assassins in the Emperor's bedroom, hens named after illustrious Romans, a Germanic general who conquers Rome with all the statistics of a

German tourist. Dürrenmatt has claimed that tyrants fear mock-ery, and *Romulus*, at first banned in both East and West Ger-many, was also closed down in France at the time De Gaulle took power.

Into his next two plays, Dürrenmatt introduces dazzling the-atrical effects. Even the titles, *The Marriage of Mr. Mississippi* (1952) and *An Angel Comes to Babylon* (1953), suggest the flamboyant proper names, the improbable plots, and the scenic exuberance that Dürrenmatt calls *Ubermut* (containing sugges-tions of both playfulness and insolence). Like his first two plays, these deal tangentially with religion; Mr. Mississippi lives by the *lex talionis*, relishing punishment for crime, and *An Angel Comes to Babylon* explores the misunderstandings and iniquities that lead to the destruction of a city. In these two plays, the influence of Brecht is manifest: *Marriage of Mr. Mississippi* is the most calculatedly estranged of all Dürrenmatt's plays, and the two main characters of *An Angel Comes to Babylon* inevitably recall those of Brecht—Kurubi and Shen Te, Akki and Azdak. Sceni-cally, both plays are more elaborate than anything Brecht at-tempted, and always the grotesque tone dominates. The cumu-lative impact of both plays, set respectively in a never-never nowhere and a never-never Babylon, proclaims that history is repetitive, and that intransigent monomaniacs will entangle situ-ations from generation to generation.

Perhaps Dürrenmatt suspects that too much scenic display can overwhelm a scenario, because he indulges in it again only in his opera *Frank V* (1959). In the plays written before and after the opera, *The Visit* (1956) and *The Physicists* (1961), Dürrenmatt subdues his scenic exuberance. *The Visit* brought Dürrenmatt fame and fortune, and it provided the swan-song, in the English-language theater, of Alfred Lunt and Lynn Fon-tanne—a swan-song that softened the hard edge of the original German version.[35]

Like *The Visit*, *The Physicists* returns to Dürrenmatt's na-tive Switzerland. Influenced by Brecht's *Galileo* and detective story suspense, Dürrenmatt incarcerates three physicists in a madhouse, then manipulates a surprise-filled plot to a mordant conclusion, which Dürrenmatt himself summarized: "Everything turns on the physicist who wants to escape into a lunatic asylum, having chosen the worst possible lunatic asylum to hide in; and on that choice, a pure chance, the fate of the world may depend."[36] In *The Meteor* (1966) pure chance seems to decide the fate of the individual. The titular meteor is death, falling where least expected. Unlike existentialist heroes who experience a feeling of absurdity when confronted with death, Dürrenmatt's protagonist, the famous writer Schwitter, experiences frustration that he cannot die. Instead, the young and healthy die; old and sick, Schwitter is resurrected again and again, crying out grotesquely at the end, "When am I finally going to croak?" Having turned his theatricality to social and moral questions, Dürrenmatt here approaches the metaphysical, but always in his idiom of the painfully comic.

Peter Weiss, in contrast, has used a different idiom for each of his eight plays. *The Tower* (1948) and *Insurance* (1952) are surrealistic in their swift, kaleidoscopic scene-shifts, but the first is lyrical, the second stripped and satiric. Thematically, the influence of Kafka is apparent in both plays; in the earlier piece Pablo, the Escape Artist who recalls Kafka's Hunger Artist, attempts to escape from a tower. In the second play Alfons, the Police President, is gradually and mysteriously victimized by the police. Both plays project a nightmare vision of a police-state.

Born in Berlin of a German mother and Czech-Jewish father, Weiss fled from Germany when the Nazis came to power, settling in Sweden at the age of twenty-two. Painter, journalist, moviemaker, and novelist, he was catapulted to world fame by his third play, *The Persecution and Assassination of Jean-Paul Marat as Performed by the Inmates of the Asylum of Charenton under the Direction of the Marquis de Sade* (1964). Through Peter Brook's staging, this play is usually said to combine the influences of Artaud and Brecht, but Weiss has stated that Brook added

Artaud; his own mentor was Brecht. The influence is apparent in calculated estrangement tehniques—play within a play, songs, narrator (The Herald), historical parallel—but the resonances of an insane-asylum setting are irrational and un-Brechtian.

Contrasting with the spectacular display of *Marat/Sade* is the statistical, reportorial nudity of *The Investigation* (1965). "An oratorio," based on the testimony at the Auschwitz trials, *The Investigation* opened simultaneously in seventeen different German theaters. Cast in the form of a legal investigation, the drama makes detailed and specific charges against all who acquiesced to the horrors of the concentration camps. Weiss condemns today's comfortable West German citizen by stealing his clichés: "Today/ when our nation has worked its way up/ after a devastating war/ to a leading position in the world/ we ought to concern ourselves/ with other things/ than blame and reproaches/ that should be thought of/ as long since atoned for" (Alexander Gross translation).

Weiss' subsequent plays cry out at injustice: *The Song of the Lusitanian Bogey* (1966) at Portuguese imperialism in Africa and *Viet Nam Discourse* (1967) at American imperialism in Viet Nam. Manipulating songs, chorus, and visual effects as Brecht did in his "epic" productions, Weiss writes learning-plays about the causes and effects of oppression. Rather than Brechtian estrangement, he seeks to encourage indignation through the theater. The plays rise above propaganda by the African rhythms and the Oriental splendor suitable to the respective background of each play.

In a sharp shift of idiom, Weiss features an Everyman clown-figure in *How Mr. Mockinpott Was Cured of Suffering* (written in 1963 but revised and produced in 1968). Finding himself inexplicably in prison, the good bourgeois Mr. Mockinpott buys his way out, but so hurried is he to leave that he puts his right shoe on his left foot and vice versa. Prison was only the beginning of his sorrows: in farcical scenes, his wife and her lover scare him out of his home, his boss will not rehire him, a surgeon cuts him up to "cure him," politicians of government speak to him in double talk, and God shakes His head sadly as Mockinpott tells him that he has had enough—his first words of rebellion against his suffering. While his companion Wurst falls into a drunken stupor, Mockinpott puts the right shoe on the right foot, suddenly enabled to walk with dignity. He is cured of suffering by changing from acceptance to rebellion. At the last "Mockinpott, winged as a dancer, as an ice-skater, moves in ever-widening arcs into the distance." The awkward clown, speaking in the rhymes that Germans call *Knittelvers*, finally wafts into silent understanding.

Although Brecht, Frisch, Dürrenmatt, and Weiss have produced impressive works, no living resident of Germany has produced a comparable body of plays. On the other hand, at the time of writing—1968—there is such *theater* ferment in Germany that it augurs excitement for drama too. Can excitement and experimentation be sustained and developed into a meaningful body of works?

The question must be left open in an introduction to dramatic originality since World War II. Various efforts have been made to fit this variety of plays into Procrustean classifications, but the plays resist such efforts. Though the shockingly new and subtly difficult dramas of the last thirty years may have lost some of their subtlety and much of their shock effect, a surprising number show their quality all the more brightly for that loss. And though the plays themselves may be radically original, standards of quality tend to be traditional—intensity, significance, integrity.

Aristotle, that teacher of critics, judged drama by its genre, its hero, and the means of production. Not necessarily because of Aristotle, these criteria are still viable for examination of groups of contemporary plays. The genre is not the same, for today's taste replaces tragedy with tragicomedy; today's heroes come in all sizes, shapes, colors, and tongues; spectacle calls attention to its own spectacularity, and dialogue calls attention to its cruel particularity. We begin with dialogue.

TWO: Dialogue of Cruelty

J UST BEFORE ENTERING THE DEEPEST CIRCLE OF THE INFERNO,
DANTE STOPS TO LISTEN TO A VITUPERATIVE DIALOGUE BETWEEN
a contemporary counterfeiter, Master Adam, and a classical traitor, Sinon the Greek. The one swollen with dropsy
and the other reeking with fever, equally matched in their capacity for cruelty, these classico-contemporary duellists so fasci-
nate Dante that Virgil admonishes him: "To wish to hear it is a
base wish." A momentary lapse on Dante's part, this base wish is
often assumed in modern theater audiences—a wish to hear lively
and deadly verbal cruelties.

In isolated scenes, verbal sparring is as old as drama—the
Tiresias-Oedipus exchange that heightens the tragic impact of
Oedipus Tyrannos, the Richard III-Lady Anne duologue that
reveals heroic villainy, the witty thrusts of Célimène and Arsinoe
in *The Misanthrope*. But Strindberg was the first dramatist to
base whole plays upon dialogues of cruelty, and several contemporary playwrights have learned verbal sadism from that master. *Inferno* is the title of one of Strindberg's semi-autobiograph-
ical novels, but his dramas etch more vivid infernoes. Laura fences
verbally with the Captain in *The Father*, Julie with Jean in *Miss
Julie*, Tekla with Gustav and Adolph in *The Creditors*; Strindberg

54

called these duels "brain battles," which led to "psychological murder." Though less deadly in Strindberg's later plays, such barbed conflicts continue—between Alice and the Captain in *The Dance of Death*, the Unknown and the Lady in *To Damascus*, the Daughter of Indra and the Officer-Lawyer-Poet in *The Dream Play*. With rapier-minds, Strindberg's antagonists wound each other, seeking what he called "soul-murder." One's pleasure is the other's pain in this fight to dramatic finish—the Captain's stroke, Julie's suicide, Adolph's apoplexy, the death of the Unknown, the return of the Daughter of Indra. In these dramas, the conflict is expressed in dialogue of mutual cruelty, whose intensity leads to catastrophe. Particularly in his pre-*Inferno* plays, Strindberg often confines such dialogue to a single act of high tension, limiting his cast to the two duelists in a claustrophobic setting.[1] Play after Strindberg play dramatizes the conflict within the couple, and that very repetition has a cumulative effect, summing up his vision of man's life on earth. Erotically sado-masochistic, Strindberg's couples express their love-hate with cruel skill, and only in his last play does such earthly pain lead to spiritual fulfillment or Nirvana, a pathos-mathos through Swedenborg and Brahma.

An admirer of Strindberg, Antonin Artaud, coined the phrase *Theater of Cruelty*, which has been mistakenly confused with verbal dispute or with violent sensationalism. Like Strindberg of the last plays, Artaud envisioned a Cruelty of wide significance and resonance. But unlike the compulsively verbal Strindberg, Artaud wished to theatricalize cruelty by stylized movement and lavish staging, de-emphasizing language. It was the highly gestural Balinese dances that inspired Artaud's conception of a Theater of Cruelty. He first uses the phrase in a manifesto for theater that is highly relevant to Strindberg's practice: "I do believe that the theater, utilized in the highest and most difficult sense possible, has the power to influence the aspect and formation of things: and the encounter upon the stage of two passionate manifestations, two living centers, two nervous magnetisms is something as entire, true, even decisive, as, in life, the encounter of one epidermis with another in a timeless debauchery. That is why I propose a theater of cruelty. . . . We are not free. And the sky can still fall on our heads. And the theater has been created to teach us that first of all"[2] (Mary Richards translation).

For all his devaluation of language, Artaud's evocation of dramatic conflict describes Strindberg's dialogue as it does that of subsequent playwrights, much of whose significance lies in their cruelty, and whose cruelty reflects a vision of the world—ethical and metaphysical.

Even Bertolt Brecht (whose determined rationalism contrasts with Artaud's emphasis on the irrational) dramatized an erotic, sado-masochistic relationship in his early play *In the Jungle of Cities* (1923). The basic metaphor of the drama is that of a boxing ring, in which "one epidermis [encounters] another in a timeless debauchery" (Eric Bentley translation). The epidermises belong to George Garga and C. Shlink, and the encounter takes place in 1912 in a semi-mythical Chicago. On stage the encounter is linguistic rather than pugilistic. Shortly before Garga drives Shlink to suicide, the latter explains their symbiotic relationship: "You have understood then, that we are comrades, comrades in a metaphysical action." This metaphysical action, like the one advocated by Artaud, exploits more than the verbal resources of the theater, but it exploits them too, in what Garga calls "the black mania of this planet—the mania for contact." Before his death, after their many verbal battles, Shlink declares: "The union of the organs is the only union, and it can never bridge the gap of speech."

In spite of Brecht's view of a dog-eat-dog capitalist society, he was never again to dramatize fights with sustained dialogues of cruelty. His Belgian contemporary, Michel de Ghelderode, on the other hand, revels in the kind of invective for which Virgil reprimanded Dante's base desire. Particularly in his plays set in

Christ's time or in the Flemish Middle Ages, Ghelderode energizes his drama with verbal shock. The women at the tomb of Christ rail at one another; Barrabas, Herod, and Pilate are masters of insult; in *Hop Signor!* physical and moral dwarfs disfigure each other with words, as do husband and wife in *Red Magic*. The most vicious dialogue in Ghelderode's drama occurs in *Chronicles of Hell*, written in 1929, but still shocking when it was produced in Paris twenty years later.

The French title *Fastes d'Enfer* puns on a double meaning of *fastes*, which may be translated as chronicles, but also as gaudy display. Ghelderode's own dramatic display is both visual and aural, shot through with farce: thunder is confused with evacuation; the regurgitation of the host is preceded by regurgitation of meat; from the lesser clergy to the papal emissary, churchmen blaspheme with vigor. Like the sadistic taunts of Dante's Inferno, the dialogue of Ghelderode's *Chronicles of Hell* is at once sin and sentence.

Ghelderode establishes his inferno in the opening scene, when the lesser clergy eat, drink, and blaspheme in celebration of the death of Jan of Eremo, Bishop of Lapideopolis (city of stoning). Simon Laquedeem (judgment by the noose), nominally auxiliary bishop, is the power behind the Inferno, and, ironically, he utters blessings; however, "*He blesses as if he were boxing your ears*" (George Hauger translation). Upon the arrival of the papal emissary, and the ceremonial entrance into Jan's death chamber, the verbal venom suddenly gives way to Simon's (mockingly?) lyrical account of Jan's saintly life. Simon Laquedeem emphatically denies a rumor that he is guilty of Jan's death, but thunder and lightning undermine that denial. In the death chamber, Jan of Eremo rises from his death-bed. After a scene of confusion and terror, Simon and Jan, as Satan and saint, wrestle, "*and all of a sudden, the drama stands still in space.*" Slowly, Jan's mother approaches her bishop-son returned from the dead; she reaches down into his throat and removes a poisoned host, which has prevented him from dying. On the point of death Jan refuses to absolve his tormentor, and his mother slaps him to his last rest. Simon rewards her satanically, forcing her to swallow the poisoned host while her son dies. In the final scene, the drama returns to the macabre farce of the opening scene; the priests have "*filled their cassocks with dung,*" and Bishop Simon crouches for the physical catharsis of which he is morally incapable.

In this drama that Ghelderode called a "tragedy bouffe," Satanism and scatology create the Hell on earth. Sometimes close to Grand Guignol, the play suggests Artaud's dictum: "Everything that acts is a cruelty."

Were one to modify that statement to "Every*one* who acts is a cruelty," it could summarize *A Long Day's Journey into Night* by Eugene O'Neill, a playwright whose forms would have been anathema to Artaud. Clumsy with dialogue, O'Neill resorts to name-calling or abstraction in scenes of hostility between his characters. Even in plays like *Strange Interlude, Great God Brown,* and *Days Without End,* which verbalize characters' unspoken thoughts, the cruelty remains largely one of intention because of O'Neill's own inability to give his dialogue a cutting edge. In *Long Day's Journey,* however, wrenched from the agony of his own past, the language is unpretentious, and the four-act accumulation of reciprocal cruelties finally dissolves in compassion.

The four members of the Tyrone family accucse one another of lying, and each is filled with blame for the others. Mary blames her husband for his penury in robbing her of a home, for committing her to the care of cheap doctors who introduced her to morphine; she blames her son Jamie for his wasted life and his suspicion of her; she blames her son Edmund because his birth ruined her health so that she resorted to morphine to alleviate pain. James Tyrone blames his family for driving him toward the poor-house, he blames Jamie for not bringing credit to his name, and he blames Edmund for following in his brother's footsteps. Jamie blames Edmund for writing better than he did. Both sons blame their father for seeking bargains at the cost of their health and happiness, and all three men blame Mary for returning to dope. All members of the family voice their blame with cruelty.

In the climactic fourth act, when Mary upstairs retreats from reality like a "mad ghost," the mutual blame reaches a climax. James, who has been drinking throughout the day, is first joined by Edmund, who has just learned that he has tuberculosis. The son accuses the father's avarice more virulently than before, and, helped by the whiskey, the father blames and explains himself in an autobiographical revelation which moves Edmund to compassion. When Jamie arrives, even drunker than the other two, he too accuses his father, but like his father, he blames and explains himself to Edmund, warning him of his own destructive drive. At the last, the three men seem to have achieved a measure of peace through their exchange of cruelties. When Mary enters theatrically, with lights, music, and costume (carried), the play's last cruelty is uttered—Jamie's "The Mad Scene. Enter Ophelia!" Though both men turn on Jamie and Edmund slaps him, the anger of both changes to pity at Jamie's own sobbing. The three men listen as Mary voices her mad recollections—as girlish as those of Ophelia.

Written only three years after Long Day's Journey, Sartre's No Exit belongs to a different theatrical world and uses cruel dialogue in a radically different way. The mutual compassion in the O'Neill play had to be earned through mutual cruelties, whereas Sartre uses cruelty as Artaud would have wished, for metaphysical exploration. Artaud wrote, "Without an element of cruelty at the root of every spectacle, the theater is not possible. In our present state of degeneration it is through the skin that metaphysics must be made to re-enter our minds."[3] Though Artaud would not have approved of Sartre's discursive dialogue, Sartre also tries to shock the audience into metaphysical and ethical meditation. Eric Bentley's phrase for No Exit, "philosophic melodrama," might describe any Sartre play, and both philosophy and melodrama are conveyed largely through dialogue.

Sartre' second play, No Exit, is patterned on Strindberg's single act of rising tension.[4] Set in Hell, Sartre's work, like Dante's, reflects its metaphysics through its physical atmosphere. As in Dante's Inferno, too, similar sinners share the same infernal circle throughout eternity, and the punishment fits the sin. Having been torturers on earth, the three characters of No Exit are sentenced to be torturers after death. Torture is as basic to Sartre's Hell as it was to Dante's, but it is more insistently linguistic. Heated recrimination replaces fire and brimstone.

In the first scene of No Exit Garcin asks the Valet, "Where are the instruments of torture?" (Stuart Gilbert translation). When Inez first sees Garcin, she takes him for the torturer. When Estelle first see Garcin, she mistakes him for the man she has tortured on earth. All three reactions will be justified by the development of the action, for Garcin will become the torturer of Inez and Estelle, and he will be tortured by Estelle and Inez. No instruments of torture are visible because each person will be the instrument of torture for the two others. Garcin will finally realize, "There's no need for red-hot pokers, Hell is—other people." Sartre's Second Empire Hell consists of two "other people" for each of the three characters. Strindberg's Hell is usually peopled by a couple, but Sartre seeks wider reverberations with a triangle, whose corners are excruciatingly verbal.

Even before the dialogue starts, we see a Second Empire drawing-room; the furnishings reflect the period—inefficient, ugly, and imitative of the past. At first glance, Hell looks "homey," like other ugly, familiar rooms. Once Garcin begins to speak, however, we gradually discover the threats in the room—a massive bronze statue, a paper-cutter, no light-switch to control the anachronistic electricity; no window or mirror; no blinking and no sleep. After the Valet leaves, Garcin tries to ring for him—in vain. He tries to open the door—in vain. The vaguely familiar room has become his prison. By the time Inez is ushered in, we know that the everyday appearance of the setting is false, as we know that Garcin's apparent calm is false. By the time Estelle is ushered in, the menace of the room renders her social etiquette grotesque. When Estelle high-handedly tells the Valet, "You can go. I'll ring for you," we have already witnessed Garcin's frenzied, futile ringing for the Valet, and we suspect that no ringing will summon the Valet again—or anyone outside the trio, a literal eternal triangle.

Once they are together, we begin to learn about their lives on earth, which Sartre only gradually reveals in a long-drawn-out exposition that functions as a subplot, at once emphasizing and contrasting with the sadistic dialogue that becomes the main plot —their condition of damnation.

In the first round of exposition, the characters feel closer to earth than to one another. Each perfunctorily mentions the form death took; then Estelle describes her funeral, Garcin his wife and newspaper office, and Inez her room. An infernal interlude is filled with veiled barbs, but as yet Hell is only an interlude. Questions follow, which lead to explicit recollection in a second round of exposition. Gradually, Estelle confesses that she married for money, Garcin that he was shot for being a pacifist; but Inez, who reveals nothing intimate, accuses the others of acting: "For whom are you play-acting? We're among ourselves—among killers. We're in hell, my pets; they never make mistakes, and people aren't damned for nothing" (my literal translation). Mocking Estelle as a "little saint" and Garcin as a "flawless hero," Inez suddenly realizes that "each of us will act as torturer of the two others." Inez understands her damnation even as she begins to fulfill it by her taunting words to the others.

And yet, even she agrees to make the effort to circumvent damnation—they will retire silently to their separate Second Empire sofas. But silence is impossible for Estelle, who rejects the amorous advances of Inez to draw Garcin back into the triangle. This time he insists that they be completely honest, and he almost boasts that he has tortured his wife with mistresses; Inez swiftly outlines how she drove Florence to murder and suicide. But Estelle has to be stung by her fellow torturers into a confession of infanticide. Sartre counterpoints these revelations against the sadistic gibes which set the infernal tone.

One by one, in the final stage of exposition, each of the three looks his last on earth, and Sartre intersperses these farewells with an exchange of affronts. Inez, the only one to be honest in Hell, is most quickly forgotten on earth; she turns from her room that has been rented to strangers, accepting the Second Empire Hell, which grows hotter and hotter. Estelle more slowly turns from the earthly lover who is seduced by her best friend, to seek an infernal lover in Garcin. And the focus centers on Garcin.

The infernal triangle is not equiangular, for Garcin is at its apex. Garcin is first on stage, Garcin brings about the climax—the opening of the door[5]—Garcin utters the realization, "Hell is—other people," and Garcin closes the play. Although all three characters have been torturers in their private lives, Garcin has committed a public sin, desertion, and though he readily admits the torture of his wife, he cannot admit that his desertion was due to cowardice.

With the revelation of Garcin's fear of fear, the infernal pattern is established. In their Hell, Garcin will be Inez' torturer when he makes love to Estelle, who in turn will torture him by her inability to reassure him, or even to understand his doubts about his courage. Garcin will torture Estelle when he refuses to make love to her, and Inez will torture him since she refuses to lie about his cowardice. By their clashing sexual predilections, Inez and Estelle will torture each other. "Naked as worms" (my literal translation), each will squirm and cause the others to squirm, repetitively, eternally, with variations of verbal cruelty.

In the final moments of the play, all three inhabitants of Hell realize that they are dead. The long exposition has brought them full circle to the awareness with which they entered Hell, but that awareness has been deepened; they are dead, which means that nothing more can happen to them. The long exposition has shown us, the audience, that their lives are what might not have been, for they were always free, while alive, to act differently. With the full exposition of their lives as lived, however, they are irrevocably damned. They can do no more than torture each other forever. Their eternal triangle is inscribed in a vicious circle: the same temporary couples may attempt to extricate themselves— Man-Woman, Lesbian-Woman, Man-Fellowman—but they soon dissolve again into their sadistic norm. Garcin's final line, "Well, let's continue" (my literal translation) emphasizes that their Hell is without climax or catastrophe, and it is paved with vituperation.

Written a few years after *No Exit*, Genet's *Deathwatch* and *The Maids* also thrive on sadistic dialogue. Like Strindberg's plays, however, those of Genet end in catastrophe. Like *No Exit*, Genet's plays contain three main characters in a single action. Both Genet plays begin close to the catastrophe, with the final deaths suggested in the opening scenes: in *Deathwatch*, Green Eyes pulls Lefranc back from attacking Maurice; in *The Maids*, the alarm-clock rings before the maids can act out the death of Claire-Madame.

No Exit is set in a literal Hell that looks like a Second Empire drawing-room. In contrast, *Deathwatch* is set in a metaphoric Hell that is not reducible to a literal prison: *"the set and costumes . . . should be in violent colors"* (Bernard Frechtman translation). In *No Exit*, each character is allowed his separate entrance, and a minimal exposition, before the infernal dialogue begins. In *Deathwatch*, we are instantly plunged into the sadistic dialogue of the prison-inferno, and the exposition is virtually completed in the first few minutes of playing time. Green Eyes accuses his cell-mates: "You've been circling around me for a long time, circling around, circling around. . . ."

Circling in word and gesture, the three characters remain in their cell-inferno throughout the play, their sadistic dialogue turning on sex and crime.[6] The two subjects often merge, for the three characters are bound in an ambivalent, love-hate, homo-heterosexuality whose highest value is murder. To some extent, too, the characters of *Deathwatch* parallel those of *No Exit*: The heterosexual couple Garcin-Estelle and the homosexual couple Green Eyes-Maurice; the inauthenticity of Garcin and that of Lefranc.

Like *Huis Clos* (which corresponds to *in camera* in English law), the French title *Haute Surveillance* has judicial overtones; the term is used for the death-watch of someone condemned to the guillotine. But though Green Eyes, the only murderer among the three prisoners, refers to his coming execution, he has not yet been tried. Maurice, the youngest of the cell-mates, offers to kill Green Eyes' girl, which would make him a candidate for "haute surveillance," and Lefranc finally does kill Maurice on stage. When Green Eyes calls the Guard, Lefranc virtually begins his "haute surveillance." Thus, the title is relevant to all three prisoners.

In the opening lines, Green Eyes warns Lefranc, "Stop the big act." But Lefranc cannot stop acting; first he lies that he wrote to Green Eyes' girl exactly as the illiterate murderer dictated. Later, he admits to having crept into Green Eyes' skin in order to write the letters. During the course of the action, Lefranc puts on Green Eyes' exterior skin, his jacket. Lefranc lies that he has been a galley slave, pointing to his ankles and wrists as circumstantial evidence, even while he claims preposterously that he has been a slave for three hundred years. Although Lefranc attacks Maurice during the day, he gives him blankets and bread at night. Lefranc refuses tobacco during the day, only to steal it at night. To vie with Green Eyes' tattoo of his girl, Lefranc has inked an Avenger on his chest. Green Eyes and Lefranc engage in a litany of the celebrated criminals of the day, but Green Eyes knows them through having associated with them, Lefranc through newspaper clippings that he hides in his mattress. Shortly before he is killed, Maurice taunts Lefranc, "Your frankness is phoney." To make it less phoney, to justify his lies, to realize his verbal cruelty, Lefranc resorts to murder. This time, when Lefranc attacks Maurice, Green Eyes does not interfere. Aloof on a basin, Green Eyes watches Lefranc kill Maurice. Sneering at the deed that terminates their mutual recriminations, Green Eyes informs Lefranc that even his murder is a lie: "You cheat to get here." Whereas Green Eyes had murdered intuitively, without premeditation, Lefranc has acted consciously, and this is "cheating." In sharp contrast to Garcin's realization that "Hell is—other people," Lefranc discovers that his Hell is solitude. He closes the drama with the line, "I really am all alone!" Crime brings no communion.

More ambiguously, in Genet's next play *The Maids*, imitation crime does bring about the communion of criminal and saint. The maids' ceremony-game is a three-step ritual: 1) adoration of the opulent beauty of the mistress, 2) blasphemy against the privileged position of the mistress, and 3) imitation murder of the mistress. Although the two maids, Claire and Solange, have often performed the ceremony, each maid taking her turn as mistress, they have never reached step three, the imitation murder through which they seek to define their identity, as Lefranc sought his in the murder of Maurice.

In his study of Genet, Sartre pointed out the parallels between *Deathwatch* and *The Maids*—the same hierarchy of crime with off-stage criminals at the top (Snowball and Monsieur), "intermediate divinities" (Green Eyes and Madame), and worshipers at the bottom (Maurice and Lefranc, Solange and Claire). Even the names Lefranc—the frank one—and Claire—clear—are similar and similarly ironic. A love-hate, homo-heterosexual relationship links the three characters of each play, who are differentiated from the off-stage divinities; in *Deathwatch* by race, in *The Maids* by sex. One-act dramas of mounting tension, each play opens with an imitation of death, and each play closes with an actual death. But though the structure of the two plays is similar, the texture is quite different in spite of the basis in verbal cruelty. The jeers and sneers of *Deathwatch* lack the tough tenderness of the dialogue of *The Maids*, with its emotional complexities.

In the opening scene, Claire-playing-Madame commands Solange-playing-Claire to remove her rubber gloves, symbol of servility; as Claire-Madame verbally torments Solange-Claire, the latter moulds her gloved hands into fan and bouquet—objects as luxuriously feminine as the lace and flowers strewn through the Louis XV bedroom. But rubber gloves and fan-bouquets are part of the same world—Madame's world and the maids' world, in which maids are possessions of their mistress. (The contrast is striking between the milieu of Genet's play and that of the bourgeois Lancelin family murdered by the Papin sisters, which was Genet's point of departure.) In a pun that cannot be translated, Solange summarizes their frustration: "Mais être bonne quand on est bonne!" (But how be good when one is a maid!) Through their social condition, the maids must define their human condition. Thus, their ceremony-ritual is a quest for transcendent goodness-sainthood through maidhood. Very differently from Dante, they too seek a Paradiso through the Inferno of their impassioned diatribes.

Though they speak in different tones, mistress and maids speak the same language; they have similar reactions to Monsieur's imprisonment—romantic visions of self-sacrifice and indifference about his guilt. The maids strew Madame's bedroom with hot-house flowers, their own garret with paper flowers. All three women play roles; they are fascinated by costumes and props. Solange and Madame both wonder whether Madame shouldn't wear mourning for Monsieur. Madame gives Claire the very same red gown that Solange has forced her sister to wear during the "ceremony." Madame rearranges her hair according to Claire's suggestion. Using identical words Solange urges Claire and Madame to be calm, to rest. Claire's use of the mirror in her "ceremony" is reflected in Madame's rehearsal before *her* mirror, of a face with which to greet Monsieur. And finally, when Claire-Madame drinks the poisoned tea, she can only repeat Madame's words when Madame refuses the tea: "And you've poured it into the best, the finest tea set."

As Sartre perceptively points out, the sadistic mistress played by Claire does not resemble the self-centered, yet solicitous mistress whom we see on stage; Sartre claims, "We do not know whether this distorted caricature tends to reveal the mistress in her true light, to expose the truth of that indifferent good-nature which may be concealing a pitiless cruelty, or whether it already wreaks an imaginary vengeance by metamorphosizing Madame, by the incantation of the gesture, into a harpy" (Bernard Frechtman translation).[7] "We do not know," and yet, by the time Madame makes a long delayed entrance on stage, we suspect that the maids' ceremony is at once a form of vengeance for their servile condition and a transubstantiation from that condition.

Madame has no name; she is her title. Her personality and possessions reflect one another, and it is through her possessions that her presence dominates the maids, even when she is physically absent from the stage. The maids talk about Madame, who is all privilege and cruelty. In *Deathwatch* Green Eyes saw the world as a hierarchy of criminals—himself above Maurice and Lefranc, Snowball above him, and "a Number One Big Shot. . . for the whole world!" In *The Maids* Claire-Madame declares that she is the Virgin Mary; the real Madame addresses the maids as her children, though she is younger than they, and, like a harassed mother, she occasionally confuses the two sisters.

As sisters, as impersonators of Madame and of one another, Claire and Solange are more closely tied than are Lefranc and Maurice in *Deathwatch*. But Claire and Lefranc seem moulded on the same form. An actress, as Lefranc is a liar, Claire bears an ironic name; yet Claire *is* clear-headed, as Lefranc is frank in his verbal cruelty. Like Lefranc, Claire writes letters; like him, she is an Avenger, boasting that she has planned the vengeance of the maids; like Lefranc, Claire is at once more practical and more extravagant than her cell-mate. Above all, Claire resembles Lefranc in perpetrating death on stage; his is murder, hers at once suicide and murder. She commands her own death, leaving Solange the only angel (*seul ange*) in the Inferno.

In the ceremony-game, when one of the sisters lapses back into reality, the other guides her with gibes into their sado-masochistic inferno. So, at the end of the drama, when Solange fails to poison Madame, Claire assumes the voice of Madame, and gives the directions that will result in the death of Claire-Madame, the death that they were previously unable even to play-act. This time, they will skip the preliminaries; there will be no adoration of beauty, no blasphemy in servility; they will repeat their ceremony, starting so close to the catasprophe that neither alarm-clock nor telephone can interrupt them.

After their crescendos of verbal violence, the cold formality of the final scene is all the more horrifying. Maid Claire-Solange is ordered to bring the tea; she protests that the tea is cold; magnanimously, Mistress-Claire says that she will drink it anyway. She sips the poisoned tea from the best tea-cup, while Claire-Solange faces the audience, hands crossed as though in handcuffs.[8] Very visibly, Claire-Solange is the criminal and Madame-Claire the saintly martyr. But since Madame-Claire has commanded the murder, she shares the crime, and thereby shares her martyrdom too with Claire-Solange. The sisters' embodiment of the criminal-saint couple, inseparable for Genet, is both individual and collective. The interpenetration of roles is sustained through the sadistic duologues to the final apotheosis.

In these dramas Sartre and Genet illustrate two possible conclusions for the one-act play whose cruel dialogue mounts in intensity: 1) the repetitive circularity of *No Exit* and 2) the abrupt catastrophe of *The Maids* and *Deathwatch*. Sartre was to shift to dramas of more linear action, in which cruel dialogue furthers the plot logically and psychologically; Genet, on the other hand, turned to a circular structure in *The Balcony* and *The Blacks*, where verbal cruelty is incorporated into the stage fiction of a performance.

Eugène Ionesco has admitted that *No Exit* is the only Sartre play he likes, and it may be that the sadistic dialogue influenced his own quite different dialogue of cruelty. Ionesco, as is well known, wrote *The Bald Soprano* through the catalyst of the Assimil method of learning English. The inanities of a language primer inspired the commonplaces, formulas, gibberish of Ionesco's first play, inhabited as it is by comic characters who speak in ready-made phrases. Though these characters rarely engage deliberately in mordant exchanges, their mechanical language strikes cruelly at an audience sensitive to devitalization. And it is this audience which is bludgeoned by Ionesco, with language that pulverizes feeling. Ionesco manipulates clichés not only to satirize the bourgeoisie but to reveal the emptiness of most verbal communication.

In *The Bald Soprano* two different couples take part in dialogues of non-communication; the Smiths reduce all people to Bobby Watson, while the Martins need circumstantial evidence to prove that they are married. But the non-substance of their dialogue tells us, the audience, that these "comic characters. . .do not exist," in Ionesco's own description. From the separate non-existence of the two couples, Ionesco moves to the non-existence of the social group. In the final scene, the automaton-characters keep repeating, "It's not that way, it's over here, it's not that way, it's over here." The concealed and undiscoverable "it" is the individual self that the comic characters have lost in their mechanically cacophonous inferno. As Richard Schechner has perceived, *The Bald Soprano* finally explodes into its theme of nothingness.[9] Thus Ionesco departs from the drama of lucid verbal cruelty, but he nevertheless uses it as a springboard. Hurlers of cliché, his characters are invulnerable to their own decimation of language, but he means *us* to be vulnerable to such verbal opacity, and it is to *us* that the tragedy of the farce is revealed through pulverization of language—what Herbert Blau has called "the virtuosity of vacancy."[10]

Ionesco has been candid about his difficulty in finding an ending for his first play. His decision to close *The Bald Soprano* on a repetition of the opening scene emphasizes the "tragedy of language"; the further decision to substitute the Martins for the Smiths (sometimes dressed alike in production) emphasizes the tragedy of farcical characters, who are expendable or replaceable because of their lack of identity. As Serge Doubrovsky aptly summarized, "Instead of men using language to think, we have language thinking for men."[11]

Ionesco's second play, labeled a "comic drama" though it ends in death, is a more violent critique of language which thinks for, even acts for man. Like *The Bald Soprano, The Lesson* is a one-act play, whose tension mounts through its cruel dialogue, but the cruelty is directed toward the pupil in the play, as well as outward toward the audience. *The Lesson* exhibits the eroto-sadism of a Strindberg play; however, the pupil-teacher couple is less evenly matched than Strindberg's couples, and the pupil's language disintegrates under the onslaught of the professor, even before he kills her. After the event, the maid discloses that this is the professor's fortieth murder, and the play ends with the entrance of Pupil #41.

Though Ionesco satirizes the bourgeois couple in several plays, he is particularly insidious in his first full-length play *Amédée or How To Get Rid of It*. For all his misogyny, Strindberg equipped his men and women with comparably sharp verbal weapons. In Ionesco's marriages, on the other hand, the women tend to be more abrasive, the men more pliable. This is evident even in so young a man as Jack in *Jack or the Submission*. Choubert collapses under the combined attack of the Police-Inspector and his wife Madeleine in *Victims of Duty*. Significantly, Amédée's wife is also named Madeleine in *Amédée or How To Get Rid of It*.

The first act presents the situation, with its metaphor of a growing corpse. There is very little rising action, but much rising passion in the asperities exchanged by Amédée and Madeleine. Because Madeleine is sharper, victim Amédée arouses sympathy, while the enoromus feet of the ever-growing corpse slide into the stage-room.

Act II is specifically concerned with how to get rid of the corpse, and yet mutual chiding keeps interrupting the plans of the couple. In a flashback that serves as exposition, we see a loving Amédée and virago Madeleine of fifteen years earlier, so that Ionesco unmistakably blames the wife for the dying marriage. Even at this late date, Amédée suggests, "Do you know, Madeleine, if we loved each other, if we really loved each other, none of this would be important. . . . Love makes up for everything" (Donald Watson translation). To which his wife replies, "I can't see love getting rid of this dead body." The couple is united only in their common wish to get rid of the corpse late at night, while the neighbors cannot see what they are doing.

In Act III, the scene shifts to the street, and the play is resolved in diffusion as the corpse is drowned, Amédée floats into the air, and Madeleine is left alone to mourn, having gotten rid of her husband with the corpse. Despite this rather fanciful happy end, the play's texture is mired in cruel metaphor and dialogue. Nor does Ionesco suggest, as does Strindberg in his last plays, that trancendent bliss is the reward of suffering through earthly cruelty.

Somewhat differently from Strindberg, Albee's first play drives toward a transcendence earned through earthly cruelty. In *Zoo Story*, Jerry delineates his pedagogic method: "Neither kindness nor cruelty by themselves, independent of each other, creates any effect beyond themselves . . . the two combined, together, at the same time, are the teaching emotion." Jerry and Peter, teacher and pupil, are not evenly matched and when Jerry's gibes fail to arouse Peter, the "permanent transient" resorts to physical violence—slapping, punching, pulling a knife. Cruelly goaded, Peter takes up the knife, upon which Jerry impales himself. Through the suicide-murder, Jerry seems to attain transcendence, or at least fulfillment: "Peter. . .thank you. I came unto you (*He laughs, so faintly*) and you have comforted me. Dear Peter." Accompanied by Peter's repetitions of "O my God," Jerry dies, comforted through his cruel pedagogy of Peter.

Albee's cruelest dialogue is contained in *Who's Afraid of Virginia Woolf?*, and in that play, too, the implication is that vituperative pedagogy leads to a kind of peace, an "exorcism." Though there are four characters in the play, scene after scene is built on eroto-sadistic dialogues à la Strindberg. Albee splits Strindberg's basic couple into two couples, but only George and Martha engage in "brain battles." Albee divides Strindberg's act of rising tension into three: Fun and Games, Walpurgisnacht, and Exorcism. Albee Americanizes the accusative dialogue, and its cruelties are the wittiest ever heard on the American stage.

George and Martha begin the play, and they end the play, alone on stage. Martha's cruelties are the first to be heard; before the other couple arrives, she calls George a cluck, Georgie-Porgie, put-upon pie, a pig, a blank, a cipher, a zero, and she informs him that he makes her want to puke. As she welcomes her guests, Martha calls George a sourpuss and a muckmouth, inspiring his comment, "Martha's a devil with language."

George's first cruelties are directed at Nick, mocking his conventional admiration of their painting, but George quickly twists this against Martha, "It's a pictorial representation of the order of Martha's mind." George goes on to a mock-lyrical account of Martha's development in drinking taste, concluding, "But the years have brought to Martha a sense of essentials . . . the knowledge that cream is for coffee, lime juice for pies. . . and alcohol (*Brings Martha her drink*) pure and simple. . . here you are, angel. . . for the pure and simple." This illustrates, too, how effectively George uses repetition in his insults. Often, mere repetition of a phrase makes a fool of the originator of that phrase.

By the middle of the first act, the mutual sneers and jeers of George and Martha have delineated a prototypical American couple, named, suitably, for our first White House couple— George, the failure in a success-oriented society, and Martha, the philanderer in a sex-oriented society. Toward the end of the act, their mutual mutilations concentrate on those two subjects, and George begins to emerge as the more able marksman, even though he designates their activities as "Humiliate the Host."

The Act II Walpurgisnacht begins with a George-Nick duologue and ends with a George-Honey duologue, during which George scatters incidental cruelties, but he rises to his full measure of cruelty only in Martha's presence. Husband and wife take sado-masochistic pleasure in their reciprocal "flagellation." They "both seem relieved. . .elated" as they declare "total war" on one another, with the telling weapon of their words.

The Act III Exorcism begins with Martha slashing cruelly at "houseboy" Nick. Soon George enters with snapdragons from the garden, in triumphant form to "play this one to the death." He has sharpened his wit to a scalpel, with which he cuts away Martha's most cherished possession—their imaginary son. George kills his son as he had killed his parents, with "a tiny chuckle." When Martha refuses to accept the death, he reiterates callously: "We got a telegram; there was a car accident, and he's dead. POUF! Just like that! Now, how do you like it?"

As he realizes how intensely Martha does not like it, however, George seems to experience some compassion for her. He announces the end of the party, and there are no more cruelties after the departure of Nick and Honey. The act's title "Exorcism" implies that cruelty has died with the imaginary child—evil spirits have been driven out. For the theater audience, however, it is difficult to imagine a purified George and Martha. Without their potential for witty cruelty, they are virtual amputees.

Samuel Beckett, Albee's mentor, does not hesitate to put real amputees on stage. And if their cruelties are less consistent than those of George and Martha, neither do they experience an optimistic exorcism. Assuming that life is a joke, Beckett's ebbing characters tell that joke, play that joke, torturing themselves and each other with its stale repetition. As aware of their insignificance as Ionesco's characters were unaware of theirs, Beckett's characters sometimes seek meaning through their cruelty to one another and to themselves. But to different degrees. Thus, the name-calling sequence of Gogo and Didi in *Waiting for Godot* is only one of their ways of passing time while waiting:

> VLADIMIR: Ceremonious ape!
> ESTRAGON: Punctilious pig!
> VLADIMIR: Finish your phrase, I tell you!
> ESTRAGON: Finish your own! *Silence. They draw closer, halt.*
> VLADIMIR: Moron!
> ESTRAGON: That's the idea, let's abuse each other.

This is fliting, a scolding-match as a game and not as a revelation of truth, either to character or audience.

In *Endgame*, the mutual recriminations are pervasive and insidious. An ambiguous antagonism is evident from the early dialogue of Hamm and Clov, revealing their cruelty and that of their situation:

> HAMM: I'll give you nothing more to eat.
> CLOV: Then we'll die.
> HAMM: I'll give you just enough to keep you from dying. You'll be hungry all the time.
> CLOV: Then we won't die.

Hamm is "shocked" that he might not have made Clov suffer too much, "relieved" when Clov assures him that he is suffering. Hamm and Nagg abuse each other; Nagg and Nell still engage in half-hearted bickering. But most of the dialogue consists of the vindictive exchange of Hamm and Clov. Though Beckett rarely explodes into the violence of Ionesco, Albee, or Genet, he can be as merciless as the single word "Corpsed." And yet, in the Clov-Hamm relationship, as in Hamm's chronicle, cruelty is a path to compassion. "Perhaps it's compassion," suggests Hamm, as the reason for Clov's obedience, "A kind of great compassion." Hamm and Clov burst into anger, deny that they feel pity; and yet an awareness of compassion threads through their dialogue, and that awareness is in turn transmitted to us.

Compassion is less evident in *Play*, where each of the three characters is convinced of his own solitude. Dead, bodiless, toneless, and each alone, the three nameless characters can express no direct animosity, as even Winnie is still able to muster in *Happy Days*. And yet, the three monologues of *Play*, begun in simultaneity, interweave cruelty and compassion. In contrast to the chaotic *closing* of *The Bald Soprano*, Beckett's torture of audience *opens* his *Play*. His trio describe their particular variant of the marital triangle, as a harsh white light falls on them. By the rules of this endgame, darkness is silence, and light is language. The play begins in verbal togetherness as the light shines on the three at once, and the result is rhythmed cacophony, cruel to a listening audience.

Almost as soon as the separate monologues are comprehensible, each of the three characters utters the verb he cannot enact: *give*.

> w1: I said to him, give her up.
> w2: Give him up, she screamed; he's mine.
> M: Give up that whore, she said, or I'll cut my throat.

Shortly afterward, the two women suppress their mutual antagonism:

> w2: Seeing her now for the first time full length in the flesh I understood why he preferred me.

and

> w1: Just a common tart.

Both women have the same suspicion that money lures the man:

> w1: She had means, I fancy, though she lived like a pig.
> w2: I sometimes wondered if he was not living with her for her money.

Though the man is "assiduous" in making love to both of them, he tortures them subtly. Though he swears to each of them that he cannot live without her, he confesses his adultery to his wife, and he complains about his wife to his mistress. He generalizes, "God what vermin women."

When they speak separately, their solitude is highlighted by the disjunction between remarks, and yet the total dialogue reveals the lovers' triangle, as each woman blames the man, then forgives and reclaims him. Their round of recollection (each character in a lone limbo) recalls the rounds of cruel dialogue in Sartre's *No Exit*. But Beckett barely sketches his harangues, usually *à deux*—two women, man and wife, man and mistress. In the story whose fragments they evoke, the man disappears, and we never learn how the trio arrived in their present state, where none of the three knows that the other is present. Hell is no longer other people, but solitude in an urn, delineated through a dialogue that works cruelly on audience nerves.

Midway through the play as printed, the light dims to half strength, the "voices proportionately lower," and the second half of the play treats a present in which each of the three characters tries to understand his life. The first half of *Play* is imitation of an action, and the second is interpretation of that action. Since none of them knows the others are dead, each imagines conversations of the other two, in which the absent member is the subject. As Sartre's trio grew more detached from the earth, to engage more intensely in an eternity of verbal torture, so Beckett's trio grows more detached from life, to be more directly and individually tortured by the half-light—"Hellish half light" as W1 calls it. She speaks of mercy and truth, of penitence and atonement— sentiments traditionally associated with Purgatory. The man, however, can ask for pardon only when he hiccups, so that perhaps his Purgatory is an eternity of hiccups. The second woman desires only darkness. Toward the end of *Play*, each of the women addresses the half-light in angry words, which she might have used to the man:

> w1: Get off me!
> w2: Go away and start poking and pecking at someone else.

The mistress wonders if she is being pitied, just as she now pities the man and his wife; the wife, too, arrives at compassion: "Poor creature. Poor creatures." The man has a fantasy of the three of them together in a dinghy. Even more deviously than in *Endgame*, the unwittingly cruel dialogue adds up to a "kind of great compassion," for the audience hears the rancor dim, with the light.

Since the play is played through twice, the elusive nuances may be perceived only on the second performance—if then. The double alternation of full light and half light suggests that the future may bring darkness, oblivion, and peace. There is a faint promise of this in the last words of the man: "We were not long together—." On the other hand, the words may be a prelude, as in the past, to still another round of monologue, to an eternity of monologue, which the audience blends into a cruel dialogue. Thus, Beckett's *Play* modifies the sadistic scene; his matched opponents do not know that they are battling one another, but their monologues are blended by the audience into the cruelty of their condition.

Admittedly influenced by Beckett, Harold Pinter modifies the scene of rising intensity by concealing cruelty beneath surface banalities, until it bursts out suddenly. In *The Room* and *The Dumb Waiter*, the victims, Rose and Gus, converse in banalities that cloak fear and hostility. *The Dumb Waiter* is probably Pinter's purest example of catastrophe erupting from conversation of mounting hostility, though the play opens with a long scene of comic pantomime. When Gus goes off stage, we hear the lavatory chain being forcefully pulled, but the toilet does not flush. When Gus re-enters the room, Ben reads aloud from a newspaper, and Gus reacts with clichés: "Go on!" "Get away." "It's unbelievable." "Incredible." As Ben continues to read, Gus complains about the room in which they are waiting to do a job—the toilet tank fills too slowly, there are no windows, the bed-linen is dirty, there should have been another blanket. Gus questions an unresponsive Ben. During the brief play, Gus asks many questions, but his most insidious and insistent line is about the questions he *meant* to ask.

As Ben continues to read sensational items from the newspaper, and Gus to complain of their surroundings, the tension rises. Through questions, quarrels, and a mysterious envelope slipped under the door, tempers flare in the windowless room. Close upon the discovery of matches in the envelope, we see the revolvers that make the pair as menacing as they are menaced. When Gus and Ben argue fiercely about whether to say "light the kettle" or "light the gas," we know that the linguistic dispute cloaks deep antagonism.

By the middle of the play, Pinter has built a symbolic world upon his realistic foundation; the dumbwaiter of the set begins to function like a mock-oracle, as exotic food commands rattle down into the basement room. Humble mortals that they are, Ben and Gus offer their laughably meagre supplies in ritualistic sacrifice. The powers above settle their language dispute, but "light the kettle" or "light the gas," Ben and Gus can have no tea since they have no shilling for the gas-meter. Gus asks pointedly, "Why did he send us matches if he knew there was no gas?" The routine rehearsal for their "job" sparks a series of questions from Gus. No longer a dumb waiter, he screams into the speaking-tube, "WE'VE GOT NOTHING LEFT! NOTHING! DO YOU UNDERSTAND?" It is evident that "NOTHING" refers to all their resources—material and spiritual.

In the last few minutes as in the first few minutes of the play, their overt hostility subsides. Ben lies down with the newspaper. Though he does not read aloud this time, the two men exchange the same cliché comments as in the opening scene, but those of Gus sound "dully," "very low," and, finally, "Almost inaudible." The antagonistic duologue is reduced to Ben's monologue. While Gus goes off stage, Ben receives the order to do his job. An unarmed, disheveled Gus enters the room through a different door; he and Ben "stare at each other," and the curtain falls. Presumably, Gus will be destroyed because he has questioned the clichés by which he lived; he refuses to continue as a dumb waiter. Seemingly harmless banalities prove to be full of harm.

Like Gus, the victims in *The Birthday Party*, *The Caretaker*, and *The Dwarfs* try to fight the good verbal fight; each of these plays, however, contains a professionally sadistic couple who riddle their victims with the clichés of our civilization: Goldberg and McCann of *The Birthday Party* sound like a parody minstrel show of the Judaeo-Christian tradition; Aston and Mick of *The Caretaker* are rarely together on stage, but they separately offer Davies the temptation of caretaking, Mick using the hard sell and Aston more bumbling; their different styles produce the same result—a cruel deafness to Davies' pleas. Pete and Mark of *The Dwarfs* are in subtle accord with the titular dwarfs, and these threatening figures are vitriolically opposed to one another as well. All three pairs converge upon their victims in dialogues of crisp cruelty.

Pinter shifts to sexual cruelty in *A Slight Ache*, *The Collection*, and *The Lover*, and his dramatic building block continues to be the duologue which is a verbal duel. Sex is at the center of *The Homecoming* as well, but the dialogue of cruelty is shared by a father, three sons, and the wife of one son—in several permutations and combinations. The titular homecoming occurs midway during the first of two acts; back home to London come Teddy and his wife Ruth. Before the appearance of the couple, however, Pinter establishes the jungle atmosphere of this home, mainly through venemous duologues between father and son (Max and Lenny, names already used by Pinter in other plays).

> LENNY: Plug it, will you, you stupid sod, I'm trying to read
> the paper.
> MAX: Listen! I'll chop your spine off, you talk to me
> like that!

Max also talks "like that" to his brother Sam, who, however, lacks Lenny's verbal dexterity. After a blackout, Teddy and Ruth come home.

The conversation of Teddy and Ruth is quite gentle, as is a first exchange between the brothers, Teddy and Lenny, who meet while Ruth is out. When Teddy goes up to bed, Lenny discovers Ruth and indulges in a menacing monologue of non sequiturs, climaxed by his accusation to Ruth: "Then you come here without a word of warning and start to make trouble." Trouble is what Ruth does start to make, arousing Lenny with "some kind of proposal," seducing Joey without satisfying him, inspiring Max's "tart," "slut," "scrubber," "whore," "disease."

Early in the play, the repetitive family pattern is mordantly summarized by Max, "One lot after another. One mess after the other. . . . One cast-iron bunch of crap after another. One flow of stinking pus after another." By the end of the play, a new family home has been formed. Teddy returns to America, Sam lies inert on the floor—perhaps dead. Lenny, a pimp, watches Ruth caressing Joey's head in her lap, while Max crawls toward her, protesting that he is not old, begging for a kiss. Through the vitriolic exchanges, mainly in scenes *à deux*, Pinter reveals that the final family harmony is a travesty of a home.

Kelly Morris has suggested that the title refers to a "veritable household orgasm" in the last scene.[12] But there is no orgasm; no one "comes"; the home is grotesquely re-formed, but the coming may never come. Recalling biblical Ruth, who was faithful to her mother-in-law, Pinter's Ruth takes the place of her mother-in-law in the home. She will serve all men but her husband, mothering them, loving them, and selling her love to maintain them.

Like Pinter's drama, the plays of Fernando Arrabal are often built on cruel duologues. In sharp contrast to the sophisticates of Pinter's later plays, however, Arrabal's characters act like children in an adult world. Tenderly, they torture and murder. Their crimes arise from no rational motive, and they give sadistic pleasure. Thus, in *Orison* Fidio and Lilbe, having killed their child, make an effort "to be good," but find it dull. In *Fando and Lys*, Fando tortures Lys to death, with occasional anger but pervasive tenderness. In *The Bicycle of the Condemned Man* Voloro and Tasla throw kisses to one another whenever a caged Paso is whipped. In *The Tricycle* Climando, Apal, and Mita plan with verve to kill a man for his money. In *The Two Executioners*, a mother and son talk of their love of husband and father, but we hear him screaming as he is tortured to death. The several characters heap cruelties on the Christlike Emmanou of *The Automobile Graveyard*. And one could go on. Each Arrabal play pivots on at least one cruelty, characterized by its own distinctive details.

In Arrabal's longer plays of the 1960's, the cruelties are dramatized more minutely and repetitively, taking on a ritual quality as indicated by the very titles *The Coronation* and *The Great Ceremony*. In the first play, Giafar, in love with Sylda, knocks at the door of her room, enters it, and finds her lying dead on her bed. Resurrecting her with a kiss, he is chained to the room, where he is subject to the verbal cruelties of Sylda herself, of a male couple, of Sylda's parents, and of a woman named Arlys, who proves to be Sylda in disguise. But the cruelties are interspersed with, and sometimes indistinguishable from games, and all the incidents tremble on the brink of dreams. The titular coronation takes place twice; two-thirds of the way through the play Sylda is crowned, and after her death, at the end, Giafar undergoes the same coronation rite. Finally, the play returns to its beginning—Sylda lying dead on her bed, and Giafar knocking at the door of her room.

In *The Great Ceremony* there is at once more cruelty and more tenderness. The hunch-backed protagonist, Cavanosa, is an anagram of Casanova; conscious of his deformation, Cavanosa cruelly repulses the beautiful Sil when she accosts him on a park bench, but agrees to signal her from his room. In his room, Cavanosa and his mother exchange cruelties interlaced with tenderness and concern. When his mother leaves, he signals Sil to come up, and he woos her with sadism—forcing her into a baby-carriage, showing her life-size dolls he has tortured, and almost strangling her. Sil's lover comes to her rescue, but under Cavanosa's orders, Sil chains and whips the lover, who flees when liberated. Sil begs to be tortured, to become the slave of Cavanosa's mother, and her request is granted. Returning to his park bench, Cavanosa meets Lys, still so young that she wears pigtails, but she pleads, as Sil did, for Cavanosa's love. Answering her cruelly at first, Cavanosa puts her into his baby-carriage, murmuring, "Your eyes are ardent for mine, your hands burn for mine, your back of pearl awaits my rods, and your voice is in mourning for your death." His "great ceremony" is to woo a woman through cruelty so that she becomes a slave to his mother, who then murders her. The police remove the corpse, and the ceremony begins again.

More spare, more intense, and much more theatrical than these two plays, Arrabal's *The Architect and the Emperor of Assyria* introduces cruelty within a dazzling spectrum of varied activities. Alone on a desert island, the Architect and the Emperor engage in a swift and imaginative series of games during which they fling insults at each other as adroitly and indiscriminately as endearments. Each is more cruel alone than in the company of the other. Thus, the Emperor plays a Carmelite confessor who speaks brutally to a pregnant nun, whose role he also plays. While the Emperor is alive, the Architect never quite measures up to his teacher in cruel finesse, but after his death, cruelty is one of the characteristics by which we recognize that the Architect *becomes* the Emperor. Though *The Architect and the Emperor of Assyria* is far more fantastic than *Who's Afraid of Virginia Woolf?*, there is an important resemblance in the manipulation of death: George kills his perhaps imaginary parents and his surely imaginary son in precisely the same kind of automobile accident; the Emperor confesses to having killed his mother and orders the Architect to kill him with precisely the same hammer-blow on the head. The Emperor also orders that the Architect devour him after death, and the Architect's soliloquy during this extraordinary meal is cruelly grotesque—perhaps the most cruelly grotesque ever heard on the stage.

More than two decades after Artaud's death (in 1948), and despite his impact, Western theater still lacks a Theater of Cruelty as he envisioned it—a cathartic and subliminal theater which would involve the spectator through his viscera rather than his mind. Though the Polish Laboratory Theater appears to fulfill such demands, contemporary Western drama has developed a dialogue of cruelty which appeals to the emotional intelligence. Unlike the horrors of Grand Guignol, this verbal cruelty is not gratuitous but functions toward revelation, and Strindberg was the great instructor in its use. In single plays, *Long Day's Journey* and *In the Jungle of Cities*, Eugene O'Neill and Bertolt Brecht wielded verbal weapons, the one to evoke compassion, the other to insist upon the metaphysical meaning of conflict. In many plays Ghelderode depicts a damnation that his characters live but do not understand. Sartre's characters in *No Exit* seek to understand their damnation, and through them we discover Sartre's definition of death as the domain in which identity is fixed forever, as in Mallarmé's famous line about Edgar Allen Poe: "Tel qu'en lui-même enfin l'éternité le change." (Eternity finally changes him into himself.) The line is valid too for Genet's criminals, whose cruelties drive them toward the death that defines them. Ionesco's characters, by contrast, are too farcical even to seek self-definition, but their verbal hysteria defines them cruelly for us. Beckett's characters elude their and our definition; cruelty is part of the idiom by which they enact their and our condition, which elicits a subtly interfused compassion. Though Pinter and Albee also try to generalize the human condition, their dialogue of cruelty has a highly national flavor. Pinter tends to begin in triviality, then allow the mounting cruelties to drive to catastrophe. Albee starts explosively but attempts to arrive at some resolution through the cruelty. Until Arrabal's latest play, he has hammered verbal cruelties more repetitively through his drama than any playwright since Ghelderode, and such cruelty is interwoven with tenderness, re-enforced by physical torture.

Apparently ignorant of Artaud's gnostic intention in a Theater of Cruelty that de-emphasizes language, Western playwrights have used *dialogue* of cruelty to shock us into an awareness of ourselves, paring away our habits and defenses. As Dante meant his readers to see their own danger in *The Inferno*, modern playwrights mean us to hear our own cruelty in the dialogue of their characters. "You're on earth, there's no cure for that," says Beckett's Hamm in *Endgame*. And since there is no cure as long as we are alive, modern dramatists have rubbed our noses, or, more accurately, our ears in the dirt, ground exceedingly fine.

THREE: The Hero and His People

IN CONTRAST TO THE CROSS-NATIONALISM OF DIALOGUES OF CRU-
ELTY IN THE MODERN THEATER, HEROISM TENDS TO HAVE A
national resonance. This is in keeping with traditional views of
the mythic hero as savior of *his* people. The hero's composite
portrait has been drawn by Joseph Campbell:

> The mythological hero, setting forth from his common-
> day hut or castle, is lured, carried away, or else voluntarily
> proceeds, to the threshold of adventure. . . . Beyond the
> threshold, then, the hero journeys through a world of un-
> familiar yet strangely intimate forces, some of which se-
> verely threaten him (tests), some of which give magical
> aid (helpers). When he arrives at the nadir of the mytho-
> logical round, he undergoes a supreme ordeal and gains his
> reward. . . . The final work is that of the return. If the
> powers have blessed the hero, he now sets forth under their
> protection (emissary); if not, he flees and is pursued
> (transformation flight, obstacle flight). At the return
> threshold the transcendental powers must remain behind;
> the hero re-emerges from the kingdom of dread. . . . The
> boon that he brings restores the world.[1]

Even if the mythological hero does not emerge from a metaphoric kingdom of dread, his trials serve to reaffirm a moral order,

and that is the boon he brings his people. Epic, tragedy, and romance are woven around such mythic heroes—Achilles, Oedipus, Galahad, for example—and a modern writer who deals with legendary or historical figures must deal with their heroic myths, if only to diminish them.

Diminishing heroes begins as early as Euripides, but it does not become widespread until the twentieth century, when aggrandizement of the Common Man is paralleled by reduction of the hero. Nor, in drama, should a mere protagonist be confused with a hero, whose actions affect the welfare of his people. A sense of *noblesse oblige* is lacking in the comic hero who thrives on fantasy, the middle-class protagonist of sentimental drama, the archsufferer of Romantic drama, the *raisonneur* of the well-made play, and the oppressed victim of the naturalistic play. None of these dramatic protagonists is a mythic hero whose deeds can mould a people's destiny. But even in our age of the Common Man, mythic heroes fascinated certain dramatists before World War II —Bernard Shaw, Eugene O'Neill, Jean Giraudoux, who marked their heroes with their own temperaments. And World War II itself suddenly endowed heroism with immediate relevance. Paradoxically, some modern playwrights returned to the Greeks so as to view their own time.

MODERN GREEKS

In quarrying Greek heroic legend, modern playwrights have been most attracted by those already dramatized—notably the royal houses of Argos and of Thebes. T. S. Eliot wrote in a 1923 review of James Joyce's *Ulysses* (which contains one chapter in dramatic form): "Myth . . . is simply a way of controlling, ordering, of giving shape and significance to the great panorama of futility and anarchy which is contemporary history." Though contemporary history is absent from Eliot's plays, he nevertheless uses myth to control, order, and give shape and significance to his plots. But he does this so deviously that the myth has sometimes been sought like buried treasure.

There is no doubt, however, of the source of Eliot's first play set in modern times, *Family Reunion*. Shortly after his hero, Harry, Lord Monchensey, appears on stage, he rephrases a sentence from the last speech of Orestes in the *Choephoroe* of Aeschylus: "You can not see them, but I see them." Both Harry and Orestes are referring to the Furies, who exact blood for deeds of blood. But Aeschylus dramatizes the *deeds* of Orestes which imperil his people, whereas Eliot dramatizes the *feelings* of Harry, which are private, and which emerge only tangentially from his deeds. We never know whether Harry murdered his wife, and it is only later and very obliquely that he murders his mother; irrelevant to and more important than his actions is Harry's sense of sin, which reveals him as a Christian beneath his worldly exterior.

As Denis Donaghue has perceptively remarked: "There are, in fact, two actions in *The Family Reunion*: a drama of 'guilt,' which is Harry's private *geste*, and a related action which is wider and symbolic. . . . Harry's consciousness (guaranteed by his recognition of the Eumenides) drives him, as hero in his own private struggle, to holiness. Another part of his role requires that, as symbolic hero, he force the inert world of Wishwood at least to acknowledge the existence of Conscience and Consciousness."[2] Harry expresses his distaste for the Wishwood world in personal rather than in public terms. Except for Agatha and Mary, he finds his family reunion a bore, and he speaks smugly to his relatives. Eliot was later to call Harry "an insufferable prig."[3] Before leaving Wishwood, Harry addresses his family arrogantly, using words that recall those of Orestes to the Furies:

> I would explain, but you would none of you believe it;
> If you believed it, still you would not understand.
> You can't know why I'm going. You have not seen
> What I have seen.

Eliot's Harry is so full of his heroic mission that he has no energy to think of his family, who remain mired in their trivial lives, unmoved by his ideals.

Though Eliot's three subsequent plays derive from extant Greek tragedies—*The Cocktail Party* from the *Alkestis* of Euripides, *The Confidential Clerk* from the *Ion* of Euripides, and *The Elder Statesman* from *Oedipus at Colonnus* of Sophocles—they become successively more private, de-emphasizing the effect of heroic action upon other people. Celia in *The Cocktail Party*, the saint-figure who succeeds Harry, is crucified because she will not leave dying natives in Africa; though these are not her people, they are the people she has chosen, and Sir Henry Harcourt-Reilly, the priest-god-psychiatrist figure, suggests that she may have had a salutary effect on those people: "Who knows, Mrs. Chamberlayne,/The difference that made to the natives who were dying/Or the state of mind in which they died?" But even this small redemptive hint is missing from Eliot's next two plays, which are confined to drawing-room worlds. *The Elder Statesman* contrasts with its model, *Oedipus at Colonnus*, in its lack of resonance; though Eliot's hero, Lord Claverton, has been a statesman, he has lost concern for his people so as to concentrate on himself. Like Oedipus, "his last hour was free and blessed," but his presence brings peace only to his daughter and her fiancé; there is no suggestion that an Athens will benefit from him.

Of Eliot's four plays derived from Greek tragedy, only *The Family Reunion* provides the possibility of heroic redemption, but his Harry-Orestes is sublimely indifferent to his people. Written four years after *The Family Reunion*, Jean-Paul Sartre's *Flies* (1943) is closer to Aeschylus in its redemptive and civic intention, but Sartre's Aeschylus is refracted through Giraudoux' *Electra* (1937). Giraudoux suggested Sartre's central metaphor of the Furies as flies, since Giraudoux' Gardener accuses the Furies: "You're just like flies." From Giraudoux, too, Sartre learned to use incongruous details, witty anachronisms, and polished dialogue that slips into dialectic—all of which he was to abandon after this first play. In *The Flies*, the very character of the Tutor, Orestes' life-guide, recalls the ironic skepticism of Giraudoux. However, as Orestes opposes his tutor, so Sartre opposes Giraudoux. In a 1940 review of the latter's novel, *Choice of the Elect* (pointedly entitled "M. Jean Giraudoux and the Philosophy of Aristotle"), Sartre describes Giraudoux' protagonist: "Man conforms to his archetype of his own free will; he is constantly choosing himself as he is." Sartre's hero, by contrast, will become what he is through choosing his deeds. Thus, *The Flies* assimilates Giraudoux' techniques to contradict his assumptions.

The very presence of Orestes in Argos is a declaration of independence from his tutor, who has advised against return. But Orestes returns in order to rid himself of a sense of exile—a feeling that he assumes is peculiar to him, and not characteristic of the human condition. Orestes is a stranger in Argos, where he was born, but he imagines a childhood, youth, and manhood that would give him possession of the Argos palace door. At the end of his musing, however, he renounces this imaginary past, comforting his Tutor: "And now I'm going to say something that will rejoice you; this is not *my* palace, nor *my* door. And there's nothing to detain us here" (Stuart Gilbert translation). Before he can leave, however, first Electra, then Clytemnestra arrive. Although they do not recognize Orestes, the two women quarrel over him, Electra urging him to stay in Argos, Clytemnestra begging him to depart for his mother's sake. Orestes decides to stay but does not reveal his identity.

In Act II Orestes is an appalled spectator at the rites of Dead Men's Day, the holiday of national atonement, sponsored by an Aegisthus who is obedient to Jupiter's order. When Orestes reveals himself to Electra, she urges him to escape from Argos, for he does not fulfill her hope of a heroic avenger. Uncertain as to his course of action, Orestes prays to Jupiter for guidance, and since a disguised Jupiter has been eavesdropping, a light immediately flashes around the sacred stone. Not for an instant does Orestes doubt its meaning: "[To obey without question. Without the slightest question.] Always to say 'Excuse me' and 'Thank you.'" (Stuart Gilbert's translation omits the important phrases in brackets.)

Abruptly, Orestes decides to defy the command of Jupiter. Nothing in the play (as opposed to subsequent philosophic commentary) explains this decision opposed by his tutor, his sister, and his god. In contrast to Giraudoux' Electra, Sartre's Orestes chooses an action instead of an archetype, engagement instead of purity, and engagement means "dirty hands"—the title of a subsequent Sartre play. Aeschylus' Orestes is obedient even in murder, but Sartre's Orestes is disobedient; he chooses the engagement of disobedience, and there lies his heroism, involving himself in the lives of others.

Though Orestes' defiance of Jupiter is sudden, his engagement is gradual. When Jupiter's light first flashes, Orestes evokes the dutiful mortal he is expected to be, and only then he rebels: "It's not for me, that light; from now on I'll take no one's orders." Instead of pride at this assertion, his overwhelming feeling is one of emptiness, before he decides to be "a guilt-stealer" for his people. Though he dislikes bloodshed, there is only one way to earn that title—murder. It is after noting his determination that Electra calls him "Orestes" for the first time.

By the final act Orestes is a harsh hero; his decision has given him a decisiveness of gesture and language. After he kills a tired and unresisting Aegisthus, after he terrifies Electra by the murder of their mother, Orestes flings his freedom in the teeth of the Jupiter whose sign he disobeyed. Leaving Electra to wallow in remorse, Orestes faces his angry people. He takes the stance of the mythic hero, who acts to free his people, but he gives them a distinctively modern kind of freedom. Proud of saying NO to Jupiter, Orestes now says NO to his people, refusing to rule his kingdom. Instead, he offers Argos his own kind of freedom—not freedom from but freedom for. By the end of the play, Orestes returns to exile; "And for me, too, a new life is beginning. A strange life. . . ." He tells the story of the flute player of Scyros, who rid his city of a plague of rats, and he draws an analogy between the rats of Scyros and the flies of Argos: "And all the rats raised their heads and hesitated—as the flies are doing. Look! Look at the flies! Then all of a sudden they followed in his train. And the flute player with his rats vanished forever. Thus." Orestes strides off stage, heedless of the Furies shrieking after him.

The first self-consciously Existentialist hero to reach the stage, Sartre's Orestes is a candidly contemporary portrait of a mythic hero. Orestes rebels against the universe of Jupiter, and he tries to force his people to rebel. He not only frees them; he challenges them to engage their freedom in a cause. And then he goes on to engage himself elsewhere.

In sharp contrast to Sartre, Jean Anouilh (who also turned to classical subject-matter during World War II) presents a hero, or, more often, a heroine, who refuses engagement, who rejects the tawdry relativism of adulthood for a childhood dream of purity. Anouilh's *Antigone* is one of his clearest statements of this recurrent theme, but earlier, Anouilh had begun to treat the Orestes story from the same viewpoint. Perhaps the success of Sartre's *Flies* hindered Anouilh from completing his play; the published fragment *Orestes* (1945) makes use of the Greek material to tell a private story, without public significance. Though the fragment is entitled *Orestes*, Aegisthus and Electra pre-empt most of the dialogue, as in Giraudoux' *Electra*. And as in Giraudoux' *Electra* too, we have a sympathetic Aegisthus. Aware of the legend in which they figure, Anouilh's characters are unaware that their fate might devolve upon their city.

In the *Atridentetralogie* of Gerhart Hauptmann, on the other hand, the house of Argos is highly conscious of its public role.

The plays of the venerable German playwright appeared during World War II: *Iphigenia in Aulis* (published 1941) in the classical five-act form, a single act each for *Agamemnon's Death* (1942) and *Electra* (1944), and a three-act *Iphigenia in Delphos* (1940). Unlike Aeschylus, for whom Orestes is the main hero, Hauptmann follows Goethe in giving this role to Iphigenia. The movement of Hauptmann's tetralogy is from the politico-military repercussions of the first drama to the intensely private involvement of the two one-act plays (from which Iphigenia is absent) to a re-emergence into the socio-political world of greater Greece. (The final play of the tetralogy was the first to be written.)

Based upon the character in Euripides' *Iphigenia in Aulis*, Hauptmann's Agamemnon is an ambitious political leader; even Clytemnestra praises him in this role: "Split, rent were the Greeks; the son of Atreus unified them to a single action, which no one else could have done." And yet Agamemnon's very power becomes the reason for his moral weakness; envious of Odysseus, threatened with revolution by his troops, he consents to their demands to sacrifice his daughter. Only briefly does he appreciate his own weakness, in a stichomythic exchange with Iphigenia:

> IPHIGENIA: You are the highest Lord of the Greeks!
> AGAMEMNON: More than that! by far their lowest slave!

In Hauptmann's drama, heroic daughter resembles heroic father, and Iphigenia meets Agamemnon half-way toward her own sacrifice—"the foremost heroine above all heroes." At the altar, a half-crazed Agamemnon, under demonic possession, plunges his dagger into the sacrificial victim, not noticing that a hind has been substituted for his daughter.

Though Hauptmann does not set gods on his stage, priests play a larger role than in extant Greek tragedies, and there is much talk of Moira (Fate) controlling the murders in *Agamem-*

non's Death and *Electra*—Agamemnon, Cassandra, Clytemnestra, Thestor, Aegisthus (killed by Pylades). These bloody deeds are linked closely with dreams, and they are performed as if under hypnosis. In killing his mother, Orestes claims: "I am only an instrument, and nothing else."

And yet, though Hauptmann shows man as the instrument of cruel, irrational forces, he contrives a happy ending for his tetralogy, and he does this without *dei ex machina*. As the fourth play opens, Orestes and Electra are haunted by guilt, hunted by an irate populace, and they seek refuge at Apollo's shrine in Delphos. Violence breaks out between them, half-crazed as they are, and between Electra and a Hekate-Priestess, who proves to be Iphigenia. With Pylades mediating between them, brother and sister are slowly restored to sanity and Iphigenia takes all guilt upon herself. Revealing her identity to Electra alone, Iphigenia tells of her life on Tauris, after she was magically saved at Aulis. There she served Hekate-Artemis, and there she nearly killed Orestes for killing their mother. In time, however, Iphigenia realized that her role was superhuman forgiveness; so now, Iphigenia accepts responsibility for all the murders, as for the Trojan War, before she disappears into the shades of Hades. Refusing Electra's plea that she reveal her identity, Hauptmann's Iphigenia offers a rational motive for her secrecy; if the Greeks learn she was not sacrificed, heroic Agamemnon would be diminished in their eyes, as would the victory over Troy. Iphigenia predicts the reaction of the Greeks:

> Thus the voice of people. And it would grow louder and louder: "This house of Atreus"—as it was then called—"is rotten through and through and must be destroyed to the very roots!" And then they would suddenly shout: "Above all, bring judgment upon Iphigenia, the murderess of so many Greek sons."

Not through reason and compassion like Goethe's Iphigenia, but through fear of popular judgment, through concern for family honor, and through justification of the Trojan War, Haupt-mann's Iphigenia sacrifices herself a second time. Raised from heroism to godhood, Iphigenia vanishes, leaving Orestes and Electra to resume a pious public life.[4]

Though they have suffered, it is at the caprice of the gods and Moira; they have learned little through their suffering. Orestes and Electra are permitted to rule Greece, though they have not earned their authority over their people, as in Aeschylus. Far from Goethe's compassionate humanism, Hauptmann's Iphi-genia acts in traditional, even chauvinistic, patriotism.

Unlike his French predecessors in the use of myth, Hauptmann emphasizes magic, dreams, madness, and Moira. In this irrational Greece, heroes are bound to their people by the cruel caprice of underworld divinities. Since such heroes act through possession by demonic powers, it is difficult to speak of moral guilt. And yet, Hauptmann specifies that the house of Atreus is morally purified by the end of the tetralogy. Hauptmann's Iphigenia takes all guilt upon herself, as a priestess of dark powers, so that the Greeks may continue to believe that the Trojan War was worth fighting and winning. Performed in Berlin and Vienna during World War II, Hauptmann's final dramas must have had reso-nances that justified that war.

In the most recent dramatization of Orestes' heroic myth, Jack Richardson's *Prodigal* (1960), there is an adroit progres-sion from a within-the-myth world to a self-conscious awareness of the theater as both theater and *theatrum mundi*, so that the actual theater audience is challenged to react to the concept of heroism.

Richardson takes liberties with the story, as did O'Neill in his *Mourning Becomes Electra*: Richardson's Orestes is older than his sister; Cassandra is not the concubine of Agamemnon, and she does not share his death; Orestes seeks an ignoble marriage to a peasant girl, and, above all, he seeks not to avenge his fa-ther's death. Indifferent to power struggles and public responsibility, Richardson's Orestes early announces: "I feel uncomfortable when included in world schemes." Though solicited by both Aegisthus and Agamemnon (after his return), Orestes resolutely turns a deaf ear to both, and accepts exile with alacrity: "I'm aware of the grand issues I leave behind me, but that's exactly where I want them to be." Bored by both Aegisthus and Agamemnon, he tells Cassandra: "Between Aegisthus' creeping, crawling, microscopic figure who's buffeted by the gods and happy to be so, and my father's fumbling giant of the future who steps in everybody's garden and on everybody's toes with good intentions, the only choice is anger or laughter. I've taken the second." And Orestes laughs all the harder when Cassandra informs him that he is doomed to be a hero.

With some difficulty, Orestes passes his own test for non-heroism; he fails to come to the rescue of his father, who goes knowingly to his death in the belief that only by such sacrifice can he enlist Orestes in his cause. Orestes stands by while his father is murdered, stands by while Electra calls for vengeance, and then flees into exile. Unlike the Aeschylean Orestes, who is haunted by grief at his vengeful deed, Richardson's Orestes is haunted by his lack of vengeance; he comes to be known as Orestes of the Unavenged Father. Even his traveling companion, the playboy Pylades, turns against him, suddenly self-righteous because his reputation has been affected by the non-action of his prince. Though Orestes' peasant bride offers to follow him, he cannot bear to make her share his hunted life. Having nowhere to turn, Orestes begins to accept his destiny. He cries out to Cassandra, also sentenced to exile: "Is there nothing else for Prince Orestes to wear but the ragged dress of still another hero?" Implicit is a condemnation, not only of traditional modes of heroism—ragged dress—but of a world that demands heroism instead of allowing each man a private destiny.

Orestes requests one last prophecy from Cassandra, and she subtly turns the theater audience into a jury, who, as in many

Brecht plays, must sit in judgment upon the case on stage. Cassandra narrates the old mythic plot, against which Orestes had vainly rebelled. Though Cassandra speaks longingly of an audience "who would see you return to Argos with feelings other than tragic," both she and Orestes know that there will never be such an audience. Orestes will play his murderous role, the prodigal son will return, he will be welcomed by his father's martial spirit, and there will be rejoicing in Argos. But Orestes acknowledges that he returns, "knowing I was not great enough to create something better." After his departure, Cassandra declares herself too old for tragedy, and leaves the stage bare "and ready for the popular and typical hero to come," which Orestes is reluctant to be. In that reluctance lies Richardson's conception of true heroism—someone who will not acquiesce to mob expectations. Though Richardson's Orestes fails, finally, *not* to be a "popular and typical hero," his struggle for a private life has weakened the traditional link between a mindless heroism and the redemption of a people.

As the matter of Argos has yielded more extant Greek plays than any other body of myth, so contemporary playwrights have been drawn to that material. The house of Thebes has been less frequently visited in recent years, and there Antigone figures heroically more often than Oedipus her father. In 1922 Jean Cocteau rendered *Antigone* in colloquial French, while remaining quite faithful to Sophocles. During World War II Anouilh used a similarly colloquial language in his free adaptation of Sophocles, and after the war Brecht adapted Hölderlin's 1804 translation from the Greek into modern German verse. Though it is uncertain that Brecht knew Anouilh's play, his version is the obverse of the French interpretation.[5]

Anouilh's *Antigone* was written during World War II, after his fragment *Orestes*. In the one, Aegisthus early predicts his own death and that of Clytemnestra; so in *Antigone* the Chorus (a single individual) early announces: "In a tragedy, nothing is in doubt and everyone's destiny is known" (Lewis Galantière translation). But these particular destinies are known because Anouilh adapts in 1942 what Sophocles dramatized in 442 B.C. Though Anouilh is faithful to the events of the legend, he robs them of any effect on the people at large. During the action of Anouilh's play, Antigone's defiance of Creon grows, but her reason for defiance disappears. Indeed, Anouilh's Antigone scarcely knows why she risks her life to bury her brother. In the opening lines the Chorus says of Antigone: "She is going to die." After her confrontation with Creon, in which Antigone learns that her brothers were both worthless, she is compelled to admit that her illegal deed is pointless. But still defying Creon, she announces that she is acting "For nobody. For myself."

Anachronistic and contemporary, Anouilh's play neither attempts to convince us of the ritual importance of burial, nor to provide a modern equivalent. Instead, the burial becomes the means of Antigone's self-destruction. In her last letter, she admits, "I no longer know why I am dying." Nor does the audience know why, for the Chorus pronounces the final judgment, "Antigone is calm tonight, and we shall never know the name of the fever that consumed her." But we can guess. Like other Anouilh protagonists, Antigone dies to preserve a purity that would be tarnished by reality. Unlike Sartre's protagonists, who must dirty their hands in order to reach existential maturity, those of Anouilh retreat from the real and dirty world. "We are of the tribe that hates your filthy hope," Antigone tells Creon, for life thrives on filthy hope, and she dedicates herself to the purity of death.

Anouilh apparently takes no sides between a pragmatic Creon and an idealistic Antigone; during World War II French resistants lauded Antigone and collaborators praised Creon. Anouilh's Creon accuses Antigone of casting herself as a heroine, but the play itself offers small indication of how her death affects her people. Antigone's only reference to them is a taunt to Creon:

"Who knows but that lots of people will catch the disease from me." But there is no indication that they do, since the final lines of the play are spoken by the Chorus: "Only the guards are left, and none of this matters to them. It's no skin off their noses. They go on playing cards." Heroic action has *no* effect upon these representatives of the people. A minor note in Anouilh's drama, such indifference is nevertheless heard with some consistency through his plays.

In *Eurydice*, the play Anouilh wrote immediately before *Antigone*, Monsieur Henri makes a speech that explains all Anouilh's heroes: "There are two races of beings. The masses, teeming and happy—common clay, if you like—eating, breeding, working, counting their pennies; people who just live; ordinary people; people you can't imagine dead. And then, there are the others—the noble ones, the heroes. The ones you can quite well imagine lying shot, pale and tragic: one minute triumphant with a guard of honor, and the next being marched away between two gendarmes. Hasn't that sort of thing ever attracted you?" (Kitty Black translation). "That sort of thing" has not only attracted Antigone; it is her *raison d'être*. She and Creon belong to separate races, speaking mutually incomprehensible languages.

In Brecht's plays, on the other hand, there is no such rigid dichotomy. Antigone is the only dramatic heroine Brecht borrowed from classic Greece, and he called her "the great figure of the Resistance." Antigone was the first heroine of Brecht's drama upon his return to Europe after World War II, and *Antigone* was the first play he directed professionally. Though he himself called his play "Die Antigone *des Sophokles*" (my italics), Brecht tightened and adapted Hölderlin's translation from the Greek. As opposed to Anouilh's Antigone, Brecht's heroine acts by free will, for the German playwright eliminates Moira or Fate. In a 1951 program note, Brecht wrote explicitly: "According to the picture of the ancients man is delivered over more or less blindly to Fate; he has no power over it. In Bertolt Brecht's adaptation this picture has given way to the view that man's fate is man himself" (John Willett translation). Accordingly, Brecht's Antigone says to the Chorus: "I beg you, do not speak of Fate. I know this: the one who harps on Fate is the one who kills me though I am innocent." Thus, all events are decided by men. Creon wages a barbaric war against Argos; his two sons turn upon one another as did the two sons of Oedipus. But Antigone defies Creon, as in Sophocles.

Brecht's prologue insists upon the contemporary relevance of Antigone's resistance, though he claims only that it "pos[es] a point of actuality and outlin[es] the subjective problem." Set in Berlin in 1945, Brecht's prologue portrays Antigone and Ismene in modern dress. The contemporary Antigone justifies her brother's desertion from the Nazi Army, though he has been hanged for it. As she prepares to cut his body down and bury him, an S. S. man enters to ask about the identity of the corpse, and the prologue ends with the question of whether to risk one's own life to bury a brother.

In the play proper, Brecht emphasizes the rational and political motivation of his characters: the tyranny of Creon, the resistance of Antigone, who, sure of her rights, feels that her defiance will inspire others, as that of her brother inspired her own. Polynices has been killed for desertion from Creon's army, and Antigone's desire to bury his body is an expression of her resistance to Creon's tyranny. She goes to her death mourning her misled country; by the end of the drama, Creon has lost both sons and the unjust war against Argos; the old Chorus has to try to rebuild Thebes. Though Brecht keeps the tragic ending of Sophocles, he expands the significance of Antigone's resistance, which has helped defeat the tyrant, and perhaps to make possible a new and better Thebes.

The Living Theatre program for its production of *Antigone* reads:

THE ANTIGONE OF SOPHOKLES
Adapted for the Stage by BERTOLT BRECHT
Based on the German Translation by FRIEDRICH HOEL-
DERLIN
Translated into English by JUDITH MALINA

Actually, however, Judith Malina does far more adapting than
either Brecht or Hölderlin. Some thirty minutes of actor-audience
confrontation takes place before a word is spoken. The audience
is introduced to Theban tyranny by mime and wailing. Though
the actors wear rehearsal clothes, Antigone and Kreon alone are
dressed in black. Once the dialogue begins, lines are muted, re-
arranged, and repeated for incantatory effect, as the audience is
forced into recognition of oppression. Since *Antigone* is the first
play of the Living Theatre's progressively liberating repertory, the
production barely hints at Brecht's minimally hopeful ending—
that Thebes may be reborn through the heroic example of Antigone.

Dürrenmatt was often influenced by Brecht, but his one ex-
cursion into Greek myth has a cynical quality that is missing from
Brecht's heroic drama. Originally conceived as a radio play, Dürrenmatt's *Hercules and the Augean Stables* was expanded for
the stage. Often a subject for burlesque in antiquity, Dürrenmatt's Hercules is depicted as a strong man who is motivated by
profit alone; his famous twelve labors are a publicity stunt of
Polybios (ironically named after the Roman historian). In other
details, too, Dürrenmatt undercuts the heroic myth of Hercules.
Despite his strength, Hercules is prevented from cleaning the
Augean stables by an inefficient bureaucracy, functioning under
a president instead of a mythical king. The sexual exploits of
Hercules are performed by a proxy, and his relationship to Deja-
neira is a Hollywood-column convenience. Nevertheless, his heroic legend fires the imagination of youth, represented by the
children of the President of Augeas, Iole and Phyleus. As Hercules moves on to the next labor invented by Polybios, Iole fol-

lows him, while their father tries to keep Phyleus in Augeas, appealing to the necessity for workers rather than heroes; "I am a politician, my son, and not a hero, and politics works no wonders." Since he could not clean the stables, the President of Augeas uses the excrement as fertilizer, creating the first garden in the wasteland of Augeas, and he urges his son to help him in converting the desert into an orchard. But Phyleus turns his back on his father's garden, hypnotized by the heroic legend of Hercules. Thus, Dürrenmatt implies that heroic legend spoils youth for the workaday world, and in his single drama based on Greek myth Dürrenmatt diminishes traditional heroism.

Using the same legend, the East German playwright, Heiner Müller, and the American poet, Archibald MacLeish, present equally ambiguous views of heroism, with minimal consideration of the effect of the hero's actions upon his people. Müller, like Dürrenmatt, focuses upon the fifth labor of Hercules, the removal of excrement from the stables of Augeas, but Müller exploits the farcical aspects of that labor. A pair of Thebans introduce the hero and cheer him on to his fifth labor, but they hold their noses while they speak; Hercules shovels with one hand and holds his nose with the other; when Zeus appears in the sky, he too holds his nose; a nude, seductive Hebe appears to inspire Hercules, and she too holds her nose. The Thebans watch Hercules at work as though he were a popular entertainer. And indeed Müller's Hercules does resemble a clown-figure—clumsy and ridiculous in his strength. Irritated by Augeas, laughingly applauded by the chorus of Thebans, enigmatically discouraged by Zeus, Hercules nevertheless manages to turn the river upon the stables, so as to accomplish his fifth labor. Though Zeus does not oppose him openly, as he does Sartre's Orestes, a mysterious frost suddenly paralyzes the river, and Hercules "tears the sun out of the sky" to melt the ice. Once the river flows again, Hercules throws Augeas into it and declares his independence from Zeus. Hercules then receives the acclaim of the Thebans, who cheer him on to his sixth labor. In the final scenic direction, Hercules "rolls up the sky and stuffs it into his pocket."

MacLeish's Hercules is a far more serious, but similarly titanic figure. He emerges only in the second act of the two-act *Herakles*. The first act serves as a frame for the Greek legend: a Nobel-prize scientist, confined to his wheelchair, comes to Greece with his wife, child, and the child's governess. The wife is scornful of her husband's monomaniacal scientific quest and his consequent fellow feeling for Herakles "Against the universe!" But the celebrated scientist proclaims, "To want the world without the suffering is all/ there is on earth to want and man's/ rebellious labor ... ultimate pride." In Act II the scientist's family visits the ruins of mythic Greece, but his infirmity prevents him from joining them. Where the oracle spoke in ancient times, first Megara appears and then Herakles, as modern mother, daughter, governess, and guide witness their drama. Megara speaks for hearth and home, in the very words the scientist's wife had used in Act I. Herakles, "a great, battered, tattered, bearded, time-scarred, triumphant man," enters in the pride of his triumph; he glories in his exploits and asks Apollo for approval. When the oracle remains inscrutable, Herakles blasphemes, and he learns that his sons are slain. Megara returns home to bury them, but Herakles continues to flout the oracle, while the scientist's wife prays to be released from "this myth remembered by a mouth of stone." In *Herakles* as in his better known *J. B.*, MacLeish shows the contemporaneity of myth—of heroes too hubristic to accept human limits and through whom all human progress is made. MacLeish follows in O'Neill's path, not interested in "the relation between man and man," but "in the relation between man and God."[6] And yet, God is known only through the hero's relationship to men; his very defiance of God leads to an ordered world for men—through Herculean labors in classical times, through Herculean science in modern times.

American playwrights venture rarely into Greek myth, and English playwrights even more rarely. German and mainly French dramatists, on the other hand, feel more at home with Greek tragic heroes; through heroic exploration of classical figures, these playwrights explore the moral situation of our own time; through these figures, the playwrights suggest a morality for our own time. Eliot's Harry, Sartre's Orestes, Hauptmann's Iphigenia, Brecht's Antigone, and perhaps even Anouilh's—these are exemplary figures; but even imperfect Hercules, and Richardson's reluctant Orestes, imply guide-lines for conduct.

PARAHISTORIC HEROES

As playwrights rewrote Greek myth in our own image, so too they rewrote history. Nor did they turn necessarily to the history of their own nation. French Joan of Arc, having attracted such major playwrights of the past as German Schiller and English Shaw, inspired German Brecht to three plays. English St. Thomas à Becket became one of Jean Anouilh's most popular subjects. German Brecht wrote one of his greatest plays about Italian Galileo. English Osborne went to German history for his Luther. English Shaffer looked to South American history for his Pisarro's conquest of the Indians. Of differing quality, all these plays reflect a search for the meaning of heroism in the modern world.

The earliest of these historical play-heroes is St. Thomas à Becket, born in 1117 and assassinated in 1170, in the cathedral of Canterbury, on orders of King Henry II of England. Thomas Eliot named his 1935 play for that deed, *Murder in the Cathedral*. Unlike Anouilh and Fry in their dramas, Eliot pares away peripheral material so as to focus on Becket's martyrdom. Like Greek tragedy, *Murder in the Cathedral* is formed of episodes separated by choral odes, so that the actions of the hero are immediately reflected in the reactions of his people, the Chorus of Canterbury Women.

Parts I and II of Eliot's play are separated by the Archbishop's

Christmas sermon, in which a single sentence sums up the play's view of the relationship between the hero and his people: "A martyrdom is always the design of God, for His love of men, to warn them and to lead them, to bring them back to His ways." Martyrs are made by God for the good of the people—a medieval belief that Eliot dramatizes with modern urgency. Part I contains the spiritual preparation for martyrdom; the archbishop confronts four tempters—sensuality, authoritarian power, popular power, and martyrdom—and he easily spurns them, commending himself to God. Part II contains the murder, after which the murderers address us directly in modern prose which parodies the double-talk of our politicians. Eliot himself admitted that these speeches may have been influenced by the final scene of Shaw's *Saint Joan*, and in both plays the saint appears even more heroic in the light of the world's pragmatism.

Anouilh's *Becket or the Honor of God* (1958) and Fry's *Curtmantle* (1961) are both based on the conflict between Becket and Henry II (who does not even appear in Eliot's play). And both plays minimize the interaction between the hero and his people; it is not even clear who *is* the hero. The two men embody opposing forces—Henry the selfish relativism of politics and Thomas the selfless absolutism of faith, which he calls the honor of God.

As Anouilh's play opens, Henry II, abject and naked, grumbles at the tomb of St. Thomas à Becket; in full panoply as Archbishop, the ghost of Thomas engages the living king in dialogue.

> KING: I said, 'In all save the honor of the realm.' It was you who taught me that slogan, after all.
> BECKET: I answered you, 'In all save the honor of God.' It was a dialogue of deaf men.
> (Translated by Lucienne Hill, who omits the last sentence.)

The play then flashes back to the beginning of that dialogue, in which Henry and Thomas seemed to speak a common language, though Anouilh's Henry is a Norman king and his Thomas is of Saxon descent (Anouilh's preface candidly admits his scorn for mere historical accuracy).

With verve and humor, Anouilh dramatizes their cynical gay times together, which suddenly terminate when Henry appoints Thomas Archbishop of Canterbury. Thomas pleads with him not to do so: "If I become Archbishop, I can no longer be your friend." This libertine, this disrespecter of priests, abruptly becomes custodian of the honor of God, whose power is vested in the Church. In *Murder in the Cathedral*, as Anouilh indicates in his preface, T. S. Eliot dramatizes the *growth* of Thomas to sainthood, but since his own Becket dons sainthood with his archbishop's robe, Anouilh confesses that he did not know how to end the play. After managing "some facile comedy lines," however, "things fell into their place of themselves, and in fifteen days I finished *Becket*."

No one but a critic would be cruel enough to use Anouilh's rare candor against him, but things did not fall into place "of themselves"; they were carefully arranged by Anouilh, who chose Becket because of his potential purity. Like Anouilh's Antigone, Becket desires martyrdom, and he taunts Henry as Antigone taunted Creon: "It's not for me to win you round. I have only to say no to you. . . . We must only do—absurdly—what we have been given to do—right to the end." Without reason, like Antigone; and without looking around to see if one has any followers.

In dramatizing the Henry II-Becket conflict, Christopher Fry was as conscientiously historical as Jean Anouilh was consciously parahistorical, and Fry's Foreword summarizes where history led him: "The play has two themes: one a progression towards a portrait of Henry, a search for his reality. . . . The other theme is Law, or rather the interplay of different laws: civil, canon, moral, aesthetic, and the laws of God; and how they belong and do not belong to each other." On stage, however, the two themes often resemble Anouilh's simplistic conflict between the king's honor and God's honor.

In production, Anouilh's king inevitably elicits more sympathy than the supercilious Thomas; Fry deliberately focuses on the multi-faceted king, for whom the play is named ("Curtmantle" was the historical Henry's nickname, "derived from the plain short cloak he wore"). Fry's Foreword suggests why Henry fascinated him: "Just as the thirty-five years of his reign contain a concentration of the human condition, so his character covers a vast field of human nature." But none of Henry's many qualities, which Fry lists and attempts to dramatize, indicate concern for his people, as opposed to his kingdom. Not simply selfish, Henry desires a kingdom of law rather than anarchy, but he will not tolerate the Archbishop's elevation of Church law over royal law. At his last meeting with Becket, Henry is conscious of his public image, and almost pleads, "I only ask him [Becket] to treat me with tolerable respect/ In front of these men who are watching us from their places." Though the meeting is calm, Henry is angered that Becket does not support his laws. Somewhat incredibly, Fry has Henry give an *unconscious* order for Becket's death. Evidently asking a rhetorical question, "Who will get rid of this turbulent priest for me?" Henry is shocked when the priest is indeed gotten rid of. With his own last breath, Henry admits the failure of his attempt at law, "It is all still to do!"

In dramatizing the events of Henry's reign, Fry specifies that "the stage is William Marshal's mind, as though he were remembering the life of Henry," and this serves to give distance, as in Brecht's Epic theater. Moreover, though the play is nominally divided into a Prologue and three Acts, the effect is rather that of a sequence of scenes, again in harmony with Brecht's Epic theater. But though Brecht also dramatized history, he always gave more attention to his hero's influence on his people.

As early as *Man is Man* (1925), before his Marxist plays, Brecht dramatizes the metamorphosis of the porter Galy Gay into a "human fighting machine," but he also dramatizes the reactions of his fellow fighting machines. Lured by a cigar, Brecht's Galy Gay is dressed in British army uniform; compromised by his profit motive, he agrees to answer to another name; after he pronounces his own funeral oration, he is carried on the Army train to Tibet. As Jeriah Jip, he adapts himself to Army rations and violence; he dominates his platoon and finally shoots away a mountain that blocks the Army entrance to Tibet. Behaving with the bravery of legendary heroes, Galy Gay virtually becomes the murderer of his followers.

After Brecht's conversion to Marxism, he remained scornful of brave heroes. Like his fellow-Marxist (at that time), Erwin Piscator, Brecht felt that "the time itself, the fate of the masses, had to be the heroic factor of the new drama" (*Political Theater*). Thus, Brecht's learning-plays are concerned with the fate of the masses, while his operas tangentially undercut heroic tradition. In his adaptation of Gorki's *Mother* (1932) Brecht dramatizes the making of a modern heroine, who redeems her people through an understanding of their common suffering. The growth of political awareness on the part of the mother, Pelegea Vlassova, leads to the Russian Revolution and the liberation of her people from oppression. Since Gorki's novel was written in 1906, the successful ideological conclusion is Brecht's invention. Gorki's character, compounded of faith and works, becomes Brecht's heroine, who learns Marxist theory and practice. Written soon after Brecht's learning-plays, *The Mother* is as much a play about learning as it is about heroism; Pelegea Vlassova learns heroism and teaches it to others. She alone in Brecht's canon accomplishes the redemption of her people in Marxist terms.

To some degree, Brecht must have conceived of the Mother as the successful counterpart of his unsuccessful heroine in *St. Joan of the Stockyards*, written a year earlier—1931. In both plays, the heroine learns about the class struggle, but whereas the Mother translates her knowledge into action, Joan fails to act. In *St. Joan of the Stockyards*, the starry-eyed visionary is plunged into a Chicago derived from Upton Sinclair's *Jungle*. Pointedly surnamed Dark rather than D'Arc, Brecht's Joan is blind to the causes of poverty; she mouths noble abstractions through which Brecht parodies traditional heroism, especially as portrayed in Schiller's *Maid of Orleans* and Goethe's *Faust*. Like Shaw's Major Barbara, Brecht's Joan wants to save souls and comes to realize that there can be no divorce of the spiritual from the material. Even when she acknowledges the primacy of the material, however, she adheres to her ideal of non-violence, and she therefore fails the strikers in their hour of need. Unlike the Mother, who understands theory *through* practice, Joan *declares* her atheism, *implies* an acceptance of Communism, but finally *does* nothing. Her dying words are muffled by the hypocritical combination of the Black Straw Hats and the Packers and Stockbrokers; too late she learns: "Only force helps where force rules,/ And only men help where men are" (Frank Jones translation). As Bernard Dukore has noticed, "Shaw's Joan of Arc is turned into a saint when she no longer threatens the powers that destroyed her; Brecht's Joan Dark is turned into a saint in order not to threaten the powers which destroy her."[7] Because Joan has not acted, her canonization will enslave the workers. Rather than a redeemer, she is, for all her good intentions, the betrayer of her people.

Though Brecht was a successful German playwright when he completed *St. Joan*, Nazi force was so feared that he could find no one to produce that pro-Communist play. On February 28, 1933, the day after the Reichstag fire, Brecht fled from Germany, to remain in exile for fifteen years. During that time, he wrote in German, a tongue foreign to his environment; with no access to a theater, he nevertheless composed about a dozen plays. In California, where he spent part of his exile, he dramatized the novel of a fellow refugee, Lion Feuchtwanger, *The Visions of Simone Machard*.

Simone Machard, a child-heroine (fifteen years old in Feucht-wanger's novel, but only eleven in Brecht's play), is the only one in France who still believes in the glory of Joan of Arc, and she translates that belief into action, blowing up the gasoline that the French collaborators intend for the Germans. Simone Ma-chard is a child who assumes the role of an adult—on stage, her clothes are too large for her—but the Nazis punish her as an adult, sentencing her to an ominous Gray House. After she is dragged away, the German-occupied Assembly-hall goes up in flames. Simone Machard's imitation of Joan has sparked the sabotage of the French Resistance. Brecht does not emphasize this as Feuchtwanger does in the novel, but the play's final line links Joan-Simone to the Resistance: "They can't have arrived at the Gray House yet. Simone will see the fire from the car" (Carl Mueller translation).

Two years before his death, Brecht again dramatized Joan's story in *The Trial of Joan of Arc* (1952). The historical trial records are followed in Brecht's adaptation of a radio play by Anna Seghers. More positively than in the case of his Chicago Joan, or even of the child Simone Machard, Brecht defines the heroism of Joan by her impact upon her people. The trial is framed in the comments of the common people in the market-place, who understand that the heresy trial is a mere pretext for political shenanigans of both French and English rulers. Joan herself is one of these common people, and she recants only be-cause she feels isolated from them, unaware that all her words are reported in the market-place. When she recants, there is the same disappointment that Brecht registered in his *Galileo*. Unlike the Italian scientist, however, Joan reacts heroically when she understands the nefarious effects of her recantation. She chooses martyrdom because of its significance for her people: "I doubted the people, thinking they would pay no attention if I died, and would continue to drink their wine. But they knew all about me, all the time, and it wasn't all for nothing." Joan's execution takes place off stage, but it is described movingly by the people for whom she sacrificed herself. In the final scene, after Joan has been burned, Brecht insists upon the inalienable bond between a hero and his people:

> BREUIL: [Joan] led France.
> LEGRAIN: Yes, but France also led her.
> BREUIL: I thought that voices led her.
> LEGRAIN: Yes, our voices.

Though the brave heroine is documented both by history and by Anna Seghers, Brecht invents the repercussions in the market-place, so as to situate his Joan in a social context. Minor Brecht, these three Joan dramas illustrate his consistent concern with her redemptive effect upon her people.

Both Anouilh and Brecht dramatized Antigone; both Anouilh and Brecht dramatized Joan of Arc. Like Brecht, Anouilh frequently draws upon legend or history for his dramas (8 of his 29 plays), but unlike Brecht, Anouilh is oblivious to the social context. Though Sartre linked Anouilh with Camus, Beauvoir, and himself in his 1946 essay, "Forgers of Myths," Anouilh has imposed the same myth instead of forging a new one in his several dramas. Beneath Anouilh's contemporary, colloquial idiom lies fidelity to a simplistic conception of heroism as absolute purity. Centered upon themselves, Anouilh's heroes rarely think of their people. Nor does Anouilh.

The Lark (1953) opens at the trial of Joan of Arc, but like *Antigone* it takes place on a bare stage that suggests timelessness. Though no one tells us explicitly, as in *Antigone*, that Joan is going to die, it is inconceivable that a modern audience would not know this, as it is inconceivable that a modern audience would come to the same verdict as her 1431 jury. In France, Joan of Arc is synonymous with a patriotism that Anouilh dresses in contemporary language, "and suddenly I had France on my hands." The first half of *The Lark* traces Joan's success as she convinces stupid Baudricourt of his intelligence, cowardly Charles of his courage, and blasphemous La Hire of his religion. The second part of the drama follows the trial records, as Shaw and Brecht did previously. Joan recants when her voices desert her, and then withdraws her abjuration. Anouilh's Joan, like his Antigone, like his Becket, dies in purity: "I don't want to live through however long this 'in time' of yours will be" (Christopher Fry translation). But Anouilh reserves a last *coup de théâtre* for us; the play closes not at Joan's burning, but at the Rheims coronation—the larks singing in the open sky. Joan's father, who had earlier tried to beat her into submission, closes the play: "I always said that kid had a great future before her" (Omitted in the Christopher Fry translation). With Anouilh's hindsight, Joan's father predicts accurately; Church Councils and dramatists have both given Joan her "great future." In closing the play on the coronation at Rheims, Anouilh insures that Joan's glory redounds traditionally on her people.

In another French dramatization of the story of Joan of Arc, Audiberti's *Pucelle (The Maid,* untranslated), Joan the heroine is lifted out of history to explore her impact upon non-historical fictional characters. Only the second of the three acts focuses on Joan. The first and third acts constitute a play concerning preparations for the performance of a medieval mystery play about St. Joan, but we do not see the mystery performed. In the long second act the poet Gilbert, who has written the mystery play of the frame, teaches "Latin, arithmetic, law. . .riding and shooting," and converts an innocent Amazonian farm girl into a heroic leader of men. However, the poet's creation outstrips his imagination, and the farm girl fashions a nation from her followers: "That's the way I want men, coming close to one another, chasing me and following me toward death, in the war for our country."

When Joan (*Jeanne* in French) departs to lead the army, her *alter ego* Jeannette stays at home, to do a woman's work.

In the third act of Audiberti's play, the mystery performance is delayed because the leading actress has been lured away by another acting company. Jeannette, now married to the boy next door, consents to play Joan; her dress accidentally catches fire, and she is burned to death, like her *alter ego* years ago. The poet Gilbert, caught up in his own creation, demands that Joan conquer again by her spirit: "Joan of Arc! Joan of iron! Joan of fire! I want those who love you to demand that flesh be even harder and purer than your metal armor." When the mystery play is over, the poet Gilbert disappears, and we are left with a duchess who played a minor role in Joan's life, and who now tries to make sense of the play: "He splits a woman in two, but I'm the one who bleeds." Seeking help, the duchess meets her old squire who had stolen her horse so as to follow Joan. Mistress and squire sing a soldiers' song that brings Audiberti's play full circle to its beginning. The combination of cynical song and the squire's empty right sleeve casts a crooked shadow on Joan's vision of a nation: "It's at war that heroes grow."

Audiberti's *Maid* presents a complex conception of Joan's heroism against the background of the nation she may have redeemed. Not only is she responsible for war heroes but for war deaths. The audience is finally uncertain as to whether Joan is visionary, fanatic, or poetic invention; whether she damns or redeems her people. Audiberti may well be the first playwright since Shakespeare to cast doubt on Joan's mission. Marxist Brecht, skeptic Anouilh, and Catholic Claudel are all agreed on her heroic role, though that role inspires her people differently in the different plays.

In his program note to the French production of *The Lark* Anouilh comments on Joan's beatification with an irony that is absent from his drama: "As regards the hypothesis familiar to Catholics, at least in France, that God had begun to worry about France and sent Joan to save her, I must point out as a matter of general interest and without drawing any conclusion therefrom that Joan was officially recognized as a saint and not as a martyr. She was canonized for 'the excellence of her theological virtues' and not because she died for her faith—her faith being identical with the cause of France, which, even in 1920, was hardly acceptable from the Vatican's point of view. Joan was thus a saint who died as a result of a political intrigue, and God did not necessarily take sides against Henry VI of Lancaster. It's a pity, but it's true."

It is a truth that Paul Claudel patently ignores in his dramatic oratorio, *Joan of Arc at the Stake* (1939). Joan, tied to the stake and facing her death, re-views her life. The scenes are presented in montage—torture by priests who are presented as animals (Cochon, her principal inquisitor, means *pig*), power politics as a card game, the voices of St. Catherine and St. Margaret, the road to Rheims, the natural beauty of Domrémy, and, finally, the aid of the Virgin, who tells Joan that she has become pure flame so that the stake-fires cannot harm her. The oratorio closes with heavenly and earthly voices chanting, "There is no greater love than to lay down one's life for those one loves." Much earlier, Joan had spoken of "these poor people whom I love." Presumably, it is for them she dies, though the montage effect conveys this as an assertion rather than a drama.

Claudel's other dramas also show how God works in mysterious ways, using heroes to shape human destiny in this world and the next. Though he draws few such heroes from history, the stories of these fictional figures are so deeply imbedded in European history that they too constitute parahistorical dramas. Claudel uses an old Portuguese proverb as one of the mottoes of *The Satin Slipper:* "God writes straight with crooked lines." Heroes and villains serve God's writing: Mara steals her sister's lover, Sygne de Coufontaine betrays her lover, Mesa effectively kills de Ciz and Ysé her child, Rodrigue rules by hatred. Descendants of the suffering Romantic hero, Claudel's heroes translate their suffering into action on a stage that represents the world.

Their action becomes history, which is part of God's inscrutable design.

From *Head of Gold* (begun in 1884) to *The Story of Tobias and Sara* (1938) Claudel creates gigantic figures, who speak in biblical rhythms, and upon whom the fate of the world turns. Such figures were too large for the realistic stages of France before World War II, and it was only after the war that most of Claudel's plays were produced. In *Head of Gold,* the titular hero, crying out in agony, inspires the return of his army, which thereupon wins the battle. In *The City* three men, frustrated by their love for the same woman, lead the city toward faith; as the woman herself is aware, she is the instrument of God's grace: "I am the promise that cannot be kept, and my grace lies precisely in that." Such grace also belongs to Ysé of *Break of Noon* and Dona Prouhèze of *The Satin Slipper,* for perfect love lies not in woman but in God. In the intensely lyrical *Break of Noon* the double deaths of the ex-seminarian Mesa and his faithless mistress Ysé carry a hint of redemptive sacrifice for heathen China.

In the trilogy of plays that traces the history of nineteenth-century France, the miscreant revolutionary Toussaint Turelure leaves a legacy of faith in an age of skepticism. His grand-daughter Pensée de Coufontaine is the final result of a series of amazing coincidences, of betrayals and counterbetrayals, of unions between aristocrat and commoner, Christian and Jew. Beloved by the twin nephews of the Pope, Pensée de Coufontaine marries the suitor she does not love, so that her spiritual mate is free to fight and die for the faith. In the grand finale of the trilogy, Claudel stops at no scenic extravagance; Pensée, pregnant by one twin, kneels before the severed head of the other, as a woman's voice sings out: "O inseparable brothers, one leads Pensée and the other has received her." The symbolism is patent: the Pope, representative of Catholicism, leads and receives the thought (*pensée*) of the world.

Plot summaries reveal the weakest aspect of Claudel's drama-turgy. When Auden wrote of him: "[Time] will pardon Paul Claudel,/ Pardons him for writing well," he neglected the enor-mous role of the stage in any such pardon, for incredible plotting can be mitigated by rhapsodic rhythms and scenic splendor. Nourished by Aeschylus and the Bible, Claudel writes large, and he peoples his dramas with giants whose every word affects the destiny of nations. In his dramas Claudel substitutes Christian destiny for Greek fate; capricious pagan gods are replaced by the unpredictability of God's grace—descending in crooked lines.

More than any other drama, *The Satin Slipper* links the small and the soaring, the unique and the universal, in the symbolist tradition. Thus, the long epic drama is named after a small satin slipper offered by Dona Prouhèze to the Virgin, praying that when she moves toward evil, she may limp. In one hand her slipper, in the other her heart, Dona Prouhèze begs the Virgin to keep her human slipper near her own immortal heart. Human and divine, literal and allegorical, are linked from the start. In this sprawling drama, unity is imposed by the tempestuous love of two titans, two heroes, Don Rodrigue and Dona Prouhèze. Though it moves over three continents, the play opens and closes at sea, a metaphor for both time and faith. It is mainly through minor characters that we are made aware of the repercussions of the heroic action of the principals; the pattern is announced in the opening prayer of the Jesuit priest: "For he is of those who can be saved only by saving that whole mass that takes form behind him."

The lovers meet only three times during their lifetime; at the first meeting in Africa, a married Dona Prouhèze nurses a sick Don Rodrigue; afterward, they are irrevocably bound in what Jacques Madaule calls a "prodigious odyssey of separation."[8] Just before Don Rodrigue becomes Viceroy of the Americas, he visits Africa to persuade Dona Prouhèze to return to Spain, and, in a remarkably staged scene, a verbal moon watches the embrace of the shadows of the two lovers. They will not meet again till shortly before the death of Dona Prouhèze.

In the interval—most of their lives—Dona Prouhèze is widowed, but Don Rodrigue does not know this. She becomes captain of the African outpost of Mogador, and Don Rodrigue acts as Viceroy of the Americas. As cruel as his king, Don Rodrigue commands men's devotion by sparing them nothing; through destruction and construction he solidifies a Catholic empire. However, when he receives a letter from Dona Prouhèze, ten years after she sends it, he leaves America for Mogador. At their meeting, aboard his ship, Dona Prouhèze is again married, and has a daughter. Voluntarily, the lovers renounce one another in a lyric rhapsody. Leaving her daughter with Don Rodrigue, Dona Prouhèze returns to Mogador; Don Rodrigue watches as the fortress blows up, killing Dona Prouhèze.

After her death, Don Rodrigue suffers a series of humiliations that Claudel eliminated from the stage version; the literal Purgatory of Dona Prouhèze is paralleled by Don Rodrigue's purgatory on earth. Like Head of Gold and Mesa, Don Rodrigue progresses from anguish to brutality to self-abnegation. Condemned to irons, he is sold to a nun for a few scraps. But not until the daughter of Dona Prouhèze has been taken aboard the royal ship, to carry on her mother's fight against the infidels of Africa. Through their personal frustration, both Dona Prouhèze and especially Don Rodrigue have spent their lives propagating their faith.

This is an anachronistic and rigid conception of redemption, as that of Brecht is modern and rigid. Polar opposites in ideology and temperament, Claudel and Brecht are similar in certain artistic aspects. Both poet-playwrights declared their art subservient to a belief to which they were "converted"—Claudel to Catholicism in 1886, and Brecht to Marxism about 1926. With completely different ideas about dramatic purpose, both dramatists enlarged their art through widespread borrowing from other arts

—music, dance, mime, painting, projections—as well as from non-realistic dramatic forms—learning-play, parable, mystery play, Noh play, total theater. Though Claudel looked toward the past and Brecht toward the future, both created dramas about extraordinarily passionate heroes.

Though Brechtians may abhor the suggestion, Brecht's Galileo has the energy of a Claudel hero. Like *The Satin Slipper, Galileo* is set in the Renaissance. But Brecht, writing in exile in 1938, warned himself against escaping into the past, and he stresses the relevance of the stage-period for our own time. Brecht wrote three versions of *Galileo*, and his attitude toward the scientist grows progressively harsher.[9] In 1938 Brecht viewed sympathetically a scientist who used his cunning to save his skin, and his first Galileo is heroic because he manages to preserve himself for science. After the atomic bomb was dropped, however, Brecht blamed a scientist who shirked political responsibility to save his skin, viewing him as a criminal. In Brecht's production notes, he emphasizes that Galileo is both a hero and a criminal, and the play dramatizes the effect of both on his people.

Brecht's Galileo has a Renaissance zest for the sensual and the intellectual, which is the source of both his heroism and his crime. Brecht's own comment is illuminating; in paragraph 63 of his *Small Organon:* "Isn't the pleasure of drinking and washing one with the pleasure which he [Galileo] takes in the new ideas?" (John Willet translation). Thus, we first see Brecht's Galileo half-naked, scrubbing down his gross body. His first line reveals his appetite both for food and for knowledge: "Put the milk on the table, but don't close any of my books." At the beginning of the second scene, Galileo is diminished by the projection: "Everything a great man does is not great." We have seen Galileo's physical greatness, heard of his intellectual greatness, and we will now witness how he uses his mind. Galileo's "not great" deed is to steal the idea of the telescope, and sell the instrument to the Venetians, buying free time for experimentation. Before Galileo perpetrates this "not great" trick, however, Brecht expresses Galileo's excitement about "a new time" and limitless exploration of "laughing continents." The projection connects this excitement with the Copernican theory. Galileo's delight is evident, too, at the social repercussions of his research. And yet, the double pressures of poverty and church force Galileo to sell telescopes to the Venetians. "I have no patience," he says, "with a man who doesn't use his brains to fill his belly" (Laughton translation). Galileo's trick, his "not great" deed, faintly foreshadows his recantation, where, by insincerely denying the Copernican theory, he again "fills his belly," but also satisfies his hunger for experimentation. Until the recantation, mention of Copernicus threads through the play, but Galileo does not feel threatened by Church rejection of the Danish scientist's theories, for Copernicus needed his calculations confirmed, whereas Galileo has empirical evidence—men have merely to believe what they see. Even when the advisers of the child duke Cosimo di Medici forbid him to look through the telescope, Galileo does not recognize that none are so blind as those who will not see.

Galileo's initial refusal to admit his dangerous position is paralleled by his initial courage in another dangerous position: the plague scene shows Galileo risking death from the epidemic in order not to interrupt his experiments. But, more coolly, Galileo refuses risks. In Rome he has a "friendly conversation" with two powerful cardinals; carrying their masks of lamb and dove, they advise Galileo against research that would shake the established order. Though Galileo holds his own in the dialogue, we soon learn that he spends the next eight years in piddling experiments; the recantation is foreshadowed by this subservience to church pressure. As Brecht emphasized in the *Small Organon*: "Does not every capitulation bring the next one nearer?"

Brecht's play implies that the Church had good reason to fear science, for Galileo's discoveries will lead to the material and spiritual emancipation of the oppressed—to "a revolutionary twist," in Brecht's own phrase. The carnival scene colorfully stages the popular interpretations of Galileo's research. Astronomy becomes the gossip of the market-place, and the scientist is called "Galileo the Bible-killer." Brecht's production notes indicate the importance he attached to his theatricalization of Galileo's teachings, and, strategically, the carnival scene precedes the Pope's reluctant order that Galileo be forced to recant. Galileo's achievements can lead to either the confusion or the redemption of his people; only his personal sacrifice can change the course of history.

But Brecht's Galileo is incapable of martyrdom. Brecht lets us know that torture is a mere threat of the Church, but Galileo does not realize this till long afterward, and he recants off stage, to the disappointment of his co-workers, of the people in the market-place, and of humankind. Brecht's projection reads: "A momentous date for *you and me*" (my italics). When Galileo returns after his recantation, his pupil exclaims, "Unhappy the land that breeds no hero." But Galileo closes the scene with: "Unhappy the land that needs a hero," which reflects on his own weakness and the weakness of a hero-oriented society.

Early in the drama, Galileo exercises cunning so as to conduct experiments; in the plague scene, he exercises courage so as to continue his experiments; in the recantation scene, where courage is demanded, he reverts to cunning, lying publicly so as to be allowed limited experimentation—and an unscathed skin. Though his student Andrea condemns Galileo at the time, the student comes to admire the teacher's subterfuge: "In the field of ethics, too, you were centuries ahead of us." Old and nearly blind, however, Galileo achieves his moral vision, the pathos-mathos of the Greek tragic hero. He accuses himself harshly, "Any man who does what I have done must not be tolerated in the ranks of science." But Andrea, fingering the *Discorsi*, protests, "I cannot think that your savage analysis is the last word." The two men have changed sides in their view of scientific heroism.

For most unprejudiced viewers of the play, there is no last word on the subject of Galileo's heroism. Galileo *does* further science through his cowardice, as he *does* stifle free inquiry through his recantation. On stage the reprehensibility of that recantation is mitigated because he do not see it; on the other hand, we hear it, and we cannot remain unmoved at its violent effect on Andrea. But on stage, too, Galileo attracts us by the concreteness of his mind and the saltiness of his language, for Brecht's Galileo has the kind of unified sensibility that T. S. Eliot also ascribed to the seventeenth century. Galileo's greatness and his weakness spring from his voracious appetites—mental and material. For a hero who is as whole a man as Galileo, there seems to be no simple way to redeem his people.

It is some indication of Brecht's own complexity that, though traditional heroes emerge poorly (Galileo, Caesar, Lucullus, Don Juan, Coriolanus, even St. Joan), his common man heroes seldom redeem their people. Matti the worker is more sympathetic than Puntila sober, but neither is made of heroic stuff. Mother Courage is neither a courageous heroine nor a clever merchant. Shen Te as Shui Ta exploits her family and friends. Grusha rescues a prince, and Azdak shelters a Grand Duke, both protagonists thus betraying their class. Even Schweik, Brecht's favorite hero, does nothing more heroic than survive.[10]

Both before and during his allegiance to Marxism, Brecht's dramas tend to center on a strong protagonist who proves incapable of a heroism that might inspire his people—Kragler, Macheath, Joan, Galileo, Mother Courage, Azdak. Two children, Kattrin and Simone Machard, become martyrs for a cause, and an old woman helps bring on the Russian Revolution. But scientist, soldier, and saint—Brecht finds them wanting as heroes of a revolution that would lead towards a classless society. On our stages, however, it is this very lack of exemplary heroism that renders Brecht's characters dramatic and even sympathetic. For despite Brecht's theories, sympathy does not preclude thought;

moved though we may be, the cumulative impact of Brecht's drama *does* cause us to meditate on the resonances of heroic action.

Brecht's strong, anguished protagonists have influenced not only German drama but English as well. Robert Bolt's *A Man for All Seasons* and John Osborne's *Luther* descend directly from Brecht's *Galileo*. The first is nominally divided into two acts and the second into three, but both plays are composed of a series of Brechtian semi-independent scenes. Though both plays contain rather large casts, they center upon a towering hero who is himself aware of his own importance. Bolt acknowledges in his introduction to the play that his style is "a bastardized version of the one most recently associated with Bertolt Brecht."

Bolt's title was suggested by a contemporary description of More: "And as time requireth a man of marvellous mirth and pastimes, and sometimes of as sad gravity; a man for all seasons." Affectionate husband, loving father, loyal friend, learned scholar, and patriotic subject of his king, Bolt's More is too consistently sunny to be a man for all seasons. Thomas More refuses to sign the oath of the Acts of Succession, which established the Anglican Church and the legitimacy of the marriage of Henry VIII and Anne Boleyn. More's act is a matter of personal conscience; he is concerned with his reputation in God's eyes, not in the eyes of the people. Unlike Brecht's Galileo, Bolt's More seems unaware of the repercussions of his action; or for that matter, of his own rigidity. Not only does he refuse to sign the oath, but he refuses to explain his refusal. To his daughter, who urges him to sign, More answers: "If we lived in a State where virtue was profitable, common sense would make us good, and greed would make us saintly. And we'd live like animals or angels in the happy land that *needs* no heroes. [The Brechtian echo is patent.] But since in fact we see that avarice, anger, envy, pride, sloth, lust and stupidity commonly profit far beyond humility, chastity, fortitude, justice and thought, and have to choose, to be human at all . . . why then perhaps we *must* stand fast a little—even at the risk of being heroes." More takes the risk of being a hero, in order to be on the side of the angels.

Despite Bolt's Brechtian devices—mainly the Common Man—his play arrives at an un-Brechtian meaning. Following Brecht's insistence upon the stage as stage and actor as actor, Bolt's Common Man changes costume and role on stage; in sequence, he plays More's Steward, a Thames Boatman, an Innkeeper, a Jailer, a Foreman of the Jury, and, finally, the Executioner. The progression indicates that the responsibility for More's death devolves upon the Common Man, whose loyalties shift with the prevailing winds. To an attractive King Henry who disappears from the play when More's position grows dangerous, to a time-serving Cromwell and a poor-spirited Rich, Bolt adds the fiictional Common Man as opponent of his hero, who never wavers from his steadfast integrity. As Jailer, the Common Man tells More, "You understand my position, sir, there's nothing I can do; I'm a plain, simple man and just want to keep out of trouble." Whereupon More cries out passionately, "Oh, Sweet Jesus! These plain, simple men!" The implication is that there would be less trouble for heroes, were plain, simple men not so anxious to keep out of trouble. After playing the Executioner of Thomas More, the Common Man interprets the play for the audience, in direct address: "It isn't difficult to keep alive, friends—just don't *make* trouble—or if you must make trouble, make the sort of trouble that's expected. Well, I don't need to tell you that. Good night. If we should bump into one another, recognize me."

As what? Executioner, time-server, *semblable, frère?*

Though it may be tenable to claim that heroes are assassinated by the Common Man, Bolt has not made that position coherent in his drama, where the king's desire, Cromwell's ambition, Rich's perfidy, and More's own intransigence all contribute to his death. In the theater, however, it is the Common Man through all his disguises who drives More toward martyrdom. Bolt declares that he "meant him [the Common Man] to be attractive, and his philosophy impregnable," but an attractive and impregnable villain diminishes More as "a hero of selfhood." Unlike Brecht's Galileo, Bolt's More is neither anguished nor ambiguous; his stance is clear from the start. But Bolt's own loyalties are mixed, attempting as he does to win us to both his martyr-hero and his charming villain.

Though Bolt is not Catholic, he chose a Catholic hero to exemplify selfhood; similarly, though Osborne is not Lutheran, he chose Luther as hero of a different kind of selfhood. Self-centered and vitriolic, Osborne's heroes suffer while causing others to suffer. Somewhat like Unamuno's St. Emmanuel, Osborne's Luther preaches in order to find his faith, for he is "an animal rubbed to the bone with doubt." After his break with the Catholic Church, after he turns upon the peasants to side with the princes, after he marries a nun, that faith is still only a hope. Luther's final words to his infant son are, "Let's just hope so, eh? Eh? Let's just hope so."

As Brecht dramatizes the scientist's insatiable appetites, as Bolt dramatizes More's intransigent conscience, Osborne dramatizes Luther's suffering, whether from constipation, self-inflicted mortification, or intellectual doubt. Only sporadically does Luther think of the resonance of his actions, but Osborne dramatizes that resonance through the figure of the Knight, who appears briefly to announce the time and place of each of the twelve scenes, and who is brought to extended speech in the penultimate scene. First he conveys the exciting power of Luther—"he fizzed like a hot spark in a trail of gunpowder going off in us, that dowdy monk." Seeing a peasant corpse, the Knight bitterly laments the course of the war. When Luther comes on stage, the Knight smears the dead peasant's blood over the Protestant leader, reproaching him for the slaughter of the peasants. But Luther refuses to accept blame: "Christians are called to suffer, not fight." After Luther's wedding (in pantomime), the Knight "smashes the banner he has been holding, and tosses the remains onto the altar." Presumably, the people reject Luther's leadership; his heroism has taken no cognizance of them. The last scene of Osborne's play focuses on a Luther who still doubts, but who still hopes to resolve that doubt. What others think, and what they think of him, is not Luther's concern. Though resembling Brecht's Galileo, Osborne's Luther is more narrowly an egocentric sufferer in a one-man chronicle; neither projection nor Carnival Scene reaches for wider relevance. Henry Popkin also makes the point that both these heroes lack Brechtian charm and complexity.[11]

Similarly, in Peter Shaffer's *Royal Hunt of the Sun*, the protagonist Pisarro suffers without charm or complexity through a spectacular succession of scenes which do not add up to a coherent drama. Unlike Bolt's More and Osborne's Luther, however, Shaffer's Pisarro is given a very tangible antagonist in the person of Inca Atahuallpa, who claims to be the son of the sun. Around that antagonist Shaffer urges his scene designer to be inspired by Artaud's scenario for a dazzling Conquest of Mexico.

Shaffer's Pisarro is a mercenary soldier who confides his dreams of glory to the audience. Atahuallpa's glory moves his subjects to bring him the gold for Pisarro's men; Pisarro's glory involves the melting down of that gold so as to divide it among his men. There is no royal hunt of the sun, since Atahuallpa is captured by trickery. Confusingly, Pisarro's publicly heroic quest for gold suddenly dissolves into his privately heroic quest for meaning, which Atahuallpa can presumably deliver through elaborate gestural hocus-pocus. Though Atahuallpa yields both gold and meaning, he is killed by the Spaniards. Pisarro breaks his word to the Inca king because he fears for the life of his followers, and yet the drama shows these followers as brutal gold-hunters. Once Pisarro has betrayed the Inca king, we are told that he is a broken man who dies soon after the end of the play. Unlike Brecht's Galileo, whose lust for knowledge was another facet of his lust for food—both of which we see theatricalized—Shaffer's Pisarro slips from quest for glory to quest for gold to quest for heroic meaning—all old chestnuts of heroism—but Shaffer's dramaturgy does not seem to be critical of such slippery heroism.

America, like England, has produced its share of recent ready-made heroes, but only the plays of Arthur Miller have received serious attention. *The Crucible* and *Incident at Vichy* are Miller's only heroic dramas, and they are his only plays to be set outside of contemporary America; *The Crucible*, based on historical documents, takes place in colonial New England; *Incident at Vichy*, entirely fictional, takes place in Nazi-occupied France. Though both plays have large casts, the central interest rarely swerves from the hero, who is a wholly good man dominating a Manichean world through his martrydom. In *Incident at Vichy* Prince von Berg's self-sacrifice saves the life of Dr. Leduc, astounds the cynical German major, but has no further repercussions. In *The Crucible*, however, John Proctor's accusers urge him to confess his witchcraft because "it will strike the village." Presumably, his refusal and hanging strike them even more strongly to reject the witch-hunters, but Miller does not elaborate on this aspect.

Like Bolt's More, Miller's Proctor is pure (adultery notwithstanding) and simple, but he wavers briefly in his heroism. In order to live, he signs the confession of witchcraft but withdraws it when he realizes it will be posted publicly. *"His breast heaving, his eyes staring, Proctor tears the paper and crumples it, and he is weeping in fury, but erect."* His last words, addressed to his wife, are vindictive against his judges and melodramatic as his gestures: "Give them no tear! Tears pleasure them! Show honor now, show a stony heart and sink them with it!" Proctor's last stage act is to catch a fellow victim who almost collapses. The hysterical histrionics of the witch-scenes dissolve into the heroism of old-fashioned melodrama—without its happy ending.

Contemporary playwrights, significant and insignificant, have returned to heroism in drama, but they have been self-conscious about that return, often seeking heroes in history and myth. Playwrights rather than scholars, they have sought theatrical excitement rather than documentary fidelity, and the most impressive of these plays are precisely those which are most relevant to us. As Jan Kott interprets Shakespeare to be our contemporary, playwrights quarry their cultural heritage for men who are convertible to contemporary heroes, who can provide moral guidance for us. Through the impact upon the people in their dramas, they reach us.

FRENCH FORGED MYTH

Greek and parahistoric heroes have appeared in the drama of many nations, but French drama after World War II was aware of its search for new myths by which to dramatize the postwar French situation. Sartre spoke for them in an essay entitled "Forgers of Myths," which was published only in English and addressed specifically to Americans. Sartre claimed that the new French playwrights were interested in the larger human condition: "We feel the urge to put on the stage certain situations which throw light on the main aspects of the condition of man and to have the spectator participate in the free choice which man makes in these situations."[12] In the dramas he discusses— those of Anouilh, Beauvoir, Camus, and himself—the situations tend to occur at crucial moments in the lives of heroes whose existential choices implicate their people. Sartre was only half right in his choice of playwrights, however, since Beauvoir wrote a single play, while Anouilh developed into France's most successful essentialist playwright, whose heroes, oblivious of their people, have their choice thrust upon them. But Sartre and Camus did try to forge myths, and they both based their first dramatic publications on classical literature—*The Flies* and *Caligula*; neither returned to the classics for their myths (though Sartre adapted *The Trojan Women* of Euripides).

Camus' Caligula, his first dramatic hero, is drawn from *Twelve*

Caesars of the Roman historian, Suetonius. Romantic in his sensitivity and suffering, Camus' Caligula claims to act, like mythical heroes, for the good of his people. One of the questions posed by the play is *what* is good for a people. Conceived before World War II, Camus' *Caligula* was not performed till the end of the war, in a revised version.[13] It is the drama of a man with a passion for the impossible; Caligula announces, "There's no understanding fate; therefore I choose to play the part of fate" (Stuart Gilbert translation). Playing the part of fate, exaggerating the Absurdity of being-in-the-world, Caligula hopes to make his people aware of the Absurd.

Camus' source, Suetonius, divides his history of Caligula into two parts, the Emperor and the Monster. The death of Caligula's sister-mistress Drusilla turns the Emperor into a Monster. Camus, however, underplays the death of Drusilla; instead, it is the quest for the impossible, the imitation of Absurdity, that turns the Emperor into a Monster. He says, "This world has no importance; once a man realizes that, he wins his freedom." Camus' Caligula is a portrait of the Emperor as Monster, but also as would-be-hero-redeemer of his people.

Like later Absurdist plays, *Caligula* is built on pattern as much as plot, repetition as much as development. Each of the four acts has a tripartite structure, Caligula dominating them all: 1) an opening crowd scene leads to the entrance of Caligula, 2) Caligula presides at a public spectacle, 3) Caligula confronts someone head-on. Within each act, as in the totality of the drama, the movement is from the dense crowd to the solitary hero.

As emperor, Caligula is Lord of Rule as well as Misrule, and he is therefore perfectly equipped to create Absurdist Chaos. As emperor, he subverts the very values on which his power rests—civil government, respect for religion, and family cohesion. In each of the four acts, it is through play and display that Caligula undermines the legal, religious, and artistic traditions of his heritage. For play is the thing that has caught the consciousness of this king: "Any man can play the lead in the divine comedy and become a god. All he needs to do is harden his heart." In the drama itself, however, Camus reveals no gradual hardening of the heart, as Shakespeare does in *Macbeth*; from Caligula's first confrontation with the Patricians, his heart *is* hard, and Caligula's hubris fits his heartlessness. Though he claims a pedagogic and heroic function, theatrical sadism is his pleasure.

In Act I Caligula drily sets a higher value on property than on life, listing an arbitrary order in which his subjects are to die. By Act II, when the Patricians grumble at Caligula's off-stage cruelties, he perpetrates them on stage, in their and our presence—forcing Lepidus to laugh at his son's death, leaving Mucius to fume while he retires to make love to Mucius' wife, poisoning Mereia on the pretext that he took an antidote against Caligula's poison. In Act III the curtain rises on a proscenium behind the proscenium, revealing Caligula dressed as Venus, to whom his mistress Caesonia addresses a parody litany. The rest of the act deals with more subtle perversions of love and faith. Insisting only on his desire for the moon, Caligula shrugs off Helicon's warning about the plot against his life. Caligula closes Act III by destroying the evidence against the chief plotter, Cherea—capriciously, absurdly, since Caligula wishes his people to be aware of Absurdity. Act IV contains Caligula's death, "a superior suicide" as Camus was later to phrase it. At the beginning of the act, Caligula's death is announced though he is very much alive. The play closes with Caligula's actual death, his last words protesting that he is still alive.

In Act I Caligula had asked Helicon for the moon, and Caesonia for her presence at a spectacle; by the end of Act IV Helicon has not brought the moon, and Caligula no longer desires the presence of Caesonia at a spectacle. Caligula strangles Caesonia because she ties him to his life; she alone affirms the possible, the frail, the fading. Before the play opened, Caligula had been brought by the death of Drusilla to an awareness of the Absurd;

at the end of the play, Caligula is brought by the death of Caesonia to an awareness of the inadequacy of imitating the Absurd, which has aroused his people's hatred but not their awareness of Absurdity.

In his preface to the American edition of his plays, Camus explains: "Caligula accepts death because he has understood that no one can save himself all alone—and that one cannot be free at the expense of others." This sounds like the restoration of a moral order, a redemption of his people through a kind of Golden Rule, but in the play itself Caligula comes to this understanding only briefly, and he accepts the inevitability of his own death before and after that understanding. However, his last words are not a calm acceptance of death, but a final defiant expression of Absurdity—"I'm still alive."

Though Cherea and the Patricians triumph in Rome, theirs is a shaky alliance. Far from restoring the moral order, the new regime can at best slow down the tempo, dull down the drama of Absurdity, in which men will continue to die and be unhappy. As Camus wrote in his first sketch of the play: "No, Caligula is not dead. He is in each one of us."

To kill Caligula "in each one of us," Camus sought further among classical heroes and re-interpreted the Greek Sisyphus myth; Sisyphus becomes his positive hero, whereas Caligula remained negative. Caligula desired the moon, but Sisyphus is condemned to a stone on earth. Caligula sought the impossible, but Sisyphus lives with his severely limited possibilities. "The gods had condemned Sisyphus to roll a rock to the top of a mountain, from which the rock would then fall by its own weight." While the rock falls, Sisyphus watches the swift undoing of his long labor; as he slowly descends the mountain before beginning his task again, he meditates upon his destiny. His only superiority over the rock lies in that meditation, in his consciousness: "The lucidity that was to torment him is at the same time his victory."

In a review of Camus' novel *The Stranger* Sartre wrote, "The absurd is a condition as well as a lucid consciousness some people have of this condition." Both Sisyphus and Caligula have this lucidity, but Sisyphus is happy whereas Caligula is histrionic about this lucidity—which is why Camus was right to put his Absurdist hero Sisyphus into an essay, his Absurdist hero Caligula into a drama.

In his subsequent three dramas, Camus splits in two the parts of Absurdist hero, treating Absurdism in *The Misunderstanding* and heroism in *State of Siege* and *The Just Assassins*. Like Caligula, the latter two plays center on heroes who are highly conscious of the public resonance of their acts. In his preface to *State of Siege* Camus tells of Barrault's desire for "a spectacle around the myth of the plague, which had also tempted Antonin Artaud." As redemptive hero, Rieux of Camus' novel *The Plague* is more complex and, ultimately, more heroically effiacious than Diego of *State of Siege*. A conventional hero, Diego conquers his own fear in order to die with his plague-ridden people. Dramatically, the plague overshadows Diego, as Caligula overshadows the *raisonneur* Cherea. The play's end is therefore unexpected: the Fisherman lyrically salutes the resurgence of life, implicitly made possible by Diego's sacrificial death.

In contrast to Diego, who learns to die, Kaliayev of *The Just Assassins* learns to kill for his suffering people, but the play raises the question of whether assassination is ever justified. In a chapter of *The Rebel* called "Sensitive Murderers" Camus discusses the Russian anarchists who failed to throw a bomb at the Grand Duke bacause there were children in his carriage. Drawing his material from *Memoirs of a Terrorist* by Boris Savinkov, Camus dramatizes their story in *The Just Assassins*. He expands upon his source in the fourth act, which is centered on Kaliayev after the bombing. Through various confrontations, doubts begin to assail the "sensitive murderer," and Kaliayev welcomes his own execution as an expiation of his action. But for his fellow anarchist, Dora, violence alone can justify violence; when she hears of his death, she volunteers to throw the next bomb.

As Rima Drell Reck has remarked, Camus' heroes seek their self-identity through the pursuit of absolutes; and they fail precisely because they do not recognize human limitations.[14] In Cherea's words to Caligula: "What I want is to live, and to be happy. Neither, to my mind, is possible if one pushes the absurd to its logical conclusions." Thus, the would-be hero is rarely a hero for Camus. In stumbling on his own rock, in conquering his own fear, Sisyphus and Diego, respectively, plead for an immersion in life, which is ultimately more redemptive than the heroics of Caligula and Kaliayev.

Like Camus, Sartre is deeply concerned about a code of ethics for modern man in a world deprived of supernatural sanctions, and more often than Camus, he committed such concerns to dramatic expression. Like Camus, Sartre confined his use of classical material to his first play, *The Flies*, and more often than Camus, Sartre examined the problem in other times, other places. Thus, *No Exit* takes place in Hell, *Death Without Burial* in the French Resistance during World War II, *Dirty Hands* in an imaginary Balkan country during World War II, *The Devil and the Good Lord* in Germany during the Peasants' Revolt. Also relevant is Sartre's adaptation of Arthur Miller's *Crucible*, set in seventeenth-century Salem. By the nature of his own ethics, Sartre poses the problem of heroism in each individual action, since man making an ethical choice chooses for all men.

In *Existentialism Is a Humanism*, Sartre wrote: "What the existentialist says is that the coward develops into a coward, the hero develops into a hero; there is always a possibility that the coward will be one no longer, that the hero will be one no longer. What counts is the total commitment, and you are not totally committed by a particular circumstance, a particular action."[15] In his first play *The Flies*, Sartre dramatizes "the total commitment" of a positive hero, but Orestes is the first and last positive hero in his drama. In his second play *No Exit* Garcin has made his commitment as a coward, and he cannot escape from cowardice since such possibilities exist only during life.

In *The Words* Sartre admits that he has always preferred reading detective stories to Wittgenstein, but most of his works combine an influence from both areas, and Eric Bentley aptly labeled Sartre's plays "philosophic melodramas." Torture, murder, rape, lynching, execution, suicide, bombing, civil and uncivil war—no Sartre play lacks such violence, and no Sartre play lacks a serious philosophic direction. Of all his plays, perhaps his third, *Death Without Burial* (also translated as *The Victors* and *Men Without Shadows*) most relentlessly combines his two tastes. More directly than *No Exit* or even *The Flies*, *Death Without Burial* poses the problem of the meaning of contemporary heroism.

The title *Death Without Burial* evokes classical Antigone, but the situation was fresh in contemporary French memory. Five members of the French underground are tortured to reveal the hiding-place of their leader, Jean. Convinced that they can redeem their people through loyalty, and not knowing where Jean is, each of the five has no choice about suffering—an adolescent and his sister, a seasoned revolutionary, a less seasoned worker, and a coward. Suddenly Jean is brought into their cell, unidentified by the collaborators, and now the decision of heroism has concrete and present point. The coward, recognizing his physical cowardice, bravely commits suicide rather than reveal Jean's identity and imperil their cause. When the boy threatens to reveal Jean's identity, the unseasoned underground worker kills him. Jean urges the other three, all of whom are tortured off stage, to make a false revelation after he is freed. Though they have felt themselves dead, the three Resistance members slowly return to thoughts of life. They give the false information, but are nevertheless shot by a collaborator who "thought it was more humane."

Despite the ironic end, however, the three survivors *have* acted heroically; they were ready to die when there was a reason to die, and they forced themselves to live, after excruciating torture, when there was no reason to die. The final outcome could not be one of the factors in their choice. In his Spanish Civil War story, *The Wall*, Sartre uses a similar climax to make the same point: a Spanish Loyalist, tortured to reveal the hiding-place of his leader, reveals a false hiding-place, which, ironically, proves to be correct. Again, the choice for heroism is made in the existent situation; what happens afterward cannot be calculated. It is a workaday, free choice arising from the situation, and not from a sudden sense of *noblesse oblige*, as in Miller's *Incident at Vichy*.

Though there was probably no direct influence, Sartre's attitudes toward heroism in *Death Without Burial* and *Dirty Hands* resemble those of Camus in *State of Siege* and *Just Assassins*. In the first play of each pair, heroic action means dying with dignity for the good of one's people; later, heroic action poses the problem of killing for a cause, which emerges as coldly abstract, when compared to the concrete person to be murdered.

Though ostensibly set in Central Europe, Illyria of *Dirty Hands* is as French as Shakespeare's *Twelfth Night* Illyria was English. Taking the form of a flashback re-enactment, *Dirty Hands* centers on Hugo, a young bourgeois intellectual who joins the Communist Party in his desire for commitment, and who volunteers to assassinate the Party chief, Hoederer, in his desire for direct action. Thus, Hugo begins very close to where Orestes arrives in *The Flies*—engagement through violence—but in this play Sartre pauses on the deed itself—murder.

Hoederer, the victim, is perhaps the most likable character in Sartre's drama; when he enters the play, it is to arbitrate between his worker-bodyguards and the bourgeois Hugo, and he does this without polemics, without sermons, preserving everyone's dignity. So that we have seen evidence by the time he tells Hugo, "And I, I love [men] for what they are. With all their filth and all their vices, I love their voices and their warm grasping hands, and their skin, the nudest skin of all, and their uneasy glances, and the desperate struggle each has to pursue against anguish and against death" (Lionel Abel translation). Hoederer understands both the aristocratic Prince who acts *for* his class, and bourgeois Hugo who acts *against* his class. He condones political assassination, but there is no evidence that he engages in it. He seeks political power for his party, which he does not equate with himself. Hoederer deliberately risks his life, so as to spare Hugo embarrassment.

Hugo shoots Hoederer only when the pretext is furnished by his wife in Hoederer's arms. But Hugo cannot, like Orestes, assume clear and conscious responsibility for the deed as a heroic act. Instead, like Garcin in *No Exit*, Hugo broods about his motives while serving a jail sentence. Ironically, it is Hugo's very uncertainty, his lack of pride in his deed, that makes him salvageable for the Party upon his release. Having shifted to Hoederer's tactics, the Party is now glorifying the dead leader and can forgive his murderer only if he denies his deed. But a Hugo that is salvageable to the Party is unsalvageable to himself; if the principles were wrong for which he killed, then the deed was wrong, and the Party was wrong. Without a cause larger than himself, Hugo's heroism collapses, and he chooses to meet death at the hands of the Party killers. Like Kaliayev of *The Just Assassins*, Hugo needs a just principle by which to act; pragmatic shifting and "dirty hands" are incommensurate with his ideal of heroism. Though neither Camus nor Sartre pronounces didactic judgment, the emotional weight of both plays is against "just" assassins who claim that their acts will redeem their people.

In only one drama does Sartre take an ironic attitude toward killing, and to do this he sets a fictional hero in the period of Germany's religious wars. *The Devil and the Good Lord* teeters so frequently between heroism and heroics that it is difficult to know how much of this Sartre intended. When we first see Goetz, bastard of a noblewoman and a peasant, he has betrayed his brother and laid siege to a city. Like Genet's characters (who fascinated Sartre at the time he wrote this play), Goetz thrives on evil. Far from caring about the redemption of his people, Goetz is exclusively interested in his relationship with God. Nor is he concerned, like Claudel's heroes, with the salvation of his soul, but rather with a hubristic dialogue with God, as between equals: "There is only God, the phantoms, and myself" (Kitty Black translation). Goetz believes that his evil deeds will damn him, but that God cannot exist without them. His zestful dedication to evil recalls Caligula's glee at playing fate: "Listen, I am going to take a nice little blood-bath to oblige the Lord." However, when the renegade priest Heinrich convinces Goetz that everyone does evil, and only good is impossible, Goetz meets the challenge: "I was a criminal—I will reform. I turn my coat and wager I can be a saint." Even the phrasing recalls Genet's inseparable couple of criminal-saint.

But pure good proves to be as difficult as pure evil; Goetz is able to found his City of Light only through lies and tricks. His almost comic dedication to good parallels his ironic commitment to evil; with his peasants he sounds like a French nursemaid, but his charges are massacred when they obediently do not fight invaders. Goetz then reverts to a private dialogue with God—fasting and flagellating himself in a parody of church martyrs: "There we are Lord; we are face to face again, as in the good old days when I was doing evil."

Self-mortification brings him no sign, as it did the saints, and the hubristic dialogue proves to be a monologue. Like Orestes before the sign of Zeus, Goetz is suddenly aware of the Absurdity of being-in-the-world: "Silence is God. Absence is God. God is the loneliness of men." Reacting to this loneliness with a desire for human brotherhood, Goetz asks to be a common soldier in the peasant army. But the army needs generals far more than common soldiers, and Goetz finally consents to return to warfare and killing: "I killed God because He divided me from mankind, and now I see that His death has isolated me even more surely. . . .

I shall make men hate me, because I know no other way of loving them. I shall give them orders, since I have no other way of being among men." Through personal need, Goetz heroically accepts the rescue of his people in spite of themselves.

Sartre's *The Condemned of Altona* deals only peripherally with the question of heroism; it carries a negative comment on a heroic action that fails to create a community of men. In *Death Without Burial* heroism was dramatized in the need to die for a cause. In *Dirty Hands* and *The Flies* heroism included the need to kill for a cause. In *The Condemned of Altona* the hero Frantz tortures and kills as a Nazi officer. Refusing to atone for his crimes when the war is over, he retires into a fiction that annihilates time, sequestering himself in the attic of the family home, and communicating only with his sister. When his sister-in-law, Johanna, intrudes upon his attic sequestration, Frantz slowly takes stock of himself and of reality. He was born into a wealthy industrialist's family, and his traditional heroism was ready-made for him; in accepting his father's world, he acquiesced to the Nazi regime and all its concommitant horrors. By the end of the play, both Frantz and his father realize that ready-made heroism and patriotic glory—inauthentic abstractions—carried within them the hideous sacrifice of individual men. Father and son can atone only by suicide, since they have committed crimes beyond the possibility of redemption.

In his first play alone Sartre dramatizes an exemplary hero, Orestes, acting for the polis like his Aeschylean ancestor. In subsequent plays, rather than presenting a *model* of heroism, Sartre dramatizes the *meaning* of heroism in the contemporary world. Sartre's whole ethical approach has been criticized as a "doctrine for heroes." When Oreste Pucciani faced Sartre with a student's question, "How can the little people be engaged?" the philosopher-playwright, instead of answering, remarked on differences between France and California.[16] But the student was a perceptive critic, for Sartre's plays are about the engagement of "big" people whose actions determine the destiny of little people, as surely as do the heroes of Claudel and Brecht. Sartre's ethical mystique also insists that "The individual's act involves all humanity. . . . I am responsible for myself and for everyone, and I create a certain image of man, which I choose. In choosing myself, I choose man."[17] The plays do not "prove" this, but they are built on deeds that involve all other men. As Jacques Guicharnaud points out: "Men are not truly men in their petty and niggardly daily acts but rather at the moment the idea of man is heroically brought into question through themselves."[18]

Today many of these plays seem theatrically old-fashioned, like the realistic problem plays scorned by these same writers. And evaluation of the plays is still influenced by the lives and dedication of their respective authors. But the most intense of the plays resonate beyond their authors' lives and beyond the particular mode—*Caligula, The Devil and the Good Lord*, whose heroes are not exemplary models of modern heroism. The last play of Jean Genet dramatizes a hero who makes the unexemplary exemplary.

In Genet's first play, *Deathwatch*, Lefranc studies Green Eyes in order to become a hero, and that study explains his failure. Green Eyes implies that heroes are born and not made; he did not plan his murder: "It was all given to me. A gift from God or the devil, but something I didn't want." Heroism was thrust upon him, like the worship of his cell-mates.

Beginning with Genet's *The Balcony*, however, heroic actions are more consciously performed against a more varied social background. In *The Balcony* the Queen rules by absence; symbolic figures conduct the practical affairs of government, and they are made symbolic by their office. Only the Chief of Police seeks to rise above his office into absence, into an abstraction of Heroism. Though he achieves his goal, his tactics have been clumsy, and his effect on his people is confined to Roger's grotesque self-castration. In *The Blacks* the hero remains off stage while the white audience is entertained by a clown show, and that white audience can never know the effect of the real black hero upon his people.

In *The Screens*, however, Genet produces the most prodigious myth of the postwar French theater. Algerian Saïd forges that heroic myth through his single-minded abjection. An Arab in a warring world, Saïd is above the battle, scarcely aware that there is a battle. As the poorest of Arab men, he must marry Leila, the ugliest of Arab women, and *The Screens* dramatizes his life from his marriage to his death.

In the opening scene, Saïd and his mother reveal their determination to be no one in particular. As ambitious for Saïd's abjection as the mother of Coriolanus for his glory, Saïd's mother impresses upon him the humiliation of his marriage to Leila: "She's left over because she's ugly. And you, because you're poor. She needs a husband, you a wife. She and you take what's left, you take each other" (Bernard Frechtman translation).

This marriage of left-overs early acquires mythic power as Saïd and his mother imitate thunder and lightning so that "The whole wedding'll be drenched." Moreover, the marriage develops into a perfect spiritual union; under the aegis of Saïd's mother, the poorest man and the ugliest woman perfect themselves in evil. Trained by Saïd's mother, Leila steals from her neighbors, and Saïd steals from his fellow workers, but they are cruelest of all to each other. Leila deliberately increases her ugliness, and Saïd increases his poverty by visits to the brothel.

Leila understands Saïd's dedication to evil, and she offers herself as an instrument toward his martyrdom. "I'll obey you," she assures him, then reveals the full measure of her devotion:

> But I want—it's my ugliness, earned hour by hour, that speaks, or what speaks?—I want you to stop looking backward. I want you to lead me without flinching to the land of shadow and of the monster. I want you to plunge into irrevocable grief. I want you—it's my ugliness, earned min-

ute by minute, that speaks—to be without hope. I want you
to choose evil and always evil. I want you to know only
hatred and never love. I want you—it's my ugliness, earned
second by second, that speaks—to refuse the brilliance of
darkness, the softness of flint, and the honey of thistles.
I know where we're going, Saïd, and why we're going there.
It's not just to go somewhere, but so that those who are
sending us there remain tranquil, on a tranquil shore.
We're here, and we're here so that those who are sending
us here realize that they're not here.

In Genet's world, the people is dependent upon a hero for its
very definition. Both Arabs and Europeans send Saïd "here" so
as to "realize that they're not here."

Prismatically, lesser heroes are reflected through Saïd: the
French Foreign Legion is trained by the Lieutenant, who is inspired by the Sergeant, who, in turn, is the beautiful mirror of
Saïd. Through Saïd, Warda refines her sacramental role, so that
Arab heroes emerge from her brothel. The Arab wise women,
Kadidja and Ommu, repeat Saïd's name as an incantation. Kadidja, on the threshold of death, prays to what is later explicitly
called a "holy family": "Saïd, Leila, my loved ones! You, too, in
the evening related the day's evil to each other. You realized that
in evil lay the only hope. Evil, wonderful evil, you who remain when all goes to pot, miraculous evil, you're going to help
us. I beg of you, evil, and I beg you standing upright, impregnate
my people."

Impregnated with evil, the Arabs rise against the colonialists.
As Leila drew a stolen clock on the screen, they draw the weapons
of their revolution. It is Saïd's treason—instructing the Admiral
to send "steamboats crossing the rye fields, . . . sailors in the al-
falfa"—that leads to Arab victory. But when the Arabs gain the
upper hand, they begin to conform to a new order that resembles
the old European order. The Arab village grows contemptuous of
prison and brothel, and the Arab army seeks Saïd as earnestly as
did the French Foreign Legion.

In the final scene of *The Screens* when Saïd arrives in the village, led by the old Arab woman Ommu, all groups—living and dead—turn to look at him. Ommu declares that Saïd's abjection is to be embalmed; he is to be deified, brow in the nebulae and feet in the ocean. But the rational Arab combatants reject such mysticism; they wish to arrest Saïd, to imitate the colonialists, and to appropriate their proverbs. The oracular old Ommu and the rational young soldiers fight over Saïd, who answers them gently, "To the old gal, to the soldiers, to all of you, I say shit." However, rejection proves difficult; Ommu urges Saïd to escape into the forest, and the soldiers order him to stay in the village. From the Domain of the Dead, Saïd's mother pleads with him to be neutral. Whether he acts or fails to act, Saïd is choosing sides, doomed to be a hero for one or the other. He hesitates, starts to leave, and is shot.

Among the dead, Saïd's mother, who has had a village square named after her (although she is nameless in the play), asks when her Saïd is coming, declares that she will wait for him. But the dead Kadidja informs her, "Don't bother. He'll no more be back than will Leila." Roger Blin's production closed on this line, but the published texts go further. "Then where is he?" asks the Mother anxiously. In the French version Kadidja answers enigmatically, "Among the dead." In the English translation, however, which Bernard Frechtman did from a revised script, the Mother asks, "Then where is he? In a song?" Kadidja *extends her palms with a gesture of doubt.*" All versions seem to agree that Saïd and Leila have gone beyond song, beyond legend, into oblivion. In early Genet works, his eternal couples of criminal-saint move from abjection to apotheosis, but Saïd, who combines criminal and saint in himself, moves from abjection through sainthood into the void, and it is by that heroic trajectory that he becomes a banner to his people. French myths forged during war are gilded in Genet's song.

HEROIC NON-HEROES AND ANTI-HEROES

Catholic, Existentialist, Marxist, and Skeptic playwrights have shown a resurgence of interest in the dramatic role of the mythic hero. Only the Greek-based heroes tend to be exemplary, but exemplary or not, these modern heroes nevertheless guide their people through their actions, and they always imply a morality for *us*, who are also their people. Legendary, parahistorical, or frankly invented, these dramatic heroes dominate their dramas, whose modern moulds retain much of the dignity of the tragic tradition. But modern drama also casts another reflection on heroism; the non-hero and the anti-hero can also influence their people; even, more rarely, redeem them through the very lack of heroism.

Eugène Ionesco seems nostalgic for heroism as a viable theme, but he dramatizes that theme within his farcical metaphysic. In his third play, *Jack—or The Submission*, Jack briefly attempts to resist a world of bourgeois clichés, but that heroism soon crumples —as indicated by the title. Ionesco's fourth play, *The Chairs*, presents a nameless Old Man with a vocation of heroism. Four subsequent Ionesco plays focus on Bérenger, a Chaplinesque figure, who proves to be a hero in spite of himself.

Concierge on an island, the Old Man of *The Chairs* has visions of a heroic destiny, and his wife has visions of the heroic careers he might have had. The theme of their pre-chairs conversation, for all its non sequitur, is a heroic might-have-been, as the theme of their manipulation of chairs is a heroic message. The Old Couple manipulate the chairs for an invisible audience, privileged to hear a professional orator deliver the Old Man's heroic message. Throughout the proliferation of chairs and the fragmentation of language, the Old Man and the Old Woman sustain their commonplace heroic vision. But one of the ironies of this "tragic farce" is that, in spite of their clichés of heroism, of obstacles to heroism, of the satisfactions in a quiet life—in spite of their obvious lack of heroism, their deaths give them dignity.

Once the Old Couple jump out of their respective windows into the moat, the chairs suddenly emerge as terribly empty. Although the heroic vision was banal, the implementation of that vision seemed to create a country for the hero to redeem. After the suicides, however, that country is abruptly inhabited by chairs instead of people, and chairs are impervious to immortal messages. But we, the real audience, are not made of wood; we, the real audience who have been watching an imaginary audience, are still waiting for the heroic message, and it is we who cannot be redeemed, since the Professional Orator proves to be mute. Thus, the heroic message is non-deliverable or non-existent, and the would-be hero is cut down still further in the Orator's final spastic efforts, and in the *"human noises of the invisible crowd; these are bursts of laughter, murmurs, shh's, ironic coughs."* The would-be hero is not only a non-hero; he is finally a non-entity. In contrast to Bérenger of Ionesco's later plays, who wants only to live his own life in a chaotic world, the nameless Old Man of *The Chairs* invents a life for his ridiculous heroic ideal.

In the Bérenger plays (*The Killer, Rhinoceros, The Pedestrian of the Air*, and *Exit the King*) the ideal of non-heroism becomes the only heroic ideal. Bérenger is a heroic non-hero. The very name Bérenger contains resonances of commoner and king, for Bérenger is the name of kings in the first millennium of French history, and it is also the name of the democratic nineteenth-century song-writer. Ionesco makes his Bérenger a nondescript, naive man of good will in his first two plays, written within a few months of each other in 1957–58. An undistinctive citizen, the Bérenger of *The Killer* has no profession, and in *Rhinoceros* he is a clerk. Neither play is named for its unprepossessing protagonist, but for the antagonists, the Killer and Rhinoceros.

Bérenger of *The Killer* is more vulnerable than his successor, for he is attracted by a radiant city, not realizing that artificially planned cities are the inevitable prey of killers. Slowly, he perceives that the Killer never strikes those who are protected by the Administration; pretty Dany is killed only when she leaves the Administration, in protest against its indifference to killing. And it is Dany's death that drives Bérenger to action against the Killer.

Bérenger of *Rhinoceros*, disheveled, hung over, is more concerned about his quarrel with his friend Jean than by rhinoceroses in the street, which are no affair of his. In contrast to Bérenger of *The Killer*, who leaves his familiar world for the radiant city where the Killer lurks, Bérenger of *Rhinoceros* tries to live only his personal life, indifferent to the epidemic of rhinoceros that is spreading through the world.

Both plays end in a confrontation of protagonist and antagonist, and in both plays, this confrontation takes the form of a monologue by Bérenger. Though Bérenger stands face to face with the Killer and pleads with him to answer, the Killer is mute; his only reply is a snicker. And such is the nature of Bérenger, protagonist of good will, that he voices a reply for his antagonist. Beginning his monologue in indignation at the crimes of the Killer, he shifts to trying to understand them, to finding reasons for them. As Ionesco indicates in his introductory scenic remarks, "Bérenger finds in himself, in spite of himself, against himself, arguments in favor of the Killer" (Donald Watson translation). Overwhelmed by such arguments, he lays down his old-fashioned pistols and kneels before the Killer's knife, closing the play: "Oh God! There's nothing we can do. What can we do. . . . What can we do. . . ." Bérenger acts by reason rather than intuition, and he is helpless before the Killer.

In *Rhinoceros* Bérenger tries to act by reason, but he shows himself more emotional than his predecessor. After experiencing the terrible loneliness of Daisy's desertion, he feels guilt about his conduct, then worry about Daisy's welfare. As the rhinoceroses roar outside, he thinks of reasoning with them, then wonders whether they are not right. And if they are right, they are handsome as well, and the human face he sees in the mirror is an ugly monstrosity. For a moment, he tries to roar, wishing he were a rhinoceros. But since he cannot perform a metamorphosis, he takes up his gun to defend his humanity: "I will not capitulate." Without reason, by nature: "I will not capitulate." Bérenger of *Rhinoceros* illustrates a famous dictum of one of Ionesco's favorite writers, Pascal: "The heart has its reasons that Reason ignores." Acting by reason, Bérenger of *The Killer* lays down his gun; acting by irrational instinct, Bérenger of *Rhinoceros* takes up his gun to resist rhinoceros; the common man becomes a hero. In neither play is there hope of spreading resistance to the people in the play, but the heroism nevertheless has redemptive resonance: if that little man can be heroic, maybe I can too, though I act for myself alone, without heroics.

Ionesco's next two Bérenger plays, written within a few months of one another in 1962, are centered around a protagonist of greater social stature—the successful playwright of *The Pedestrian of the Air*, and the King of *Exit the King*. In contrast to *The Killer* and *Rhinoceros*, agons with overpowering antagonists, the two later plays focus on the emotional life of Bérenger. Significantly, the first two plays are titled after the antagonists, the second after the protagonists, for Bérenger walks on air in *Pedestrian*, and he is a king in *Exit the King*. The *Pedestrian* is remarkable in its scenic variety—bombardment, acrobatics, other-world scenes—whereas *Exit the King*, nearly twice as long, is remarkable for its intensity—the reactions of a man as he dies.

So divergent and surrealistic are the events of *The Pedestrian* that it is difficult to follow its theme of death. Bérenger has come to England because his creative powers are dead. During the course of the play, his wife Josephine learns but refuses to accept the news that her father has died. Among the characters are a Funeral Attendant dressed in black, an Inhabitant of the Anti-world who resembles a ghost, hooded executioners, a John Bull who shoots two children, a gallows to which an executioner tries to tempt Josephine, and Bérenger's apocalyptic vision of universal death. Such enumeration, however, imposes a unity that is not apparent in the play, which ends with the small family huddled together, temporarily spared by death.

Early in *The Pedestrian* Bérenger tells a journalist that he is paralyzed because he knows that he is going to die. In this paralysis lies the entire action of *Exit the King*. The subject of man facing death constitutes one of the major strands of medieval drama, the Morality Play, whose best-known example is *Everyman*. Far from the medieval psychomachia, however, as a result of which the soul is eternally saved or damned, Ionesco dwells upon the process of dying, with the implication that life is all, and there is nothing beyond. Man dying is symbolized by the king who loses his hold on his kingdom.

In *The Pedestrian* Bérenger conquers space only to learn that death exists even beyond the earth; in *Exit the King* Bérenger is conquered by time, for it is in time that death claims man. The spatial effects of the first play contrast with the grotesque temporal effects of the second. Very literally, Ionesco calls attention to the remaining time of the play, which exactly equals the time that the king still has to live. He dies at the end, and the set disintegrates and disappears. Our world dies with us.

The cumulative effect of the four Bérenger plays suggests what none of the four does singly—a Portrait of the Determined Non-Hero. In the first two plays, a private individual faces powerful forces (social or metaphysical); it takes heroic stature to oppose these forces, and little Bérenger rises to such stature, in spite of his natural timidity. Through his intuitive assertion of a moral order, Bérenger shows himself capable of redeeming his people, though the plays actually end on his solitude. Non-heroic, he fights. In the second pair of plays, Bérenger is an uncommon man —writer and king—who has to face that most common human experience death. Refusing cliché heroics, he rebels against the Absurdity of being-in-the-world; against death. Unheroic, he is inspired by fear to fight death itself.

More socially than metaphysically oriented, Dürrenmatt's protagonists are also non-heroic, sometimes taking a directly *anti*-heroic stance. In his book on Theater Problems, Dürrenmatt groups his non-heroes, though he does not designate them by that word: "The Blind Man, Romulus, Uberlohe, Akki are all men of courage. The lost world order is restored within them" (Gerhard Nellhaus translation). These Dürrenmatt characters are loyal to a past that has been rejected by a forward-moving society. The Blind Man, Romulus, Uberlohe, and Akki refuse heroic action in a time of action. Hostile to heroism, they are literally anti (opposed to) heroes. Their courage lies in not performing brave deeds; for Dürrenmatt the true hero does nothing. In inaction alone lies a moral power which can save a people.

Dürrenmatt's *Blind Man* is about a hero who sees further than those with sight. Written shortly after World War II, *The Blind Man* is set in the Thirty Years' War. A blind duke reigns tranquilly in "the peace of [his] country and the peace of [his] soul." However, an Italian invader arrives to disturb both peaces, subjecting the duke to a series of misfortunes which recall those of biblical Job. Though the duke suffers loss of son, daughter, and dukedom, he remains convinced of God's greatness and the order of His world. Such faith finally disturbs the cynicism of his conqueror, who, admitting defeat, returns to the war at large; his last lines summarize the paradoxical heroism of the blind duke, who triumphs through inaction:

> I yield to you, groping like a blind man.
> You did not resist me and you conquered me.
> I was destroyed by one who did not defend himself.
> I leave you now, as Satan left Job, a black shadow.

The Duke blesses his "black shadow." Though the Duke is left with a Wasteland, there is peace in that land.

Subsequent Dürrenmatt heroes take a similar stance of peaceful non-resistance, but none of them takes it so blindly and completely. They are aware of the anachronism of their position—

nostalgia for a "lost world order"—in a time of power politics. Dürrenmatt, like Shaw and Giraudoux, sees history as repetitious in pattern, and in *Marriage of Mr. Mississippi* the corpses arise to enunciate this explicitly: "We return again and again as we always returned." Dürrenmatt traces fictional history through *Romulus the Great*, a Roman play, *Marriage of Mr. Mississippi*, a contemporary play in a fictional country, *An Angel Comes to Babylon*, a play of biblical Babylon, and *The Visit*, a contemporary play set in an imaginary Swiss town.

Of these four plays, only *Romulus the Great* (subtitled "an un-historical comedy") deals even remotely with real history, set as it is on the Ides of March, 476, date that the historical Odoacer forced the resignation of Romulus Augustulus, Rome's child emperor. In Dürrenmatt's play, however, the child is replaced by a man of fifty, who is more devoted to his chickens than to his warriors. Romulus displays no concern that the German armies are marching on Rome, for Rome's emperor, a more determined anti-hero than the blind duke, has deliberately married a Roman princess in order to dissolve a corrupt empire. "You are Rome's betrayer," his wife accuses Romulus, but he replies, "No, I am Rome's judge" (Gerhard Nellhaus translation). The soldiers call him Little Romulus (*der Kleine*), but Dürrenmatt's title *Romulus THE GREAT* (my emphasis) indicates his sympathy for an emperor who sets hedonistic humanism above military glory. In the final act, German Odoacer is revealed as similarly humane, and the two rulers vie with one another in a gamesmanship of gracious surrender, but even as they do, the goose-stepping Theoderich is biding his time to replace them both. "He is a hero," Romulus describes Theoderich, and, later, "People want heroism." At best, the two middle-aged humanists can borrow a civilized respite for their peoples, in spite of their respective peoples.

Though Dürrenmatt groups the blind duke, the peaceful Roman Emperor, Uberlohe, and Akki in their devotion to a lost ideal, it is some measure of his own increasing pessimism that the anti-heroic Uberlohe and Akki play lesser roles in their respective dramas. Uberlohe, in the final scene of *Marriage of Mr. Mississippi*, appears as Don Quixote, futile and comic. Not even a pawn, he is a fringe nuisance in the power struggle between Mississippi, an absolute Calvinist, and St. Claude, an absolute Marxist. We see Uberlohe only in comic guise, "often beaten down, often laughed at," literally charging at a windmill as the curtain falls— saving no one, not even himself.

In *An Angel Comes to Babylon*, on the other hand, Akki the beggar does not forget the wider resonances of his moral stance. He remains a beggar because he sees corruption in all but the humblest occupations—begging, prostitution, poetry, and—grotesquely—execution. Highly skilled in begging large sums of money, Akki throws his wealth into the Euphrates in order to relieve the world of its riches. Openly, he espouses an inverted morality favoring the humble: "Heroic deeds are senseless." When King Nebuchannezzer condemns to death the innocent maiden who loves him and is loved by him, beggar-executioner Akki flees with her. A sandstorm engulfs the mighty city of Babylon with its goals of power and glory. As beggar and maiden, the only survivors of Babylon, make their painful way through the storm, Akki voices hope that a new city may be built.

Patterned on Azdak of Brecht's *Caucasian Chalk Circle*, the Swiss-Babylonian Akki is more sentimental and less influential. Azdak never preaches morality, but as judge he condemns the oppressive and the humorless, so that "The people of Grusinia did not forget him but for long remembered/ The period of his judging as a brief golden age/ Almost an age of justice" (Eric Bentley translation). Since Babylon is destroyed, Dürrenmatt's Akki leaves no such impression, and there is only a faint hope that a new city may contain his somewhat sanctimonious concern for the underprivileged.

In Dürrenmatt's later plays (written after *Theater Problems*), the 1958 Visit, 1959 Frank V, and 1961 Physicists, Dürrenmatt's anti-heroes provide no hope for their people. The Visit contains a near-tragic hero in a drama that Dürrenmatt designates as "a tragic comedy." Though set in a fictional village of contemporary Switzerland, the drama ends like Greek tragedy, with a choral ode (original version only). Dürrenmatt's chorus, as so often in Greek tragedy, proclaims the calm after the catastrophe, but the moral resonances are quite differently bitter.

In his Afterword to the play, Dürrenmatt writes, "If Claire Zachanassian is unchangeable, a heroine from the very beginning, her old lover has to develop into a hero" (Patrick Bowles translation). This is Dürrenmatt's only play that traces the *growth* of a hero; Alfred Ill has to earn the inactive resignation with which other Dürrenmatt heroes begin. He earns it by slowly understanding that his people will allow Claire Zachanassian to buy his life for them and from them: "The town's getting into debt. The greater the debt, the higher the standard of living. The higher the standard of living, the greater the need to kill me." By Act III Ill is resigned to his death; neverthless, he refuses to commit suicide and thus to relieve the town of its collective responsibility. He recognizes both his own guilt and that of his townsmen, admonishing the Priest, "Pray for Güllen."

After Ill's execution the Gülleners join as a Chorus, but unlike a Greek Chorus, which draws the moral lesson of tragedy, they are an immoral Chorus, who learn no lesson. Though Ill's death has enriched the Gülleners materially, they do not mention his name. Instead, they sing the praises of their benefactress, who demanded Ill's death. Ill's own moral recognition has taught his townspeople nothing; his heroic descent into the kingdom of dread, his heroic inaction, has redeemed no one.

In subsequent plays, Frank V and The Physicists, the more typical Dürrenmatt hero of resignation appears from the start— Frank V, who resigns himself to the corrupt banking practices of his forefathers, and Möbius the physicist, who resigns himself to living in an insane asylum rather than facing the fearful results of his research. In neither of these works do the resigned heroes achieve redemption of their people, who fall victim—to an immoral banking heir in the opera, and to an insane psychiatrist in the melodrama. In Dürrenmatt's dramas, heroic action emerges as lack of action; in the later plays, however, even inaction brings small hope, but such inaction always elicits Dürrenmatt's admiration. The cumulative impact of his drama suggests that a land may be *un*happy if it breeds a thundering hero.

Dürrenmatt's countryman, Max Frisch, is also concerned about modern attitudes toward heroism. Frisch's protagonists are usually unheroic, but their non-heroism is implicitly condemned; the result of accepting the status quo, such non-heroism leads to the moral damnation of their people. The Contemporary in *The Chinese Wall*, at first afraid to speak out against injustice, is applauded as a clown when he dares to protest. In *Biedermann and the Firebugs* the Chorus of Firemen call Biedermann a hero, but he is unheroic in placating the firebugs so as to protect his property. Andri in *Andorra* is an exceptional and exemplary Frisch hero, who accepts martyrdom as a Jew, but his people are neither educated nor edified by his death. Kürmann in *Biography* deserts his mulatto mistress, who charges him with cowardice; he nevertheless risks (and loses) his professorship by joining the Communist Party. But there is no suggestion that his acts have any public effect. The collective impact of Frisch's plays is skepticism about the results of action or inaction, heroism or nonheroism.

Recent German documentary dramas tend to focus on a strong central protagonist whose action or inaction has wide social repercussions. Weiss' Marat fails to triumph in the French Revolution, but his selfless revolutionary dedication inspires revolt among the inmates of Charenton. Rolf Hochhuth's controversial *Deputy* portrays a Pope who rejects heroic compassion for political opportunism, but the martyr Father Fontana comforts the Jews and inspires the Christians; both are his people. Heinar Kipphardt's Oppenheimer chooses inaction, deciding not to do atomic research, because his responsibility to humanity is greater than his obligation to his country's defense. Günther Grass' Boss, modeled on Brecht, estheticizes a workers' uprising, and, like Brecht's Joan of the Stockyards, betrays the workers through inaction.

Among these variously heroic plays, America is only scantily represented—perhaps because of its more determined Cult of the Common Man. Even Richardson's Orestes wishes to be a common man, and Tennessee Williams glorifies the Common-Man myth in his *Camino Real*. He combines characters of history (Lord Byron, Casanova) and fiction (Marguerite Gauthier, Esmeralda the Gypsy, and above all Don Quixote) as background for the adventures of Kilroy. A synonym for GI Joe during World War II, Kilroy has a very brief myth, confined to the sentence "Kilroy was here." In Williams' play, Kilroy is a twenty-seven-year-old light heavyweight champion, with a heart of gold as big as a baby's head. The metaphor sums him up—guileless, generous, and vulnerable.

In the play's intricate structure, Kilroy appears in Don Quixote's dream. A Golden Gloves winner, Kilroy finds himself on the Camino Real because of the size of his "ticker," forcing him "to give up liquor and smoking and sex." And, incidentally, the boxing ring and his One True Woman. On the Camino Real, Kilroy is forced to play a patsy; he is beaten and mocked and finally downed by the funereal Street-Cleaners. But he rises from the dissecting-table, still, in his own words, "the chosen hero of the big fiesta." Kilroy finally joins forces with the newly awakened Don Quixote, who leads him off stage with the inspirational idea, "The violets in the mountains have broken the rocks!" Not in the play as played, perhaps, but in the symbolic union of the two idealists, who redeem all people through their invincible ideals.

Before the turn of the twentieth century, Shaw wrote, "Depend on it, the miserable doctrine that life is a mess, and that there is no way out of it, will never nerve any man to write a truly heroic play west of the Caucasus."[19] "A truly heroic play" has probably not been written since the seventeenth century, but despite "the miserable doctrine that life is a mess," heroes have fascinated many contemporary playwrights, and plays have often focused on how the hero establishes a moral order for his people; the traditional descent into the kingdom of dread is no longer sufficient.

Except for Hercules, heroes of Greek ancestry tend to be model figures as they rarely were in extant Greek tragedy: Eliot's Harry may be rude to his family, Sartre's Orestes may disobey Zeus, Hauptmann's Iphigenia may sanction war, Anouilh's Antigone may taunt sister and uncle, but they rise high in their plays to point the straight moral way. Parahistorical heroes, in contrast, are often lost in the dark, so that they cannot illuminate the way for their people or us—Henry II of Anouilh and Fry, Joan of Brecht and Audiberti, Osborne's Luther. On the other hand, Anouilh's Joan accomplishes a coronation at Rheims, and Claudel's Joan accomplishes a coronation in Heaven, both redounding to the glory of their people. Eliot's heroes achieve an off-stage redemption, with uncertain repercussions. But Brecht's heroes fail to redeem their people—Joan of the Stockyards, Galileo, Shen Te, Azdak. Conversely, Claudel's heroes redeem their people obliquely, because of their eventual mastery over themselves. Variously unsuccessful are the Existentialist heroes of Sartre and Camus, anxiously balancing life and death, asking for a justification of dying or killing. Comparably torn, but less self-conscious, the heroes of Dürrenmatt and Ionesco are exemplary in their non-heroism, through which their people attain some slim chance of happiness.

Frankly heroic, Genet's Saïd dedicates himself to immorality. As the traditional hero is loyal and brave, Saïd is a coward and traitor. Though the word *anti-hero* is widely used today, Saïd alone fulfills it to the letter, and he has no rivals among mere heroes or non-heroes. Not exemplary like Orestes; not holy like Thomas à Becket; not flamboyant like Caligula; not zestful like Galileo or Don Rodrigue; not, finally, charming and ridiculous like Bérenger, Azdak, Akki, or Kilroy, he touches upon their heroic qualities in order to embody his own anti-heroism. Saïd is anchored in history, and he soars into myth; he scorns his people, but he redeems them. Romantically anguished and classically civic, Saïd is our contemporary who dies into song.

FOUR: The Mixed Mood

IN CONTEMPORARY DRAMA TRADITIONAL HEROES ARE RE-VIEWED, AND TRADITIONAL GENRES ARE RE-FORMED. TRAGEDY, IN WHICH heroes figure so prominently, virtually disappears from the contemporary stage. Dürrenmatt calls his *Visit* a tragic comedy, Beckett calls his English translation of *Waiting for Godot* a tragicomedy, and Ionesco calls his *Chairs* a tragic farce. By these labels, the playwrights emphasize a modern mixture of moods, but some degree of blending is as old as Western drama. The Athenian tetralogy consisted of three tragedies followed by a satyr-play that strikes us as comic. Within the individual tragedies, there are occasional comic characters like the Nurse in the *Choephoroe* and the Messenger in the *Bacchae*. Several tragedies of Euripides contain comic scenes, and several end happily—to Aristotle's distaste. In Plato's *Symposium*, Socrates tells Agathon, the tragic poet, and Aristophanes, the comic poet, "that the genius of comedy was the same as that of tragedy, and that the writer of tragedy ought to be a writer of comedy also" (Benjamin Jowett translation). But Socrates does not say that the qualities of tragedy and of comedy should appear in the *same* play.

Plautus seems to have coined the word *tragicomedy* in the Prologue to his *Amphitryon*, when the god Mercury announces high-handedly: "Faciam ut commixta sit: tragicomoedia." Mercury's mixture, however, is a social mixture—gods and a slave appearing in the same play—while the mood is unrelievedly comic. From late classical times through the Renaissance, however, comic and tragic elements have often been combined in the same play, and that mixture seems only tangentially related to sporadic use of such genre labels as *tragicocomoedia, comoedotragoedia,* and *comoedia tragica.*[1] During the sixteenth and seventeenth centuries, the word tragicomedy most often referred to a melodrama with a happy ending, which *might* contain comic scenes (as might tragedy). Thus, Giovanni Battista Guarini in Italy and John Fletcher in England zealously defended their respective pastoral tragicomedies, in which the comic element is exceedingly thin. Dryden's *Essay on Dramatic Poesy* (1668) suggests that a comic scene in tragedy may provide "relief." And, beginning with the eighteenth century, many serious plays provided their audience with some comic relief, but self-conscious Romantic writers demanded that the serious be mixed with the comic as in life. By that period—early nineteenth century—the word "tragicomedy" suggested a mixed mood rather than a particular form, a texture rather than a structure.

Modern drama is often ambiguous as to what is comic and what is tragic. Playwrights such as Ibsen, Strindberg, Chekhov, and Pirandello evoke complex audience reactions, and more recent playwrights follow their lead. Far from comic relief in a serious play, contemporary tragicomedy can inspire fear and pity through laughter.

Despite the efforts of Aristotle, Horace, Hegel, *et al.,* there has been small critical agreement on a definition of tragedy *or* comedy. Tragedy is sometimes discussed in terms of authorial vision, and comedy in terms of audience reaction, but the tragicomic is even thornier to define than either tragic or comic. Contemporary playwrights, more than their predecessors, blend the funny and the fatal, and contemporary critics try to characterize that blend, experiencing more difficulty with the tragic than with the comic aspects. Trying to maintain perfect balance between the two, Karl Guthke finds in modern tragicomedy "reciprocity of the interaction of the tragic and the comic."[2] Eric Bentley, on the other hand, suggests that the distinctively modern form of tragicomedy is comedy with an unhappy ending.[3]

The circus has long provided tragicomedies in miniature, which combine Guthke's criterion with that of Bentley. The circus clown, especially as delineated in the mid-nineteenth century, provoked laughter by calculated clumsiness and ineptitude. Arousing laughter, the clown prefigured his final failure through his sad face. Dramatists as different as Ghelderode, Brecht, Weiss, and Genet have absorbed the tradition of these Clowns of Failure.

Ghelderode's Folial, who appears in several plays, is a fool-protagonist in the tradition of the suffering clown. In such plays as *School for Buffoons* and *Escurial*, suffering dominates clownishness, so that laughter is only rarely aroused. In *Pantagleize*, however, Ghelderode immerses a clownlike protagonist in scenes of social satire, mixing comedy and pathos. On his fortieth birthday, the fool-hero Pantagleize, a philosopher who writes for a fashion magazine, strolls to his habitual cafe and remarks to the assembled customers, "What a lovely day!" (George Hauger translation). Instantly there is panic; the innocent exclamation proves to be the signal for the start of a revolution. In swift scenes patterned on silent film comedies, Pantagleize is kidnapped by a Jewish Mata Hari, persuaded to appropriate the national treasure from an army vault, and finally captured by government forces. At the end of the day, the revolutionaries are summarily tried and executed. Shot without understanding why, Pantagleize lies down near his friends, unaware that they are dead. The Officer fires a final shot into the back of Pantagleize's neck, and the fool-hero dies, uttering the phrase that sparked the revolution: "What...a...lovely...day!"

In his *Epitaph for Pantagleize*, written for the 1957 English production of this "farce to make you sad," Ghelderode explicitly links his protagonist to Charlie Chaplin, the film avatar of the victimized clown: "Pantagleize is a distant relative of the great circus, invented and codified by England, a fugitive from the circus which gave the world that other poet of action called Chaplin."[4] Ghelderode's execution falls short of his intention; his clown-figure lacks the extraordinary verve of the English "poet of action," and our sadness is thereby diluted. Nor is the Revolution a convincingly farcical milieu, as in *The Good Soldier Schweik* or *Catch-22*. In spite of his sentimental attitude toward Pantagleize, however, Ghelderode's play is a clear example of the modern desire to mix the farcical with the sad.

Remaining within the framework of farce, both Brecht and Weiss rely upon the circus clown tradition, intending to cast retrospective sadness upon our laughter. Brecht was directly influenced by Karl Vallentin, author and performer of clown-plays. One of his acts is adapted in Brecht's 1929 *Baden Learning Play*. Three clowns take part in the "number"—a complaining Mr. Smith and his two "helpers." When Mr. Smith's left foot hurts, they saw it off; since his right foot begins to hurt, they saw it off too. So that Mr. Smith will not have to hear the clowns say that he cannot stand, they twist his ears off, one by one. Upon further complaints, they relieve Mr. Smith successively of his arm, the top of his head, and, finally, his whole head. When he continues to complain, the helper tells him, "Well, Mr. Smith, you can't have everything." Brecht's intention in this learning-play was to show the farcical nature of help in the corrupt capitalist world, but in production, we laugh and sympathize with Mr. Smith, whose every compaint inspires a comico-pathetic cure. A skit rather than a play, the scene is simultaneously pathetic and farcical, ending unhappily.

Though Peter Weiss uses similar techniques in *How Mr. Mockinpott Was Cured of Suffering*, a happy ending lightens the final effect. Written in 1963, while Weiss was working on *Marat/Sade*, the clown play uses the *knittelvers* (rhymed couplets) of the Herald in the longer play—a verse with an immediate comic effect. The clown-protagonist bears the ridiculous name of Mockinpott, and he is accompanied in his adventures by a Mr. Wurst, whose name links him to the old German Hans Wurst slapstick tradition. But for all the comic associations, eleven scenes of the play farcically dramatize the *sufferings* of Mr. Mockinpott. Inexplicably finding himself in jail, Mr. Mockinpott buys his way out, at the price of all his money. Freed, he puts his left shoe on his right foot and vice versa, so that he walks through the rest of the play like a clumsy clown. Returning home, he is kicked out by his wife and her lover. Feeling ill, he is operated on by a doctor who moves his heart to the other side of his chest; after the operation, he occasionally loses control of his limbs—in comic clown routine. Appealing to figures of authority, he is spurned. Finally, appealing to God, Mr. Mockinpott finds that his complaints turn into condemnation: "I won't listen to your deceitful stuff;/ Once and for all I've had enough." Tripping over his mismatched shoes as he leaves the presence of a cigar-smoking God, Mr. Mockinpott takes time to examine his feet. Understanding his plight, he puts the right shoe on the right foot, and the left on the left; he leaves the stage in arabesques of grace. More satiric than Brecht's clown-play, Weiss' *How Mr. Mockinpott Was Cured of Suffering* nevertheless shows a similar interaction of the comic and pathetic; only in the final moments does Weiss lighten his mixture.

In Genet's *The Blacks*, which he subtitles *"une clownerie,"* the tone is ambivalent to and through the conclusion of the play. Unlike the retrospective pathos of Brecht or the retrospective comedy of Weiss, Genet keeps his mood balanced, like the tightrope-walkers he so admires. *The Blacks*, the only Genet play so perfectly balanced, is also his only play to draw—however obliquely—upon the clown tradition.

Bernard Frechtman translates Genet's *"clownerie"* as "clown-show," and a difficult word it is to translate. French *"clownerie"* is far more commonly used than English "clownerie." French *"clownerie"* refers to life rather than art; it is never used about circus clowns, but about preposterous conduct or a farcical situation. *"Clownerie"* is a pejorative word, implying trickery or hypocrisy. Genet's *Blacks* is thus a trick or hypocritical communication involving the black race. While the white audience watches a farcical spectacle, the real life of the blacks remains a mystery to them. While the white audience laughs at the comic surface, the black actors reveal real rage. Through the mixture of moods, Genet casts subtle shadows on the nature of racial reality.

In a brief foreword, Genet explains that the play is written for black actors, to be played before a white audience, even if that audience is represented by a single person. "But what," Genet asks, "if no white person accepted? Then let white masks be distributed to the black spectators as they enter the theater. And if the blacks refuse the masks, then let a dummy be used." These few sentences suggest Genet's own clown techniques in *The Blacks*. Instead of white-face clowns, five Negroes wear white masks. Midway through the play, a Negro preacher dressed in blond wig, white mask, white gloves, and skirt, will give birth to five dolls—dummies of the five Negroes who play a white government.

The intricate play and by-play of roles and reality is better examined in the context of theatrical self-consciousness, but what must be stressed here is the extraordinary quality of the comedy by which Genet jars us into tragic awareness. Early in the play, Archibald Absalom Wellington "severely" admonishes his cast, "The tragedy will lie in the color black! It's *that* that you'll cherish, *that* that you'll attain, and deserve. It's *that* that must be earned." A little later he warns his most recalcitrant actor, Samba Graham Diouf, who plays the white woman, "Sir, if you have any intention of presenting even the most trivial of their [the whites'] ideas without caricaturing it, then get out!" But just as the Negroes' negritude shows around their white masks, so the Ne-

groes' tragic reality shows around their comic poses. White civilization has treated their life as a clown-show, and they will
"therefore be it to the very end, absurdly."

No other major modern playwright derives directly from the
tradition of the tragicomic clowns, but moods are mixed in
different ways. Ionesco's remarks on such mixture are most
helpful in analysis of his own plays.

> For my part, I have never understood the difference people
> make between the comic and the tragic. As the "comic" is
> an intuitive perception of the absurd, it seems to me more
> hopeless than the "tragic." The "comic" offers no escape.
> I say "hopeless," but in reality it lies outside the boundaries
> of hope or despair.
>
> Tragedy may appear to some in one sense comforting, for
> in trying to express the helplessness of a beaten man, one
> broken by fate for example, tragedy thus admits the reality
> of fate and destiny, of sometimes incomprehensible but
> objective laws that govern the universe. And man's help-
> lessness, the futility of our efforts, can also, in a sense,
> appear comic.
>
> I have called my comedies "anti-plays" or "comic dra-
> mas," and my dramas "pseudo-dramas" or "tragic farces":
> for it seems to me that the comic is tragic, and that the
> tragedy of man is pure derision. The contemporary critical
> mind takes nothing too seriously or too lightly. In Victims
> of Duty I tried to sink comedy in tragedy; in The Chairs
> tragedy in comedy or, if you like, to confront comedy and
> tragedy in order to link them in a new dramatic synthesis.
> But it [is] not a true synthesis, for these two elements do
> not coalesce, they coexist: one constantly repels the other,
> they show each other up, criticize and deny one another
> and, thanks to their opposition, thus succeed dynamically
> in maintaining a balance and creating tension.[5]

Though Ionesco claims "balance" in his plays, his dramatic
texture is comic and crookedly traditional: comedy of situation
becomes banal situation; comedy of character becomes non-
character; comedy of language revels in sound play that under-

mines the significance of language. To these traditional domains of the comic, Ionesco adds proliferation of objects and decimation of logic. Richard Coe describes Ionesco's linguistic hodgepodge as "non sequiturs, false syllogisms, deductive and inductive arguments divorced equally from valid first principles and from any relevant evidence, a pattern of false analogies, arbitrary conclusions, incongruous associations, transferred causalities, irrelevancies, anomalies, anachronisms, and plain impossibilities, forming a sort of looking-glass universe which is the direct opposite of that with which we are normally familiar."[6] But it reflects pointedly upon that with which we are normally familiar.

Similarly, Ionesco's dialogue—filled with onomatopoeias, puns, spoonerisms, neologisms, repetitions, inversions, alliterations, rhymes, and off-rhymes—echoes our daily speech, emphasizing its inadequacy as a means of communication and expression. In Ionesco's early plays, language and logic are mechanical monsters, proliferating like eggs, cups, and furniture; and people are extensions of objects. Serge Doubrovsky summed it up neatly: "In our awkward moments, Bergson saw what he called a mechanical something grafted upon life: in our best moments, we discover ourselves to be but a living something grafted upon mere mechanism."[7] And we discover this through laughter at Ionesco's tragic farces. Rather than a tension between tragic and comic within the play, there is a tension between the farcical world on Ionesco's stage and our awareness of its tragic relevance to our world off the stage, however imprecisely we define tragic, comic, and farcical.

In the stage directions of *Jack* Ionesco writes, "Everything must arouse in the spectator a painful feeling of shame and uneasiness" (Donald Allen translation). This combination of easy laughter and uneasy shame may function correctively, as in the classical conception of comedy. Thus, someone with miserly tendencies, laughing at Molière's miser, presumably exorcizes these tendencies; similarly, someone with cliché tendencies, laughing at the cliché dialogue of *The Bald Soprano*, may exorcise those tendencies. If clichés are man-made, they may be unmade by man, as Ionesco occasionally implies in his essays. If, on the other hand, clichés are an ontological prison, then linguistic farce is irrevocably tragic, and no correction is possible, as Ionesco suggests with equal frequency. In plays and pronouncements, Ionesco mixes social comedy (which can function correctively) with metaphysical comedy (which cannot). Thus, *The Bald Soprano* parodies the English bourgeoisie, but it also suggests that human identity may be metaphysically absent: "It's not that way, it's over here, it's not that way, it's over here." As the bald soprano of the title has no existence in the drama, so the characters with names have no existence either. In his comments on the play, Ionesco stresses the interchangeability of the two comic couples, who lack individual identity.

> The Smiths and the Martins no longer know how to talk because they no longer know how to think, they no longer know how to think because they are no longer capable of being moved, they have no passions, they no longer know how to be, they can become anyone or anything, for as they are no longer themselves, in an impersonal world, they can only be someone else, they are interchangeable: Martin can change places with Smith and vice versa, no one would notice the difference. A tragic character does not change, he breaks up; he is himself, he is *real*. Comic characters are people who do not exist.[8]

And that is their tragedy—a far cry from the noble fate of heroes.

By Ionesco's own account, he tried to drown the comic in the tragic in *Victims of Duty*, and the tragic in the comic in *The Chairs*. If this means that the comic dissolves into tragedy in the one play, and the tragic into comedy (or farce) in the other, his analysis fits *Victims of Duty* more closely than *The Chairs*. Like *The Bald Soprano* and *The Chairs*, *Victims of Duty* opens on a comic couple, Madeleine and Choubert. A detective interrupts the domestic scene, excusing himself politely. Courtesy changes abruptly to rudeness as the detective questions Choubert about a mysterious Mallot. Comedy disappears when the detective adopts Gestapo methods of interrogation, with Madeleine supporting the detective against Choubert. After developing the terror on stage, Ionesco dissipates it as the focus shifts from the detective's examination to Choubert's dreamlike actions—swimming, climbing, descending, and rhapsodizing. Threading through both comic and threatening exchanges are references to theater, heard in *our* theater. Before the entrance of the detective, Choubert has defended the avant-garde theater. In the presence of the detective, Choubert acts like an actor. After Choubert's "number," a nameless lady enters, to serve as a silent on-stage audience for all subsequent action.

With the entrance of the fifth character, Choubert's friend Nicholas d'Eu (pronounced *deux*), comedy and menace are tightened into a more dynamic balance. The detective orders Madeleine to serve coffee, and she proceeds to carry in a farcical series of coffee-cups. Comically, too, Choubert begins to behave like a child who is, however, seriously intimidated by the detective-father-doctor. The detective forces Choubert to eat bread in order to "stuff the holes of memory." While Choubert is being tortured to chew and swallow the bread, the detective and Nicholas d'Eu engage in a dialogue about the theater, and Nicholas replaces Choubert as the defender of the avant-garde. Nicholas sounds a little like Ionesco when he declares that he wants no more drama, no more tragedy for "the tragic's turning comic, the comic is tragic, and life's getting more cheerful." But on stage, life is not cheerful. Even while Nicholas declares that he need not write dramas because "We have Ionesco and Ionesco is enough," Choubert manages to swallow his way through to speech. Abruptly, Nicholas assumes the savage fury of the detective, stabbing the latter to death. The detective's last words protest that he is a victim of duty. With his body still warm, Nicholas and Madeleine begin to interrogate Choubert about the mysterious Mallot. Farcically but menacingly, Nicholas replaces the detective in forcing bread upon Choubert. Then, each of the three characters, protesting that he is a victim of duty, orders the other two to chew and swallow. The nameless lady thereupon breaks her silence, ordering all three to chew and swallow. In the last savage scene, the comic is combined with terror, as in the final scene of *The Bald Soprano*—a terror which is related to tragedy.

Ionesco suggests that *The Chairs* offers a contrast to *Victims of Duty* since the tragic is submerged under the dominant comic mode, but the movement is similar in the two plays—from farce to a catastrophe that is not free of farce. In the earlier play, the proliferation of the titular chairs is the comic device that reveals the tragic hollow in the lives of the Old Couple, for the "tragic farce" dramatizes the emptiness of their lives. Even before the hilarious chair scene, however, Ionesco forecasts the invasion of the human by the inert. The stage set reveals eight doors and conceals two, through which the Old Couple continually enter and exit. Yet the suicidal exits take place through high windows, so that the Old Couple are comically awkward at their most tragic moment.

Early in the play, Ionesco establishes the comic mood. Though the Old Couple are in their nineties, the Old Man sits in the Old Woman's lap, and in this ridiculous position they exchange the non sequiturs of their conversation. The Old Man commands the Old Woman to drink her tea, though there is no tea. He calls her "Sémiramis, ma crotte," juxtaposing the legendary and the excretory. In response to her request, the Old Man imitates the month of February by scratching his head like Stan Laurel, the film comedian. The Old Man's story is full of sound play and sentence fragments. Giggling childlishly, crying like an infant, the Old Man incongruously gives free rein to his

dreams of grandeur; to hear his immortal message, he has con-
voked a vast audience, animate and inanimate.

The guests are invisible, but their approach is audible, and at
first the Old Man and Old Woman utter similar platitudes of
hospitality. Gradually, however, their attitudes diverge. The Old
Man and the Old Woman, though in their nineties, adventure
erotically among the guests, the Old Man addresses romantic
sentimentalities to the Belle he loved when young, and the Old
Woman tries to lure the Photo-Engraver. A few minutes later,
the Old Woman speaks of their lost son, while the Old Man,
announcing that they never had any children, speaks of the
ungrateful son he has been to his dead mother.

As the invisible guests continue to arrive, the Old Woman
continues to carry chairs through the several doors, her pace increasing as she protests, "I am not a machine." But the scene
must be played as though she is a machine in this Bergsonian
farce. Ionesco writes in the stage directions that "[the Old Cou-
ple] *appear to be gliding on roller skates*"; motions and sounds
are farcically mechanized.

When the stage is full of rows of chairs (which mirror the rows
of seats in a theater), and the air is full of social inanities and
sotto voce mutterings (which echo the mutterings of a theater
audience), the play momentarily becomes a parody of theater,
with the Old Woman selling programs and refreshments, and the
Old Man trying to impose order on the unruly audience. At the
end of this scene of comic confusion, the Old Man and the Old
Woman arrive at their respective windows. Fearfully, they realize
that they are separated from one another by the invisible crowd
on stage. But the pathos of their realization is soon undercut by
their comic non sequiturs and by their exaggerated subservience
to the invisible Emperor, who is almost a deity figure.[9] They
revert to mechanically comic puppets until the arrival of the
Orator; at that point, their reactions coincide with that of the
real audience:

OLD WOMAN: It's really he, he exists. In flesh and blood.
OLD MAN: He exists. It's really he. This is not a dream!

Although we do not yet know that the Orator is mute, it is already comically incongruous that he should give autographs while the Old Man indulges in elaborate salutation to the audience. Expressing his trivial dreams of glory, the Old Man builds to the climax of martyrdom, but even his martyrdom is ridiculous, for it offers "the supreme sacrifice *which no one demands*" (my italics). Other heroes become a legend because of their deeds, but the Old Couple will "die in order to become a legend" and have a street named after them. Despite this comico-pathetic vision of glory, the old people do commit the double suicide that interrupts the farcical tone. Even though the mute Orator ignores their gesture, the fact of the suicide gives them a dignity they lacked in their life on stage. And yet, the play's end is not tragic. The audibility of the invisible audience and the silence of the visible Orator return the play to its dominant comic mode. There is, however, a half-mocking hint of serious significance in the only intelligible words of the Orator: *Angel*food and *Adieu* (my italics). After the departure of the Orator, we are left with the confetti-strewn, chair-filled stage, as empty as the life of the Old Couple; so that the cumulative impact of the drama is tragicomic, the tragic resonances having risen from and subsided into farce.

In Ionesco's *Exit the King* (in French, *The King is Dying*) the emotional weight is more gravely tragic, for King Bérenger is dying in his throne-room. Ionesco's earlier Bérenger plays (*The Killer*, *Rhinoceros*, and *The Pedestrian of the Air*) leave Bérenger in a perilous position, but in this fourth play he actually dies. In a "vaguely dilapidated" throne-room, a crack in the wall (inspired, perhaps, by Poe's "Fall of the House of Usher") grows as the king's life-span shrinks. Though Bérenger's kingdom once numbered millions of inhabitants, it has dwindled to a few thousand. Climate and crops, armies and arts—all are dying; the kingdom is "full of holes like an immense Swiss cheese" (Donald Watson translation).

The approach of death has even affected the stage economy: though the king has two wives, they are served by the same maid, Juliette. Bérenger's beautiful young wife Marie wishes to protect him, but his scolding old wife Marguerite insists that King Bérenger know about his coming death. The king's physician is also his surgeon, executioner, and astrologer. Since the king is dying, the physician sees him as a clinical case. At unexpected intervals in the action, the Palace Guard issues news bulletins, which comment comically upon that action, in a parody of Brechtian projection-commentary.

Even though we know that the king is dying, he is a comic figure when he first steps barefoot on stage, complaining peevishly about his ailments. When Marguerite informs him that he is going to die, he reacts selfishly, impatiently, incredulously. Only when she links his death directly to his theatrical presence does he believe her: "You will die in an hour and a half, you will die at the end of the show." Once King Bérenger grasps this fact, he rebels, he reasons, he cries like a child. Before our eyes, his hair turns white; people and planets cease to obey him; he loses the use of his limbs, falling down and getting up in what the scenic directions describe as "tragic guignol." He comes to envy the miseries of his maid, for they are miseries of the living. During this development of tragic intensity at the knowledge of imminent death, there are two main sources of comic nuance: the Palace Guard and the maid Juliette. But their comedy provides no relief, contributing instead to the king's anguish. The Guard summarizes the scenic action with ironic inadequacy: "His Majesty is delirious." or "The King finds some consolation in literature!" The maid reduces everything to the material and the elemental —sweeping, spider-webs, and cooking. Though the king in his fear cries like a baby, he is not so comic as the Old Man in *The*

Chairs, for we know that King Bérenger has death to cry about, whereas the Old Man's suicide is unexpected.

When the king accepts the fact of his coming death, he tries in vain to learn resignation through ritual, and this casts a dubious light on the solace of ritual in Western civilization. A similar shadow is cast upon Western civilization itself as the Guard summarizes Bérenger's monumental accomplishments: stealing fire from the gods; writing *The Iliad, The Odyssey,* and the plays of Shakespeare; inventing the automobile and the airplane. Incongruously, however, this archemythic king can think only of his pet cat, who died too soon. In the royal presence, members of the court begin to speak of King Bérenger in the past tense; the crack on the wall deepens. Bérenger is finally abandoned by all the characters except his stern old wife Marguerite, who prepares him for death. There is scarcely any comic undercutting of her final fantastic requiem, during which she leads him from his wheel-chair back to his throne. Saying, "useless agitation, wasn't it?" she summarizes his life and all life (my literal translation). The king dies, Marguerite departs, and the throne-room disappears. In the last scenic direction, *"The King sitting on his throne should remain visible for a short time before fading into a kind of mist."* Though the play's action is basically tragic, comic details have increased the poignancy of Bérenger's "useless agitation," which resembles Sartre's well-known description of man as a "useless passion."

Between Ionesco's early plays and *Exit the King* (more than a decade later), his conception and theatricalization of uselessness changed. At first, uselessness was conveyed farcically through the decimation of language and logic, the proliferation of people and things. Stage plenitude revealed profound emptiness. In *Exit the King,* the "useless agitation" is one of emotion more than motion. Only in the death scene does Ionesco return to the visual and verbal effects of his early plays—Marguerite's long soliloquy and the physical disappearance of the throne-room. No longer so farcical, these devices place a period on the agitation that was life.

Though Dürrenmatt's vision is different from that of Ionesco, he too is haunted by death, and like Ionesco's early plays, those of Dürrenmatt thrive on techniques of farce. The critic Reinhold Grimm finds that Dürrenmatt's dramas are the best contemporary example of the grotesque, which Wolfgang Kayser characterized above all by its disorientation from the familiar world.[10] Because the horrible and the comic are intertwined in Dürrenmatt's drama, as are the familiar and the fantastic, he arouses a sense of disorientation. But as in the plays of Ionesco, such disorientation implicitly suggests meaninglessness in our world. And like Ionesco, Dürrenmatt demonstrates both visual and verbal ingenuity in building his grotesque world. He is fond of scenery that rises up into the flies; his people often act like puppets, plants, or animals; his names have comical sounds or meanings—Maximilian Bleibeganz (stay whole), Gnadenbrot Suppe (Gracebread Soup); Florestan Mississippi and Frédéric René Saint-Claude fight over the nearly dead body of Bodo von Uberlohe-Zabernsee; the characters of the entourage of Claire Zachanassian all rhyme in *oby*; and the eunuchs' real names are Jacob Chicken and Louis Perch.

In an often quoted passage from his *Theater Problems,* Dürrenmatt indicates his view of the modern mixture of moods: "We can achieve the tragic out of comedy. We can bring it forth as a frightening moment, as an abyss that opens suddenly" (Gerhard Nellhaus translation). In the plays themselves, however, the frightening moment tends to occur after the curtain falls, for comically dehumanized characters can arouse fright only in retrospect.

Dürrenmatt's puppet-like characters move in a vaguely familiar social context—religious wars, Roman invasion, ancient Babylon, which have their counterparted features in our world and time. The humor of his farce is socio-economic rather than metaphysical. In *It is Written, The Marriage of Mr. Mississippi, An Angel Comes to Babylon,* and *The Physicists,* death and parody are intertwined so that our immediate reaction tends to be laughter. Only in *The Visit* does Dürrenmatt "achieve the tragic *out of* comedy" (my italics). He labels *The Visit* as a tragic comedy, which his Postscript implicitly defines as a "comedy with a tragic end."

The first act of this three-act play is largely comic, with only hints of the play's gravity up to the time of Claire Zachanassian's climactic announcement: "A million for Güllen if someone kills Alfred Ill" (Patrick Bowles translation). Act III, in contrast, moves relentlessly toward Ill's murder, with parody sharpening the tragedy. The relatively short second act, combining the comic and the tragic, provides our deepest insight into Ill's feelings, as we watch his development from a fatuous buffoon to a self-conscious hero (discussed in the preceding chapter).

Dürrenmatt opens the play with a swift succession of comic devices—the old mechanical mime of "head movements from left to right," glorious resonances in the names of trains whereas the name of the town means excrement, cliché nostalgia for the past, cliché explanations for Güllen's present poverty, cliché small-town preparations to welcome the local girl who made good. Only in retrospect can we appreciate the irony of Ill's praise of Claire—her generosity and her love of justice.

When Claire arrives in Güllen before she is expected, her high style is comic—she pulls an emergency brake, she flings her money around, she commands people as though they were dogs, she thanks the mayor for a speech that has been drowned out by the noisy train. She quickly undercuts the sentimentality of her reunion with Ill: "You've grown fat. And grey. And drink-sodden." Nor will she accept Ill's attempt at gallantry, declaring that she too is old and fat, displaying her artificial leg. Claire's artificiality reaches out tentacularly; though her seventh husband is named Pedro, she calls him Moby to rhyme with Boby, her butler's name: "You get your butlers for life, so husbands have to be christened accordingly."

As the welcome continues, Claire suggests with comic cynicism that the policeman may have "to wink a blind eye to things," that the priest may have "to comfort the dying." Grotesquely comic, but comic, are the details of her entourage—the sedan-carriers she bought from Sing Sing, the eunuchs who chirp in doublets, and the elaborate black coffin. After the open scene-change, the contrast is pointed between Claire's wealth and Güllen's poverty, for which we learn that she is responsible. Her belongings invade the drab town hotel, significantly named Golden Apostle, for the ever-present sign of the Golden Apostle suggests that Claire is a messenger clothed in her gold. Only the Schoolmaster suspects her tragic function: "She made me think of an avenging Greek goddess; her name shouldn't be Claire; it should be Clotho." But it should be Claire as well—in the lucidity of her vision, the purity of her vengeance, and, ironically, in her impure influence on Güllen.

In a parody of German romantic love scenes, Claire and Ill exchange modern horror stories—the horror of their respective lives. The scene ends grotesquely, as Ill learns that Claire's hand, which he has just kissed, is made of ivory. After the tediously comic official welcome for Claire, she reveals the story of her betrayal and her desire for revenge. No comic notes relieve that tale, though the double phrases of the eunuchs provide a gro-tesque refrain.

Once Claire has made her demand for Ill's life, the tragic per-meates the comedy of Act II of *The Visit*. Before the dialogue of that act begins, Claire's thugs, chewing gum, "bear wreathe and flowers as at a funeral." The increasing anxiety of Ill contrasts with the triviality of the dialogue on the balcony of the Golden Apostle. Claire, living richly at the hotel, is paralleled in the low comedy of consumption in Güllen—her cigars by their cigarettes, her whiskey by their cognac, her gold-digging husbands by their

yellow shoes (associated with pimps in Europe). The new prosperity in Güllen is shown through repetition of "on account."
When Alfred Ill hears this phrase and sees his fellow citizens
wearing yellow shoes, he begins to fear for his safety, and Dürrenmatt conveys that fear grotesquely, for Ill suddenly speaks in
the doublets of the eunuchs: "How are you going to pay? How
are you going to pay? How? How?"

Claire utters the horrible summary of town activity: "Haggling
over the price of meat." As Ill seeks help from the Policeman, the
Mayor, and the Priest, Claire prepares for a mammoth Güllen
wedding with Husband VIII. While the three town officials will
not admit to Ill that they are falling into Claire's trap, Husband
VIII complains of the dullness of Güllen, with its "carefree
peace and contentment and cosy comfort. No grandeur, no
tragedy." Slowly, however, Ill rises to the grandeur of his tragic
role. In the final scene of Act II, all of Güllen surrounds Ill at
the railroad station; though no one touches him, they speak in
the doublets of the eunuchs. It is left ambiguous as to whether
they would stop Ill if he tried to escape on the train. But he
collapses in fright.

In Act III, all the comedy is grotesque, arousing our horror at
Ill's fate. Mass media and Greek chorus, incongruously juxtaposed, heighten Ill's tragedy. Wearing her wedding-gown, Claire
refuses the pleas of the townsmen to free them from debt. Even
Ill's store reflects the town's debt-ridden prosperity, and the new
sanctimoniousness of the citizens makes it clear that they will
accede to Claire's condition. Ill's wife has his portrait painted,
"You never know what might happen, it's a comfort to have a
souvenir." Only the Schoolmaster urges Ill to woo the press, but
Ill has accepted his guilt and his fate: "It's all my work, the Eunuchs, the Butler, the coffin, the million. I can't help myself and
I can't help any of you, any more."

Before Ill's execution, there is a grimly comic scene in the
Güllen town meeting. Radio and Press report surface facts,

knowing nothing of the moral gravity of the subject. Ill agrees to accept the town verdict, and the Mayor calls for a vote: "All those pure in heart who want justice done, raise your hands." The pure in heart vote for murder. The Mayor and the citizens exchange phrases that recall the stichomythic exchange between Choregus and Chorus of Greek tragedy. But the contemporary phrases are piously hypocritical, and each phrase is repeated, like the doublets of the eunuchs, castrated for their hypocrisy. When Ill screams his single, "My God!" the insensitive Pressman asks for a retake because the "news-reel camera jams." But Ill does not cry out again; he has moved beyond the parodied town and the doublet refrain of guilty corruption. Ill goes to his death by strangulation, sinking to his knees as his townsmen close in upon him. The doctor declares that he died of a heart attack, and the Press echoes the Mayor's declaration that Ill "died of joy."

The final scene contrasts grotesquely with the opening. At the railroad station of the now prosperous town, the Gülleners form a Chorus to chant their happiness. Claire appears "like an old stone idol" and is praised in phrases that recall prayers of Greek tragedy. No one mentions Ill, but the town sings: "She bears a precious charge." Literally, that charge is Ill in the coffin, but metaphorically, it is the burden of a wealth that has petrified the morality and humanity of the town, where trains now stop. Allowing himself unbridled use of the grotesque, Dürrenmatt has pointed it toward Ill's tragedy, which is also the moral tragedy of the town.

Biedermann and the Firebugs by Max Frisch resembles *The Visit* in its dramatization of an evil which first appears in comic guise. In *The Visit* the hero alone is aware of his tragic situation; in *Biedermann*, on the other hand, the hero alone is *un*aware of his tragic situation. In *The Visit* the hero and the audience come to simultaneous recognition of the inevitability of his fate; in *Biedermann* we recognize Schmitz as a firebug almost at once, and Biedermann fails to recognize him only by deliberate refusal.

Frisch's first sketch for the drama, in his diary, is entitled "Burlesque," and the play retains a heavy-handed form of comedy, manipulated to its tragic ending in this "learning play without a lesson."

In the first sketch of the material, Biedermann has no name; he is what we might call the narrative *you*.[11] As you admit the firebug, invite him to your table and then into your attic to sleep, you may be suspicious of the stranger, but you tell yourself that your suspicions are unjustified and unworthy. Even though you smell the gasoline which the firebug and his partner (who has appeared from nowhere and from prison) stock in your attic, you refuse to admit your suspicions. And the vindication of your silence comes each morning as you awake from a drug-induced sleep: "Just look, your house is still standing." Finally, however, when the inevitable catastrophe occurs: "Just look, you're burned out, and you can't even be surprised."

In the drama, one of the firebugs ironically reflects Frisch's own tragicomic technique: "Joking is the third best camouflage. The second best is sentimentality. . . . But the best and surest camouflage I find is still the pure naked truth. As a joke. Nobody believes that." (My translation is more literal than that of Mordecai Gorelik). The tragicomic ambivalence of Frisch's drama springs from the pure naked truth which Biedermann forces himself to call a joke. He lies himself to death, and—even more important in his own view—he lies his property to destruction.

The name of Frisch's protagonist is ironic—Biedermann, which is a type-name like Babbitt; Biedermann shares with his American cousin a middle-class Philistinism, but his name places more emphasis upon his dull honesty. Frisch's Biedermann, however, is dishonest to others and above all to himself. Against this mock-hero, Frisch plays a Chorus of Firemen in a city where fires are spreading like the plague. Hero and Chorus are staples of classical tragedy, but Frisch undermines the tragic suggestions. In the opening scene, for example, the hero lights a cigar, and the

Chorus expresses itself cryptically, casting doubt on the power of Fate: "Not everything that burns is Fate" and "Fate [is] given that name/ So that you don't ask how it happens" (Mordecai Gorelik translation).

After the opening choral ode, the action begins swiftly, for Sepp Schmitz enters Biedermann's house in spite of orders not to admit him. The powerful firebug combines threats, flattery, and piety to obtain food and shelter from Biedermann, who remains firm in his refusal to admit his employee, Knechtling. In spite of his original intention, Biedermann installs Schmitz in the attic, and Babette Biedermann says to the audience: "Gottlieb, my husband, promised to go up in the attic every evening, personally, to see if there is any firebug up there." When Schmitz comes down for breakfast the next morning, he wears a sheepskin—an obvious wolf in sheep's clothing, but the wolf acts like a lamb, playing sentimentally upon Babette Biedermann's sympathy, so that she does not ask him to leave, and the maid announces Willi Eisenring, firebug number two.

It is above all in the third scene that the truth is treated as a joke. Finding that there is gasoline in his attic, Biedermann orders the firebugs to leave. They pay little attention to him, and when the Policeman announces the suicide of Knechtling, Biedermann's own guilt prevents him from denouncing the firebugs for their guilt. Together, firebugs and Biedermann lie to the policeman that the gasoline is hair tonic, and Biedermann's advertising slogan rings out ironically, "Man can breathe a sigh of relief."

But so *un*relieved is the Chorus of Firemen that they confront Biedermann on his way to work: "Far be it from us the Chorus/ To judge a hero of drama. . . ." Instead of judging, they plead with him to drive out the firebugs. Pretending innocence, Biedermann summarizes his investigations, which lead him to conclude that he smells no gasoline in his attic. Like Greek Choruses, this one laments its fate, for its hero is "so soon accustomed to bad smells."

By the next scene, Biedermann no longer cares whether his "guests" are firebugs. He listens to Eisenring's candid betrayal of their activities, which he treats as a joke, inviting the sinister pair to dinner, so as to protect his own property. The last two scenes—preparations for the dinner and the dinner itself—push to farce Biedermann's determined non-recognition of his danger. Insisting on his democracy, he orders the maid to hide linen and silver; the goose is to be served in the pot in which it was cooked. Then, turning to the audience, Biedermann admits that his guests are firebugs, but asks, "What would you have done? If you were in my place, for God's sake? And when?"

This single expression of anxiety is forgotten in the final scene. Biedermann doubles up with laughter at the joke that oil waste burns better than sawdust. But Biedermann's sense of humor will serve him no better than his proletarian aspirations; as the firebugs casually mention the fires they have seen, the maid brings out the linen and silver, to which the firebug-guests are partial. An ex-actor, Sepp Schmitz drapes the linen tablecloth around himself, distorting the lines from *Everyman* to "Gottlieb Biedermann, dost thou hear me?" Though Babette recognizes Sepp as Death, Biedermann argues that he might be the ghost from *Hamlet*, or *Don Juan*, or *Macbeth*. On the brink of death, Biedermann-Everyman refuses to recognize the danger that threatens him.

Sepp goes on to sing an old German children's song: "Fox you stole that goose. Give it back or the hunter will come after you with his gun" (my literal translation). The song is ironically relevant to the situation of Biedermann; rather than steal his fowl, however, this fox in ghost's clothing is offered the goose by the very hunter who should come after him with a gun. When the fire sirens approach, Biedermann is relieved that his house is not burning. Both firebugs assure Biedermann that they are firebugs; a third firebug, the Professor, after a speech drowned out by the sirens, assures Biedermann that they are firebugs; but Biedermann neverthelesss gives them matches: "If they really were firebugs, do you think they wouldn't have matches?" The play ends in explosions and flames, the Chorus wailing, as in Greek tragedy, "Woe to us! Woe to us! Woe!"

The rather long Epilogue that Frisch added for the German production of the play attempts to heighten and generalize the parody of tragedy. The Policeman of the main play sprouts wings, Schmitz becomes Beelzebub, and Eisenring, dressed like a bishop, passes freely from Hell to Heaven. The Biedermanns are not certain whether they are in Hell or Heaven, damned or saved. The ineffectual Chorus, who extinguished no fires on earth, is ordered by Eisenring to extinguish the fires of Hell, because the biggest sinners are all going to Heaven. As the firebugs ride gaily off to earth, the Biedermanns kneel. "Do you think we're saved?" asks Babette, and Biedermann replies, "Yes, I think so." Perhaps they are big enough sinners to have earned a place in Heaven; pointedly, Biedermann has been christened Gottlieb—beloved of God. The ironic tragedy of the drama is capped by the ironic comedy of the epilogue; there may be a happy ending for the Biedermanns, who have caused human tragedy in this "learning play without a lesson."

Frisch and Dürrenmatt use comedy and farce to underline the suggestion that these catastrophes could have been avoided. Both plays, like Brecht's parables, use comic techniques to reveal social immorality. Brecht depicts characters who are inextricably entangled in a system, whereas Frisch and Dürrenmatt move through specific immoral acts to disaster. Our horror is aroused because the individual could have avoided such disaster, had he behaved differently—in any social system.

Like the two Swiss plays, those of Harold Pinter begin in comedy, but end in disaster. Like the comedy of Frisch and Dürrenmatt, that of Pinter is based on social reality, but, most unlike the Swiss playwrights, Pinter takes no social or moral side. Frisch mixes the tragic and the comic, when Biedermann's comic blindness leads to disaster; Dürrenmatt caricatures the background of his increasingly tragic hero; Pinter builds menace upon a comic language, which is the perfect reflection of a milieu—cliché Cockney patter in *The Room, The Birthday Party*, and *The Dumb Waiter*; smart suburban chatter in *A Slight Ache, The Collection*, and *The Lover*. Pinter compresses his early plays into fetid rooms into which fear creeps through the conversations. The pattern moves from comedy to catastrophe: the cheerful platitudes of Meg and Petey in *The Birthday Party* lead to Stanley's disintegration; the hesitant insecurity of Aston and the crisp confidence of Mick lead to the despair of Davies in *The Caretaker*; the memories of sex and success lead to Edward's replacement by the match-seller in *A Slight Ache*; the sophisticated banter of *The Collection* leads to the permanent insecurity of James. In the earlier plays the lower-class clichés contribute to the destruction of the individual; in the later plays the middle-class clichés contribute to the destruction of the couple. In *The Homecoming*, sexual clichés contribute to the travesty on family life. After tea and cakes and ices, Pinter's Prufrocks *are* confronted with crises.

All Pinter's plays have realistic settings, and almost all of them begin in conversations of comic realism, but colloquialism, repetition, or staccato rhythm imply the menace to come.

> ROSE: Here you are. This'll keep the cold out. It's very cold out, I can tell you. It's murder. *(The Room)*
>
> MEG: It that you, Petey? *Pause.* Petey, is that you? *Pause.* Petey?
> PETEY: What?
> MEG: Is that you?
> PETEY: Yes, it's me.
> MEG: What? *(Her face appears at the hatch.)* Are you back?
> PETEY: Yes.
> MEG: I've got your cornflakes ready. *(She disappears and reappears.)* Here's your cornflakes. . . . Are they nice?
> PETEY: Very nice.
> MEG: I thought they'd be nice. *(The Birthday Party)*

Just as their breakfast conversation comically reveals the dead complacency of the Petey-Meg marriage, so *their* breakfast conversation comically reveals reciprocal hostility in the Edward-Flora marriage of A *Slight Ache*:

FLORA: Have you noticed the honeysuckle this morning?
EDWARD: The what?
FLORA: The honeysuckle.
EDWARD: Honeysuckle? Where?
FLORA: By the back gate, Edward.
EDWARD: Is that honeysuckle? I thought it was . . . convolvulus, or something.
FLORA: But you know it's honeysuckle.
EDWARD: I tell you I thought it was convolvulus. (*Pause.*)
FLORA: It's in wonderful flower.
EDWARD: I must look.
FLORA: The whole garden's in flower this morning. The clematis. The convolvulus. Everything. I was out at seven. I stood by the pool.
EDWARD: Did you say—that the convolvulus was in flower?
FLORA: Yes.
EDWARD: But good God, you just denied there was any.
FLORA: I was talking about the honeysuckle.
EDWARD: About the what?
FLORA: (*calmly*) Edward—you know that shrub outside the toolshed . . .
EDWARD: Yes, yes.
FLORA: That's convolvulus.
EDWARD: That?
FLORA: Yes.
EDWARD: Oh. (*Pause.*) I thought it was japonica.
FLORA: Oh, good Lord no.
EDWARD: Pass the teapot, please. *Pause. She pours tea for him.* I don't see why I should be expected to distinguish between these plants. It's not my job.
FLORA: You know perfectly well what grows in your garden.
EDWARD: Quite the contrary. It is clear that I don't.

One might summarize A *Slight Ache* as the progressive menace of what Edward does not know is growing in his garden. Later in the play, Edward himself suggests the ambiguity of the tragi-comic tone, unable to decide whether the silent matchseller is laughing or crying: "—don't weep—. . .—please stop crying— . . . You're laughing. Your face. Your body. Rocking . . . gasping . . . rocking . . . shaking . . . rocking . . . heaving . . . rocking. . .You're laughing at me! Aaaaahhhh . . ." This ambiguity precedes the substitution of the match-seller for Edward. The comic dialogue has led to a tragic loss of identity.

In *The Collection* menace is already present in the slightly comic opening conversation:

> *Harry approaches the house, opens the front door and goes in. He switches on a light in the hall, goes into the living-room, walks to the telephone and lifts it.*

> HARRY: Hullo.
> VOICE: Is that you, Bill?
> HARRY: No, he's in bed. Who's this?
> VOICE: In bed?
> HARRY: Who is this?
> VOICE: What's he doing in bed?

That question summarizes *The Collection*: what does Bill do in bed, since he lives with Harry and has perhaps had an affair with James' wife, Stella?

Any Pinter play provides similar passages, the comic rhythmic repartee leading to a crisis, sometimes subtle and sometimes violent. This integration of threat into comic dialogue is part of our *Zeitgeist*, or, more precisely, *Zeitstimme*. Though it would be too facile to single out T. S. Eliot or Harold Pinter as typical of his decade, the two playwrights do exemplify a shift in dramatic tone. Pinter's *Birthday Party* (1957) and *Homecoming* (1965) may be viewed as skew reflections on Eliot's *Family Reunion* (1939).[12]

All three plays contain a mixture of moods ranging from the trivial to the tragic; all three plays make religious suggestions through small talk. The titles suggest the tragic import: Eliot's *Family Reunion* is about the reunion of the Christian family; called together to celebrate a homecoming and a birthday, the family finds itself present at a death, but Christian belief views death as spiritual rebirth. Pinter's *Birthday Party* also dramatizes a birthday for which a party is promoted by a pair who recall the Judaeo-Christian tradition in stale cliché. The morning after his birthday, Stanley Webber is reduced to an automaton in morning-clothes (which puns on mourning); his spiritual death leads to what may be his redemption but is more probably his damnation, in the "special treatment" promised him at a mysterious Monty's. Despite the biblical name of the female protagonist—Ruth—in Pinter's *Homecoming*, the family reunion is based on her willingness to serve as prostitute for her male in-laws. Pinter's biblical suggestions are oblique and ironic, confirming the comment of John Russell Taylor about Pinter's theology: "The Fall of man is more like Humpty-Dumpty's than Adam's and Eve's, resulting in a situation where nobody, oneself or another, can hope to put all the pieces together again into a perfect and coherent whole."[13]

In mixing the tragic and comic, Eliot works differently from Pinter. Classicist though he claimed to be, Eliot includes comedy in his dramas, which border on the tragic. Much of the comedy in *Family Reunion* is assigned to the Chorus of uncles and aunts, whereas Pinter distributes clichés among the several members of his family. Although Eliot was later to disparage his play because his actors had to move in and out of the Chorus, they are caricatures both individually and collectively, so that their choral response has seldom disturbed audiences as much as it has their author. Moreover, the caricature Chorus is important to Eliot's theme. As in Greek tragedy, Eliot's Chorus reflects the feelings of the audience; for example "We all of us make the pretension/ To be the uncommon exception/ To the universal bondage." Or "I am afraid of all that has happened, and of all that is to come." Or "We must listen to the weather report/ And the international catastrophes." Or, finally, "We have suffered far more than a personal loss—/ We have lost our way in the dark." And yet, because Eliot contrasts his Chorus with his protagonists, the audience cannot identify with them in their moments of fear—unlike Pinter's characters, who evoke fear *through* their comic conversation.

Eliot's fearful protagonist, Harry, Lord Monchensey, speaks of his brother, John, who has had an automobile accident: "A brief vacation from the kind of consciousness/ That John enjoys, can't make very much difference to him or anyone else." Much of the time, the consciousness of the Chorus is at a similar nadir. In patronizing them through Harry, Eliot risks patronizing his audience, for he implies that most of us live our lives as comic caricatures who can derive dignity only from the martyrdom of saints and heroes.

In Pinter's plays, there is neither dignity nor redemption. Though Stanley of *The Birthday Party* retorts both to the sexual domestic clichés of Meg, and to the socio-religious clichés of Goldberg and McCann, he is finally pulverized into semiparalysis. In *The Homecoming* there is no clear line between victim and villain; Ruth brings both temptation and ruth, discord and harmony, into the all-male household. The savagely comic dialogue subsides into an ambiguous equilibrium at the end of the play.[14]

As a critic, Eliot hoped that contemporary poetic drama would not retreat into artificiality but that "our own sordid, dreary daily world would be suddenly illuminated and transfigured" by such drama.[15] In the repetitive rhythms and evocative images of poetic prose, Pinter has illuminated our sordid, dreary daily world *as* sordid and dreary; instead of transfiguring it, he has revealed that darkness and ambiguity lie on the near side of comedy.

Like Pinter, Edward Albee uses colloquial comic dialogue to reveal a serious, even a tragic, sense of human experience. In two

plays, particularly, *Zoo Story* and *Tiny Alice*, comedy dissolves
into menace, which in turn erupts into violence of transcendental
resonance. In both plays, as in those of Pinter, the comedy lies
almost entirely in the dialogue.

The play-long contrast of Peter and Jerry in *The Zoo Story*
begins in the opening lines. Though Jerry calls Peter "a richly
comic person," it is Jerry whom the phrase fits. In the first few
minutes of playing time, Jerry characterizes Peter in his own
distinctive idiom, "Well, *Time* magazine isn't for blockheads."
Through Jerry's mounting threat to Peter, his techniques of comedy are repetition, colloquialism, and incongruity—all of them
employed with hostility. The following lines depend upon repetition for their comic effect: "Say, what's the dividing line between
upper-middle-class and lower-upper-middle-class?" "This colored
queen has rotten teeth, which is rare, and he has a Japanese kimono, which is also pretty rare; and he wears this kimono to
and from the john in the hall, which is pretty frequent." "Under
which...weighed down...are some letters...please letters...
please why don't you do this, and please when will you do that
letters. And when letters, too. When will you write? When will
you come? When?" Jerry's suspenseful dog story is comically undercut through repetition: "I was...well, how would you put it
...enticed?...fascinated?...no, I don't think so...heart-shat-
teringly anxious, that's it; I was heart-shatteringly anxious to
confront my friend again. . . . Yes, Peter; friend. That's the only
word for it. I was heart-shatteringly et cetera to confront my
doggy friend again." Even the threat of the knife fight is comically
shaded: "You fight, you miserable bastard; fight for that bench;
fight for your parakeets; fight for your cats; fight for your two
daughters; fight for your wife; fight for your manhood, you
pathetic little vegetable."

By repetition, Jerry converts the realities of their conversation
into metaphors of Peter's conformity. But Jerry's own metaphors
are colorfully colloquial: "That particular vaudeville act is playing

the cloud circuit now" for the death of his parents; "her most constant companion . . . among others, among many others . . . was a Mr. Barleycorn" for his mother's promiscuity and dipsomania; "But that was the jazz of a very special hotel" for his own homosexuality.

The comedy is severely limited once Jerry's knife is visible, but even his death scene is not free of comic suggestion. After the stabbing, Peter can only repeat incessantly, "O my God." Earlier in the play, Peter had responded to Jerry's descriptions with a prissy "Oh my," and Jerry had sneered "O your what?" By the end of the play, the two men are linked through their common utterance of the phrase "O . . . my . . . God." And Albee's scenic direction indicates that Jerry speaks these last words in *"a combination of scornful mimicry and supplication"*—a summary of the mixed mood of tragicomedy.

The tragicomic direction of *Tiny Alice* is similar to that of *The Zoo Story*, or, for that matter, to Pinter plays—from comic surface to tragic dominance. The opening scene of *Tiny Alice* is a triumph of comic hostility between the Cardinal and the Lawyer. The central joke rests on grammar—the Cardinal's rare shifts from *we* to *I*, which the Lawyer mockingly notes. Both opponents make adroit use of repetition and pause. The Lawyer taunts the Cardinal, "Your Eminence was not always so . . . eminent." And he admits abandoning the church for the law: "A common-law marriage, for I am at law and, as you say, common." Playing upon a metaphor, the Cardinal tells the Lawyer ironically, "Pure. You're pure. You're ringed by stench, but you're pure. Theres [sic] an odor that precedes you, and follows after you're gone, but you walk in the eye of it . . . pure." Though the Cardinal slips from *we* to *I*, he never deviates from formal speech, whereas the Lawyer is capable of pointed colloquialisms: "You'll grovel, Buddy. (*Slaps his hip hard*) As automatically and naturally as people slobber on that ring of yours." Or "Of course, we were at an age when everyone diddled everyone else. . ." Or "the hand, the kissed hand palsies [pun] out . . . FOR THE LOOT!!"

Once Brother Julian enters on scene, however (and he is in every subsequent scene but one), the comedy of *Tiny Alice* is considerably reduced. The others play upon Julian's profession, but he seems ignorant of the pun on *lay* brother, as he seems ignorant of the double entendre in his remark, "The organ is...in need of use." Though the Lawyer comments that Alice was "never one with words," she and her two companions, the Lawyer and Butler, milk several words for sexual suggestion: "Odds and ends," "if you're not to queer the whole business," "Little bird, pecking away in the library." After Julian is shot, Miss Alice asks the Lawyer, "You want me to go now?" and he replies monosyllabically and suggestively, "Come."

There is further linguistic play—Butler as name and profession, for example[16]—but Julian's tragedy dominates the tone increasingly. Under his comically colloquial cloak, however, the Lawyer reveals two profoundly tragic meanings of the play. On Julian's wedding-day, the Lawyer sneers, "Julian, you are indeed a fortunate man, today. What more cheering sight can there be than Frank Fearnought, clean-living, healthy farm lad, come from the heartland of the country, from the asylums—you see, I know—in search of fame, and true love—never fortune of course." In spite of Julian's pleading, the Lawyer intensifies the mockery through repetition: "And see what has happened to brave and handsome Frank: he has found what he sought...true..love; *and* fortune—to his surprise, for wealth had never crossed his pure mind; and fame? . . . Ooooh, there will be a private fame, perhaps."

When the Lawyer checks the cartridges in his pistol, Julian begins to live that private fame—of martyrdom—and, with colloquial pungency, the Lawyer summarizes the theme of *Tiny Alice*, which we will see dramatized in Julian's long death scene, "Face the inevitable and call it what you have always wanted. How to come out on top, going under." After Julian is shot, the Lawyer's hard surface remains unperturbed and imperturbable. Tragedy hangs in the air, and yet the context of the play confers a hint of mockery on Julian's final crucifixion position, and his final incorporation of Alice-Truth into his Christian belief. Even Julian, dying, is aware of the "awful humor" of the reality of abstraction, but at the last he puts it from him "com[ing] out on top, going under."

Though the comedy in Albee's plays intensifies the tragedy, the tragedy does not, as in Pinter, grow out of the comedy. Both playrights fulfill Bentley's definition of tragicomedy as a comedy with an unhappy ending, and they occasionally illustrate Guthke's criterion of mutual interaction between the comic and the tragic. The most perfect blend of the two moods occurs, however, in the plays of Samuel Beckett, where almost any line can be viewed both tragically and comically. Though the English translation of *Waiting for Godot* is the only one of Beckett's works explicitly designated as "Tragicomedy," the mixed mood permeates his creation, which is channeled into poem and pantomime, fiction and drama. Beckett's earlier works, written in English, have a comic surface that is woven of such sophisticated devices as allusion, quotation, pun, macaronic, paradox. Upon Beckett's shift to French, however, which was accompanied by his resurgence of interest in the dramatic medium, he turned his back on his own erudition, much as Eliot, in his drama, spurned his own lyric gift. Rather than urbanity, Beckett's comedy rises from slapstick, obscenity, incongruity, and ignorance—which he converts into aspects of the human tragedy.

Traditionally, dramas show humor in plot, character, dialogue, and stage business. Beckett uses all of these, but he glides into them softly, moving plot toward arrival and departure, characters toward an immediate presence, and speech-gesture toward repetition. This diminution is itself a comic comment on the complicated plot, complex psychology, and inflated rhetoric of various forms of drama; even more pointedly and generally, his drama forms a tragicomic commentary on the complicated plots, psychological complexities, and inflated rhetoric of our daily world.

The skillful dramatist of the realistic tradition informs us swiftly and unobtrusively of the "facts" of his plot; with Beckett there are no such facts. It is not that we cannot verify facts, as in Pinter, or that facts become farce, as in Ionesco; rather, Beckett's action pounds facts into pattern. Though obvious in outline—the two acts of *Godot, Happy Days, Play*; the circular movement of *Endgame, Krapp's Last Tape, Come and Go*—the pattern is subtle in texture. More than in pattern or texture, however, Beckett's humanity resides in his tragicomic characters. Many critics have generalized about Beckett's characters—bums, clowns, human flotsam, crepuscular beings, dying gladiators, stoic comedians, disintegrated men—and his fictional protagonists are hard to tell apart. In contrast, his dramatic characters possess a fierce and concrete individuality.

They have no character, if we demand the logical and psychological consistency of traditional drama. On the other hand, unlike Ionesco's characters, those of Beckett are not interchangeable: even blind and mute, Pozzo and Lucky remain as separately identifiable as they are eternally bound; even dressed alike, Gogo and Didi have distinctive idioms and stage postures. It is largely through his characters that Beckett conveys the tragicomic mixture of *Waiting for Godot*, and he introduces the ambivalent tone as swiftly and unobtrusively as the conventional skillful playwright delivers his exposition.

Unlike most tragicomedies, *Godot* remains tragicomic throughout its duration. As Geneviève Serreau has perceptively commented: "The text of *Godot* and its scenic directions re-enforce ...clown suggestions: derbies for all characters; the spectacular entrance of Pozzo and Lucky, the latter using a whip like a circus animal-trainer; Pozzo's generous offer of Lucky's burlesque recitatif as a dependable entertainment that has stood the test of time. Or the hat pantomime (three hats for two heads) which Gogo and Didi enact with the seriousness of acrobatic jugglers; or the slapstick fall of all four actors piled up on one another."[17] But each of these comic incidents has tragic resonance.

The tragicomic mixture is evident from the beginning, and the inconclusive conclusion combines comedy of repetition with the tragedy of what is repeated. When the curtain rises, the pathetically bare tree—the whole setting—contrasts with Gogo's comic business—trying to take off his boots. Gogo's physical struggle must be played for laughs, and his opening line, "Nothing to be done" usually brings laughter too—laughter at his frustration and at the declaration of inaction to open a drama, which is an imitation of an action. At intervals in the action, moreover, the phrase will be repeated, undercutting Beckett's action with denials of the possibility of action.

Didi's "short, stiff strides" should be played for laughter; his opening words are a reply to and a comic misunderstanding of Gogo's remark. At the same time, they reveal a difference between the two friends. Gogo's "Nothing to be done" refers to his material condition—the boots stick to his feet. Didi's reply refers to their metaphysical situation, upon which he ponders even before he "broods, musing on the struggle." It is not the words alone that carry Beckett's tonal mixture, but Didi's seriousness as opposed to Gogo's comic business; yet Gogo himself is serious, and Didi's walk borders on the slapstick.

As we follow the conversation of the two friends, we respond to their quick shifts in mood, and yet our mood is not a mere reflection of theirs. After Didi's first meditation, most of the dialogue is comic—meeting, beating, remembering, suffering, urinating—until his introduction of the two thieves who were crucified with Christ. By that time, still early in the play, Beckett has established the misery of the two tramps through their funny dialogue, and they express their misery so that we laugh *at* them and *with* them. Both Gogo and Didi have exclaimed angrily: "Hurts! He wants to know if it hurts!" Even as we smile at the complaints of each tramp, we know that it does hurt, physically and metaphysically.

We laugh at the way Didi and Gogo misunderstand each

other, at the indefiniteness of their references, at their pat phrases in doubtful situations. But after our first exposure to the play, these laugh-lines emerge as a sustained tragic theme—the inadequacy of language to express thought and feeling. This inadequacy is not, as in Ionesco, the fault of farcical characters who accept ready-made phrases; nor, as in Pinter, is cliché a camouflage for mysterious menace. In Beckett's work, all language is unsuited to all men; yet words are all we have, and we are compelled to use them, comic though they and we appear.

Upon first viewing *Godot*, we can only cumulatively perceive the tragicomic erosion of language and thought, whereas we can respond directly to the tragicomic qualities of the two friends. They share the wait for Godot, but they wait together in partial solitude, Gogo fretting about the creature comforts and Didi pondering their metaphysical situation. While Gogo eats and sleeps in comic gestures, Didi expresses a tragic sense of life. Gogo is funnier and more endearing; Didi attains an ironic view of himself and his situation.

On stage, they are dressed alike—as clowns—but they are concretely different. Didi knows the details of their appointment with Godot, whereas Gogo forgets even his name. Didi is the more eloquent and inventive of the two, Gogo the more physically active—running, dancing, limping, falling, sitting, lying, miming. Gogo's stage business revolves around his boots and Didi's around his hat; when Pozzo cracks his whip, Gogo drops a boot, Didi a hat; Gogo stinks from his feet, Didi from his mouth; Gogo wants Lucky to dance, Didi to think. Yet the friends never engage in a Mind-Body debate.

Different as they are, they are inseparable on stage. Both Gogo and Didi engage in specific mental and spiritual exercises to pass endless time; they react similarly to Lucky's monologue. They both express their misery, and they both take part in a hat-juggling routine; both sprawl farcically and helplessly on the ground, with Pozzo and Lucky. The antics of the tramps, singly and together, are a stylized parody of the actions of our life—comic in the short run, tragic in the long run.[18]

Only after we laugh at the farce and sympathize with the fears of Didi and Gogo, only after we appreciate their friendship and their loneliness, are we confronted with a different pair of characters—Pozzo and Lucky. The master-slave couple contrast visually and verbally with the ragged friends: rope and whip oppose the clumsy embraces; Pozzo's chicken and wine replace the root diet of Gogo; the free conversational exchange of the friends continues against the new background of a silent Lucky and a loquacious Pozzo; the compulsive waiting of the one couple is opposed to the compulsive wandering of the other.

Though we learn a good many details about Pozzo and Lucky, these details rarely arouse our sympathy. Because we never see Pozzo and Lucky alone, because they speak in formulae, we view them with critical detachment, laughing at Pozzo's pretentiousness and, perhaps, at Lucky's logorrhea. We can imitate the tramps in feeling sorry for Lucky, though Didi's comparison "like a banana skin" undercuts his and our pity. We may even pity Pozzo as Didi does, but we do not feel pity *while* we laugh, as we do for Gogo and Didi. However, as Jean-Jacques Mayoux points out, Lucky is not only a pitiable object; he is also "the man about whom the others make their comments, and through whom they observe their own situation."[19] Ironically, the friends' pity for Lucky quickly shifts to concern for themselves, even as our own tends to do.

Only in Act II, when the four characters are sprawled on the ground, can we pity them all at once, while laughing at them. Only then do we see that the four characters are "of the same species," symbolized simultaneously by their attachment to the ground and by the bowler-hats they all wear. Associated with ceremonious occasions, these hats also suggest clown-victims, such as Charlie Chaplin, or Laurel and Hardy; but unlike Brecht, Weiss, and Genet, Beckett merely suggests that tradition.

Like Didi and Gogo—"We're inexhaustible"—Beckett's works are inexhaustible. *Godot* above all has evoked widespread enthusiasm because of the widespread appeal of the two tramps who are on stage almost all the time. Like Shakespeare's fools, they ape their betters until we question whether their betters are any better or better off than they—or we. Günther Anders has written perceptively that the two clowns know they are playing, while we do not know we are playing in our lives. Thus, they become our betters; we laugh loudest, but they laugh last, for they know that they can do no more than "find something to give [them] the impression [they] exist," whereas we believe directly and naively in our own existence.[20]

That "something" takes comic form on stage—gesture and language, slapstick and "wordy-gurdy," faint recollection and fainter prediction, mastication, defecation, and play. But the more one plays, the less fun it is. And sure only that they are waiting, the two friends have doubts about time, space, and memory. This doubt is expressed with comic violence which weakens our own foundations of belief. Significantly, their doubts begin in their first conversation about Godot: "He said by the tree. Do you see any others?" Didi worries at once: "What are you insinuating? That we've come to the wrong place?" A moment later, he asks, "You recognize the place?" and Gogo has to admit, "I didn't say that."

Even more perilously, time is subject for doubt: "He [Godot] said Saturday. (*Pause.*) I think." When Gogo suggests that it may not be Saturday, that they don't know what day it is, Didi *"look[s] wildly about him, as though the date was inscribed in the landscape."* The indicative *was* strengthens the link between date and landscape, time and place. During the course of the play, time disintegrates through comic overinsistence on its units —hours, days, seasons, years, decades, but the distintegration itself is tragic. Pozzo's Act I lyricism mocks the chaos of time; by Act II, having lost his watch in Act I, Pozzo has also lost his sense of time, and he reacts furiously to the question, "Since when?" Growing calmer, he expresses a tragic view of life in time, which Didi will echo (with minor modifications) after Pozzo is gone: "They give birth astride of a grave, the light gleams an instant, then it's night once more." Nevertheless, Pozzo jerks on Lucky's rope, and they move grotesquely on through the gleaming instant.

If apparently objective time and space are undependable—tragically undependable but comically discovered as such—human thought is an ephemeral farce. A. J. Leventhal has noted that Beckett's tragicomedy is based on the axioms of Gorgias the Sophist: "1) Nothing is. 2) If anything is, it cannot be known. 3) If anything is, and cannot be known, it cannot be expressed in speech."[21] Memory, which plays so large a part in human thought, is utterly untrustworthy: Pozzo admits to a defective memory, but the two friends and Godot's boy (if he is Godot's boy) also forget easily, denying even the events we have witnessed on the stage. We laugh at their absent-mindedness, but through that laughter we come to a dismaying awareness of the futility of presence of mind.

Beckett's characters can scarcely make a statement without retracting it, contradicting it, qualifying it, building questions upon it. Names, colors, vegetables are as uncertain as places or days of the week. Though the friends urge each other to action, they do not act. On the one hand, they seek the *mot juste,* and on the other, they bury meaning in synonyms or sound play. Early in Act I, Didi exclaims to Gogo: "Nothing is certain when you're about." By the end of the act, Gogo agrees wearily, "No, nothing is certain."

Beckett's most insistent comic device, which contains his most tragic meaning, is repetition. He repeats the scenic direction for repetition: *As before* (in French, more pointedly, *même jeu*). Verbally, Lucky's monologue is the most stunning example of repetition, with its obscene stutter: "Acacacacademy of Anthropopopometry," its opposition of "for reasons unknown" to "be-yond all doubt," and "but time will tell" to "not so fast." The other characters also repeat themselves; each of the tramps echoes the other in such phrases as "Nothing to be done," "It's inevi-table," "I'm going." In their verbal duets, Didi's variations are counterpointed against Gogo's repetitions. In Act II, Didi echoes Pozzo's phrases, and he feeds lines to Godot's Boy, so that they replay the Act I scene.

There are about half a dozen comic repetitions in Act I, em-phasizing the pitiable condition of Lucky: "Why doesn't he put down his bags?" and "Do you want to get rid of him?" Largely in Act II, but also in Act I, there are some dozen repeti-tions of "We're waiting for Godot" before Gogo's climactic "*I'm* waiting for Godot" (my italics), in which the variation on the repetition is comic, but the sudden declaration of loneliness is tragic. Similarly, repetition of biblical motifs culminates in one of the funniest, bitterest comments on the human condition in a Christian framework:

VLADIMIR: But you can't go barefoot.
ESTRAGON: Christ did.
VLADIMIR: Christ! What has Christ got to do with it? You're not going to compare yourself with Christ?
ESTRAGON: All my life I've compared myself to him.
VLADIMIR: But where he lived it was warm, it was dry!
ESTRAGON: And they crucified quick.

In addition to verbal comedy of repetition, Beckett arouses laughter from Gogo's repetitious stage business with his boots, Didi's with his hat. The hat-juggling of the friends repeats the phrase-juggling of their minds. Pozzo's comic losses of Act I result in his tragic loss of sight in Act II.

Farcical obscenity and poignant anguish are juxtaposed near the beginning and the end of the tragicomedy: early in Act I, Gogo calls Didi's attention to his open fly; just before the end,

Didi tells Gogo to pull his trousers up. Early in Act I, the two friends talk of hanging themselves to attain an erection; near the end, they test Gogo's rope-belt in a vain hope of hanging themselves to attain death.

The round song which Didi sings to open Act II summarizes the repetitive tragicomedy of the dogs' life, the play, and the human condition.[22] More frequently than language or gesture, however, occurs the repetition of the scenic directions *Pause* and *Silence*, precisely because one of the fundamental meanings of the play is that, in Gogo's words, "There's no lack of void." And the more we engage in repetitive efforts to fill the void, the more void there is.

The tragicomic suggestions of infinite games through infinite waiting in an infinite void, conveyed dramatically through many forms of repetition, are contained in the two-act structure of *Waiting for Godot*. Just as "It rains and rains" suggests endless, repetitive rain, so the two acts of *Godot* suggest endless, repetitive waiting.[23] Each act closes with identical words, but the lines are spoken by a different voice:

> Well? Shall we go?
> Yes, let's go.

Since they do not move, all acts close in the tragicomic paradox of contrapuntal immobility.

Though Beckett reserves the designation *tragicomedy* for *Godot*, all his drama reflects a tragic sense of life which is riddled by comic detail. In his one-act plays the tragic drive is more insistent, and the comedy is grimmer. The two plays that repeat *Godot*'s two-part structure, *Happy Days* and *Play*, provide more humor both by and within the repetitions. Winnie of *Happy Days* chirps about her happy day, and the Man of *Play* hiccups requests for pardon in his purgatory. Like Didi and Gogo, Winnie and the Man may be desperate, but they do not despair. Though they do not quite find something to give *them* the impression they exist, they still convey that impression to us.

An oddity for Beckett, Winnie is femininely bourgeois to the hat on her lady-like head; she is baked into the earth's crust, her possessions within reach and her family within call. Possessions and family have the usual Beckett comic economy: a husband, a parasol, and a sack of miscellaneous objects. As Didi and Gogo continue to wait for Godot, so Winnie continues to count her blessings—against all evidence and reason—aging while we watch. As in *Godot*, we respond first to concrete characters, and only slowly perceive the tragicomic pattern whose dialogue begins with "again" for Didi, with "another" for Winnie. Even in Act I, Winnie's field of activity is a marked reduction upon that of the tramps in *Godot*. Buried to the waist, Winnie can kill time only with hands and words. But she does so with a will, taking inventory of her material possessions and allowing her consciousness to stray from prayer, to optimism about her surroundings, to personal and literary recollection. Though she makes no point of it, Winnie's quotations from great English poets stress a union of joy and woe—almost defining tragicomedy.

Through Winnie's resolute expressions of joy, she reveals her tragedy. The visible objects of grooming and her invisible groom are both sources of comedy, and yet their human inadequacy is tragic. Winnie first speaks of her happy day after looking at an off-stage Willie, naked in his boater. She repeats cliché words of cheer about her own cheerless condition. She describes her references to time as "old style." Toward the end of Act I, she announces that "sorrow keeps breaking in" on her determinedly happy day. When she puts her belongings away, she turns to Willie again and re-reads the toothbrush inscription which she has been at pains to decipher: "Genuine pure fully guaranteed hog's setae." Winnie worries about the meaning of *hog* (one of the invectives of *Godot*), and her invisible husband, in his longest speech, defines the word with comic cruelty: "Castrated male swine. Reared for slaughter." The definition, which reflects as much upon the definer as upon the thing defined, inspires Winnie's most rhapsodic exclamation on her happy day.

Act II of *Happy Days*, like Act II of *Godot*, moves nearer to tragedy, and that movement is immediately evident, for Winnie has sunk up to her neck in the scorched earth. Sack, parasol, and revolver are now forever beyond her reach, since her hands are buried. She is entirely dependent on words to help her kill the light of day, and they, too, are beginning to fail her. In Act II, she no longer prays; her quotations are fewer and feebler. But she babbles on in the weariness of her determination to end another happy day. Even more insidiously than Gogo and Didi, she doubts time ("Then...now...what difficulties here, for the mind"), memory ("The look...What look?"), and her own body ("My arms... My breasts...What arms?...What breasts?") As her world runs down, she invents a second story, then returns to the one she began in Act I. Both stories veer toward catastrophe. Winnie prepares to sing to end another happy day, when Willie suddenly crawls into sight *"dressed to kill—top hat, morning coat, striped trousers, etc., white gloves in hand."* This is the most startling climax in all Beckett's drama, and it is a comic climax by virtue of the incongruous costume for a man on all fours. Winnie's immediate reaction is genuine pure fully guaranteed delight, but even she comes to wonder about Willie's intention. Willie says only, "Win," as when he asked Winnie to marry him. Winnie asks whether Willie has come for a kiss, but we see his hand near the revolver. Kiss or kill, the choice is never made on stage. Winnie's last words are the sentimental lyrics from the Merry Widow waltz, a title that binds joy to viduity. Her happy expression fades into a smile, and that smile also fades. Finally, Winnie and Willie look at each other in the inconclusive conclusion to *Happy Days*.

In such inconclusive conclusions, which suggest a repetition of the action *ad infinitum* and *ad plus absurdum*, Beckett's dramas differ from the catastrophic ends of the tragicomedies of Ghelderode, Eliot, Ionesco, Genet, Dürrenmatt, Frisch, Pinter, and

Albee. These playwrights use comedy mainly to intensify the final tragedy whereas Beckett's tragedy is continuously dramatized by his comedy. In this contemporary mixture of moods, all the playwrights are ungrateful children of a marriage between Romanticism and Realism. Romanticism called for a blend of the comic and the tragic, and Realism called for an end to sentimental happy endings. Their children fulfill both demands, but rebel against the self-conscious rhetoric of the one and against the photographic rigidity of the other. Contemporary dramatists thrive on slang and slapstick, incongruity and invention. Using techniques of mass appeal, on the one hand, and of esoteric Symbolist poetry, on the other, these tragicomic playwrights have attracted sizable audiences for their variously philosophic dramas. With a black humor that is no longer the exclusive province of Surrealism, these playwrights have dumped us into awareness of the debris of our civilization, so that we can hardly recall a harmonious whole.

Classical comedy dramatizes social aberration—a soldier who brags more than he fights, a slave who schemes more than he serves, a pedant, a hypocrite. Classical tragedy dramatizes a noble solitude from which society eventually benefits. The modern blend of tragicomedy, however, attempts a union of opposites that often leaves us more aware of the opposites than of the union. In a tragicomic context, Jan Kott has linked *King Lear* and *Endgame,* but Edgar says in *King Lear:* "The worst is not/ So long as we can say, 'This is the worst.'" Contemporary playwrights say "This is the worst" in very funny ways, but they leave it to us to decide if "the worst is not."

FIVE: The Role and the Real

ALMOST AS SOON AS THERE WAS A THEATER, THE WORLD WAS COMPARED TO A STAGE, AND ITS INHABITANTS TO ROLE-players.[1] The metaphor occurs in the writings of such pre-Socratics as Democritus, Heraclitus, and Pythagoras. Plato uses the comparison in several dialogues. It appealed to both historians and poets, though no extant Greek tragedy contains a world-stage reference. The Stoics turned the comparison to moral instruction:

> Remember that you are an actor in a drama, of such a kind as the author pleases to make it. If short, of a short one; if long, of a long one. If it be his pleasure you should act a poor man, a cripple, a governor, or a private person, see that you act it naturally. For this is your business, to act well the character assigned to you; to choose it is another's.
> (Epictetus, *The Enchiridion* XVII. W. H. D. Rouse translation)

Christian writers early appropriated the world-stage, man-actor metaphors, using them even during times for which we have no record of theater. By the twelfth century, John of Salisbury, blending classical tradition with Christian conception, broadened the *scena vitae* to a *theatrum mundi*, with God as audience-judge. Other medieval writers used the world-stage metaphor, but it is not found in medieval *drama*, for audience and actors were participating in a re-enactment rather than an imitation of an action; the stage was emblematic of essential reality—Heaven and Hell—and between them was the ephemeral moment of life on earth. Since the medieval makeshift stage contained religious reality, dramatic reference to a world-stage would have diminished that reality by giving undue importance to events of the temporal world. In the illusionist drama of the Renaissance, in contrast, we find many reflections on dramatic illusion—from the world-stage metaphor to such devices as song, masque, and play within the play.

Though plays within the play occur in the interlude *Fulgens and Lucrece* (1497) and the religious play *Mary of Nimigen* (c. 1500), the combination of this theatrical device with world-stage imagery appears only in fully developed secular illusionist drama. The Renaissance frequency of this combination testifies to an involvement in a world of shifting appearance, even while adhering to the theocentric belief that that world is no more than illusion. For roughly a century, the metaphor and inserted play appear in dramas of England, France, and Spain. In these dramas the old world-stage metaphor attains a new resonance through being spoken by an actor on a stage. As might be expected, Shakespeare is given to both the image and the device. Through variants of the world-stage metaphor and of the play within the play, Shakespeare called attention to his plays *as* plays; perhaps he convinced his audiences of the Globe Theatre motto: "Totus mundus agit histrionem."[2]

It was not Shakespeare, however, but Calderón who dramatized the old world-stage metaphor in a Christian context. In *The Great Theater of the World* God plays the role of spectator while man is an actor whose deeds result in either his salvation or damnation. Where Shakespeare's tragedies and comedies suggest the idea of play and the problematic nature of a reality beneath roles, Calderón's *auto sacramentale* emphasizes reward or punishment for the playing of an earthly role, which is the temporal reality we know.

Late-comers on the theatrical scene, German writers appropriated both world-stage metaphor and device of the inserted play. Wolfgang Kayser, in his study of the Grotesque, has shown the importance of the puppet-image in the plays of Lenz, Büchner, and Wedekind. The very basis of Tieck's dramaturgy is the destruction of dramatic illusion; thus, the third act of *The Topsy-Turvy World* contains four concentric plays reflectively ridiculing one another. Just as the ironic strain is stronger in German than in any other Romanticism, so the self-consciousness of the stage is stronger in its drama. Reflections on the artifice of roles are made by allusions to the play as only a play, to actors as mere actors, to technical and framing devices, and by variations of the play within the play. Büchner commented on a theatricalized world through his Danton, who remarks, "We are always on the stage, even though we are finally stabbed in earnest" (Carl Mueller translation). In the nineteenth century, the play within the play is used only sporadically, but is carried on to the twentieth-century German stage by two Viennese dramatists, Schnitzler and Hofmannsthal. After World I, a German-educated Sicilian, Luigi Pirandello, worked the device so deeply into the fabric of his drama that subsequent playwrights were marked by it, mainly in France.

Early in the twentieth century, even before turning to drama at the age of forty, Pirandello examined the theory of role-playing in a series of lectures later published as *Humor* (1908). Some of these thoughts might have served—did perhaps serve—as the springboard for his own dramatic practice.

> Humor is the feeling of polarity aroused by that special activity of reflection which doesn't hide itself, which doesn't become, as ordinarily in art, a form of feeling, but its contrary, following the feelings step by step, however, as the shadow follows the body. A common artist pays attention

> only to the body. A humorist pays attention to the body
> and its shadow, sometimes more to the shadow than the
> body. He sees all the tricks of the shadow; it now assumes
> length or width, as if to mimic the body, which, mean-
> while, doesn't pay any attention to it. (Teresa Novel
> translation)[3]

When Pirandello turned to drama, he found in contemporary
Italian Theater of the Grotesque a conflict between suffering face
and social mask, opposing each other in situations of nineteenth-
century melodrama. Pirandello deepened both face and mask,
body and shadow.[4] Especially in his Theater Trilogy, he sets
on stage "real" characters as well as the actors who play the roles
of these characters, and among the audience he sets other actors
to identify with the real audience. In *Six Characters in Search
of an Author* (1921) the real characters seek an author to defend
them against the stereotyped roles in which the actors try to
imprison them.[5] In *Each in His Own Way* (1924) real characters, challenging the actors for whom they are mere roles, interrupt a performance, and they leave unfinished both the play
within the play and Pirandello's own play. In *Tonight We Im-
provise* (1930) the actors themselves are haunted by the life
of the characters they portray, so that they rebel against the
director wishing to cast them in familiar roles. In all three plays of
the Theater Trilogy, the face-mask conflict of the Theater of the
Grotesque is deepened to a conflict between the living being
and the rigid role, in situations revolving around sexual fidelity.
The betrayal of the characters by the actors becomes the inevitable
betrayal of living experience when it is committed to art. Usually
(though not necessarily), the play within the play—*Hamlet* is
the best-known example—enhances the reality of the frame play
by the very artifice of the inserted device. In Pirandello's dramas,
the boundaries between frame and inner play are more fluid; his
play within the play is a betrayal of the outer play, which he
fictionalizes as not-play. The dramatic not-play is itself a form

of fiction, and it is a form that adroit playwrights subsequently incorporated into their repertory of techniques.

Though Ghelderode has disclaimed having any knowledge of Pirandello's work before he wrote his own theater-reality plays in the 1920's, he too interweaves the real and the role. He too uses lovers' triangles as the background for real-role conflicts. In *The Death of Doctor Faust* (1925) the real Faust's seduction of Marguerite is paralleled by the actor Faust's seduction of the actress Marguerite. The crowd, believing that Faust has murdered Marguerite, lynch the actor in his Faust costume, after which the real Faust shoots himself, and the real Marguerite falls prey to the real devil (named Cretinus). This "tragedy for the music hall" ends when an authorial figure, Diamotoruscant, keeps repeating, "Imbecile! Imbecile! Imbecile!" Ghelderode's Faust play thus dramatizes the eternal return of myth in the form of dramatic roles. A year later (1926) Ghelderode wrote *Three Actors and Their Drama*; in a play within the play, a jealous husband shoots his wife and her lover. The actors playing these parts rise up hale and hearty, only to learn that the author has shot himself. The real intrudes incongruously upon the role.

Working far from large theaters, Ghelderode was nevertheless interested in theatrical problems, as he confirmed in his Ostend Interviews: "I was only trying to open a door, a window, to raise the curtain on something new, to extend a formula that was a little too closely tied to its period, to break the conventional frame of the theater" (George Hunter translation). In this, he succeeds, though Pirandello probes more subtly and persistently into the relationship between the role and the real.

Soon after their original productions, Pirandello's plays were presented in France, and "Pirandellism" became a synonym for theatrical relativity, or drama which searched beneath the illusionist stage, behind the actors' roles. Such playwrights as Henri Lenormand, Armand Salacrou, Marcel Achard, and above all Jean Anouilh take up Pirandello's main themes—role-playing and the consequent relativity of truth—in conventional realistic forms. Anouilh frequently creates self-dramatizing characters who call attention away from the plot to focus on their roles.[6] Rarely, however, does their spirited role-playing reflect upon the nature of roles. Rather they play for the love (and success) of play, and only cumulatively do the many disguises in Anouilh's plays suggest his insecurity about the stability of human personality and the nature of reality. His characters tend to be comfortable in their consciously assumed roles. Thus, in an individual play like *The Rehearsal*, there is ambiguity about whether certain lines belong to Musset's play within the play or to Anouilh's own play, but suffering is not betrayed by ready-made roles.

Probably Anouilh's boldest examination of roles occurs in one of his less popular plays, *Poor Bitos*. The frame play is a wig-party in which contemporary characters make up faces only, including wig, to resemble those of leading figures of the French Revolution. The party masks the desire of World War II collaborators to avenge themselves upon the public prosecutor, Bitos, who plays Robespierre at the party. Act I uses *The Rehearsal* device of ambiguity as to whether certain lines belong to the frame play or the charade. In Act II Anouilh shifts to the real French Revolution, in which the real Robespierre, dying from a gun-wound in the jaw, reviews the causes of his own pitiless revolutionary activity. Anouilh intends to illuminate Bitos through these scenes from the life of Robespierre. In Act III we learn that Bitos, whom we believed shot, has been hit by a blank cartridge. Anouilh's title is ironic; his "poor Bitos" merits no pity; instead, the modern Robespierre will live out a vengeful life, pitiless in his public prosecution. As in Pirandello's *Henry IV*, history is reduced to a personal vendetta. But whereas Anouilh's Bitos recapitulates a cliché Robespierre, Pirandello's protagonist is richer than his role as Henry IV.

With entirely different theatrical results, Bertolt Brecht began to examine role-playing at about the same time as Pirandello. Brecht's first play, *Baal*, began as a parody of Johst's *Lonely One*, and parody is predicated upon critical examination. At the period of his conversion to Communism, Brecht wrote musical parody and learning-play, both in reaction against the dominant illusionist stage of his time. In developing his *Verfremdungseffekt*, Brecht did not declare that his plays were simply *fremd*—strange —but *verfremdet*—made strange, so as to provoke examination. Brecht's theoretical writing confirms his estranging practices as director—harsh white light, projections, masks, well-worn props, interpolated songs, revolving stage. All these techniques serve to increase the spectator's awareness of being in the theater.

Brecht derived this approach from Diderot's *Paradox of the Actor*, which declares that the actor moves his audience only by remaining unmoved in his interpretation of a role. To keep his actors unmoved, Brecht insisted that they be conscious of acting. He had them recite their parts before mirrors, or in the third person, or with stage directions; occasionally actors exchanged roles. As dramatist, Brecht wrote estrangement into his plays —prologue, epilogue, lack of suspense, direct address to the audience, reference to himself as author, reference to the play as a play, scene interpolated within a scene, and trial scenes in which the audience is challenged to judge the actors or situation, rather than empathize with the actors in their roles. Since Brecht considered his plays as lessons, meditations, or parables, rather than imitations, he had little use for the world-stage metaphor. On the contrary, he insisted upon the stage as stage, upon actors as actors, but by such insistence, he teaches that the stage is a parable for the world. What looks like play is really real.

Only once does Brecht use the device of the play within the play—in *The Caucasian Chalk Circle*. It is interesting that, at about the same time that Brecht wrote that play, Paul Claudel adapted *The Satin Slipper* for Barrault's production, enlarging the comic role of his epic Announcer. The French Catholic and the German atheist were attracted to the same epic theater device, to different ends. Claudel is Calderón's successor in creating a theater of *theatrum mundi* for our instruction, whereas Brecht invites our judgment through his dramatic instruction. For such judgment, Brecht dramatizes the chalk circle trial (familiar in both Hebraic and Chinese culture), about which he had already written a short story set in his native Augsburg. Even in this first version, Brecht turns traditional material topsy-turvy, for both King Solomon and the Chinese Judge award the child to the real, biological mother. In Brecht's story and play, on the other hand, the child is given to the woman who best fulfills the role of the mother. In *The Caucasian Chalk Circle,* as opposed to Brecht's earlier story, that role and its hazards are dramatized by the old-fashioned device of the play within a play.

Brecht began *The Caucasian Chalk Circle* when he was a refugee in California, while Russia was suffering heavy losses in World War II, though German defeat at last seemed possible. The outer frame play of *The Caucasian Chalk Circle,* set in Soviet Russia, contains a sense of wonder at having survived the war at all, and for this reason, perhaps, the dramatic conflict is genial, untinged by bitterness or hatred. After the Nazis were expelled from a Caucasian valley, fruit-growers took possession of it. In the new time of peace, there is a dispute as to whether the valley should revert to its old owners, the goatherds, or should be given to its developers, the fruit-planters. After the decision is made for the fruit-planters, everyone retires to be fed and entertained. As Eric Bentley emphasizes, *"The Caucasian Chalk Circle* is not an *enquiry* into the dispute over ownership presented in the Prologue but a *celebration* of the assignment of the land to 'those who are good for it.' "[7] The celebration takes the form of a play within the play, or, rather, plays within the play, for, as the Story-teller explains, "It's really two stories" (Eric Bentley translation).

Both stories are set in the very valley that is being disputed in the frame play, and this provides some unity between the two parts, as do the wagon of Mother Courage and the shop of Shen Te in other Brecht plays. The Story-teller's name, Arkadi, indicates the Arcadian quality of the inner action, which differs markedly from that in Brecht's earlier short story on the same subject. Both of the two plays within the play cover the same semi-historical ground, with the Story-teller manipulating time and place. For all the obvious artifice of plays within the play, narrated by a Story-teller, the central character of each of the plays looms large, human, and humorous—Grusha, who mothers the abandoned child, and Azdak of Robin Hood heart, Sancho Panza or Schweik head, and contemporary emotional complexity. Each of the plays within the play is a protagonist-centered drama, and although they provide us with different views on the civil war, both views take the side of the underdog, who has nothing to gain and everything to lose when princes fight. And yet both the protagonists, after their respective hair-breadth adventures, lose nothing and gain a good deal, in this mellow play of a never-never Golden Age. In the Epilogue that links the two plays, the Story-teller emphasizes the fairy tale aspect, reciting on a stage full of dancing couples:

> And after that evening Azdak disappeared and was not seen again.
> The people of Grusinia did not forget him but long remembered
> The period of his judging as *a brief golden age*
> *Almost an age of justice*
> [my italics]

Despite the ravages of war, despite the cruelty of the aristocrats (unfeeling behind their stage masks), despite the selfishness of those with a little property, a Utopian quality pervades Brecht's adaptation of the chalk circle story. Since the story is familiar, there is no suspense as to the final reunion of Grusha and the child; instead, we respond sympathetically to the perils of Grusha the loving and of Azdak the cunning, who demonstrate, respectively, folk goodness and folk wisdom.

To this old story, Brecht gives a new vigor through diversity of his language. In the play's dialogue Brecht shifts from the disciplined dryness of the Soviet officials, to the salty cynicism of the peasants (feudal or Soviet), to the staccato telegraphese of the Grand Duke, to the Rabelaisian lyricism of Azdak. Like the Story-teller, both Grusha and Azdak break into verse at moments of intense excitement. Like Azdak, Simon Sachava knows his folk sayings, and the final Chalk Circle judgment is both predicted and delayed when the two men address each other in a sticho-mythic exchange of proverbs.

Brecht's linguistic variety functions thematically as well as dramatically, for beneath the explicit theme of use establishing ownership is an implicit suggestion of the grace of art. When the play within the play is first suggested in the opening scene, the Soviet Official and the Girl Tractorist are impatient of such a waste of time. Earlier, the Old Goatherd knew that he had lost the valley when the young Agronomist brought out projects for planting orchards. The frame play depicts and gently mocks an efficiency-oriented society that "can't resist machines and projects." But the two inner plays, empty of machines and projects, dramatize familiar legends, and find them still of emotional relevance. Thus, Brecht subverts the traditional use of a play within the play, just as he subverts the traditional use of a chalk circle trial. The outer action is dry and undramatic, but we respond to and sympathize with the protagonists of the inner plays, Grusha and Azdak. The roles of folk heroes are emotionally realized, whereas the contemporary realistic characters emerge as mere roles.

Brecht's plays are almost always more complex than his theories, and *Verfremdungseffekt* is a less than adequate summary of his dramaturgical skill and his emotional power. Though Brecht used Aristotle as a whipping-boy, Aristotle himself said nothing about empathy or estrangement, and it is only later theoreticians, mainly German, who closely linked Aristotelian catharsis to empathy (*Einfühlung*). Brecht reacted against an esthetics of empathy, as his recommendations for actors reacted against the histrionic style of German acting. The theory of estrangement arose from Brecht's own creative needs, but like all theories it can be disastrous if rigidly practiced—despite Marxist lip service to a union of theory and practice.

Rationally, every member of a theater audience knows that he is in the theater, and yet he shares certain emotions with certain characters. Probably the suspension of one's own reality to enter that of another is a highly personal experience for each member of an audience, perhaps for each time that person goes to the theater. Understanding the experience would demand psychological analysis of the individual and of the group, but the province of the drama critic must remain the drama. Brecht named devices for inducing Verfremdungseffekt—songs, slides, lights, narrator. The Caucasian Chalk Circle uses a narrator, and yet that device does not serve to preclude empathy for the protagonists. On the contrary, the Story-teller helps us feel with Grusha and Azdak, but our main response to simple Grusha and complex Azdak is evoked largely by their own stage words and actions—as audience response has been evoked since the Greeks. And it may be doubted whether any device can guarantee distance, or, conversely, whether an illusionist stage can guarantee empathy.

The device of the play within the play, however, necessarily calls attention to the actor as actor. Whereas Renaissance playwrights usually achieve empathy for characters of the frame play, who are rendered more convincing by the inserted artifice, Brecht resembles Pirandello in focusing on the inner plays. Like Brecht of The Caucasian Chalk Circle, Thornton Wilder favors the epic device of a story-teller, but Our Town and Skin of Our Teeth lack an external frame; the inner play is the whole play, epically distanced. Experimental as Wilder's plays may have appeared at the time of their first Broadway productions (1939 for Our Town and 1942 for Skin of Our Teeth), their self-consciously theatrical tricks reflect little light on the relationship of roles to reality. The Stage Manager of *Our Town* functions much like an omniscient author in a novel, but he does not suggest that his characters are actors, nor that there is any reason, despite the lack of props, to question the reality and solidity of the characters on stage, even those who are dead. On the contrary, the characters are more real than things, because they are present on stage whereas things are not. In *Skin of Our Teeth* omniscience seems to be somewhat diluted. However, several of the characters refer to their roles as roles. Sabina, the "other woman," uses her real name as an actress and delivers asides to the audience. Yet no one tells us that the actors on stage play recurrent roles in human history, as Wilder's characters muddle through history and legend. In both his plays, Wilder stresses the familiar rather than the strange, but he uses unfamiliar, unrealistic stage techniques to present us with the prototypical in *Our Town*, with the symbol-typical in *Skin of Our Teeth*.

The English dramatists John Osborne and Robert Bolt, writing in the late 1950's, seem to be more influenced by Brecht than by Wilder. Nevertheless, they recall some of Wilder's effects when they introduce narrators into *A Subject of Scandal and Concern* and *A Man for All Seasons*. The former play, written for television, dramatizes the trial of the atheist George Holyoake, who stated publicly that he did not believe in God. A Narrator introduces the scenes and cryptically interprets them. Osborne's Narrator seems to demand a verdict from his audience: "If it is meaning you are looking for, then you must start collecting for yourself. And what would you say is the moral then?" Actually, however, Osborne's Narrator seeks sympathy for his protagonist.

In *A Man for All Seasons*, Bolt creates a comic Narrator, the Common Man, who addresses the audience directly. Unlike Osborne's legalistic Narrator, the Common Man also demands sympathy for himself, but he does so at the expense of the hero. In his preface to the play, Bolt points out the dangers of mechanical use of what he calls alienation (and I have been designating as estrangement): "When we use alienation methods just for kicks, we in the theatre are sawing through the branch on which we are sitting." Whereupon Bolt proceeds to saw. His Common Man, who changes hats to change his roles, and who comments ironically on the action, undercuts our sympathy for the hero without giving us sufficient basis for judgment. Even through the Golden Age atmosphere of *The Caucasian Chalk Circle* Brecht leads us to condemn the ruling class in its unfeeling masks. But Bolt condemns neither Henry VIII (who appears only briefly in the play) nor corrupt intermediaries, nor the "System." Moreover, since the Common Man is absent from climactic scenes, his ironic comments function somewhat like comic relief from such scenes.

The Common Man is modeled on such dramatic characters as Azdak, Schweik, Sancho Panza, all of whom we laugh *with* more than *at*. But Bolt's Common Man becomes jailer and executioner of the hero, whose conduct Bolt finds flawless. Whereas Wilder's narrators furnish us with dramatic facts rather than food for thought, Bolt's Common Man furnishes us with laughs at the expense of moral conviction; his role is theatrically viable but dramatically incoherent.

Perhaps Brecht's influence is difficult to translate, for it achieves greater coherence among German language playwrights than among English.[8] In Zurich, both Brecht and Wilder were produced in the 1940's, and Max Frisch's third play, *The Chinese Wall*, reflects their staging techniques, but dramatizes his own obsession with caricature-roles imposed by society. Like *The Skin of Our Teeth*, *The Chinese Wall* contains several levels of time: today's world represented by the Contemporary, China at the time of the Great Wall, and a timeless world in which legendary figures mingle with those of history treated as legend. It is through this third realm that Frisch reflects on the meaning of roles, for masked figures represent Romeo and Juliet, Napoleon, Columbus, Pontius Pilate, Don Juan, Brutus, Philip of Spain,

Cleopatra, and Mary Stuart. But no sooner does the Contemporary present these figures than a fictional character, Olan, introduces herself: "I am the eternal mother who plays no part in the great history of the world" (James Rosenberg translation). And the Contemporary remarks in an aside to the audience, "Naturally, she says that now, because later, as we shall see, she will play a most decisive role." Into that aside, Frisch compresses an ironic reflection on the nature of roles—in history as in drama, we stereotype them too readily, even while disclaiming them.

The main plot of *The Chinese Wall* takes place in a fictionalized China which, like that of Brecht's *Good Woman of Szechwan*, reveals aspects of contemporary social conflict. But more explicitly than Brecht, Frisch relates this China to our own civilization, haunted by the atom-bomb. It is partly through his fantastic tales of modern science that the Contemporary attracts the Chinese Princess, who is bored by the warrior-suitor chosen for her by her father. For a while the Contemporary appears to be the poor man of the fairy tale, who wins out over the prince. But Frisch writes a fairy tale without a happy ending. In the rebellion against construction of the Chinese Wall, the Emperor's soldiers seize the mute son of Olan, mistaking him for the rebel ringleader. Since he is mute, he cannot protest, and the Emperor orders him tortured until he confesses his subversive activity. Powerless to interfere, our Contemporary loses the respect of the Princess. All his imaginative tales dissolve to cowardice; he remains silent while an innocent mute is tortured. When the court convenes, the Contemporary attempts to bear witness to the inevitability of social revolt, to the innocence of the mute, and to the calamity of war. But his courageous speech is applauded as mere poetry; he is decorated as an entertainer, for his most impassioned sincerity is viewed as his artistic role. When the broken body of the tortured mute is given to his mother, Olan, and the Contemporary urges her to identify him as her son, Olan perpetuates the lying legend, determined to play a decisive role as mother of a hero. Civil war results, and in the next scene, which reveals the stage as a stage, *"Brutus and his two companions* [a modern in tail coat and a modern in cutaway] *come in as if to view the ruins."* In the cynical indifference of these "noble citizens with hollow hearts," Brutus sees Octavius and Marc Antony. Stabbing them, he cries out, "As species, you will still survive!" The Contemporary announces that, though the play is over, the farce will be played again. At the beginning, the figures of legend and history enter in masks, acting caricature roles. In the final scene, the Contemporary tells the tattered Chinese Princess that he has achieved nothing by speaking out. The play ends, with everyone but the Chinese-contemporary couple in rigid masks, and the tattered Princess tells our Contemporary, "Now it is you who are mute." Ironically, he is mute because he is unheard, even though he has spoken out.

Designated as a farce, *The Chinese Wall* is set "in an era when the building of Chinese Walls has become . . . a farce." It is our time—the Atomic Age—that makes farce of Chinese Walls, European history, and stereotyped legends. And it is we who render them doubly farcical by our deafness, by treating Frisch like Cassandra. Though the eternal return of legend is one meaning of the drama, it is not—as with Anouilh or Dürrenmatt —the whole or most important meaning, for the Chinese-Contemporary couple do not represent mere historical repetition, and there is some suggestion that people need not be locked in roles for which they are cast by history or legend. In *The Chinese Wall*, most roles are repeated between the time of ancient China and our time; yet the underlying hope is that the audience may learn about a real and individual commitment, through but beyond the stage roles.

In other Frisch plays which focus on legendary figures—Don Juan or Count Oderland—there is no within-the-play awareness of the repercussions of legend. In *The Chinese Wall* a Don Juan who loves geometry says directly to the audience, "I come from the hell of literature." When Frisch devotes an entire play to Don Juan, he shows how literary legend becomes the hell of the lover of Seville. Frisch's Afterword to his play stresses the unchangeable character of literary legend, so that one cannot imagine a Don Juan who is old or a father. Though the real Don Juan may prefer the abstractions of mathematics to the sweetness of seduction, he is imprisoned by his legendary role.

Any serious use of legendary material necessitates an examination of roles, but only certain playwrights are disturbed by a cleavage between such roles and reality. Frisch does not share Pirandello's obsession with this theme, but he does imply that the rigidity of roles—legendary or social—betrays individual honesty and commitment. Frisch's Don Juan rebels in vain against his role; Frisch's Biedermann pays lip service to anti-arson, but proves to be an accomplice of the firebugs. Similarly, the Andorrans of Frisch's *Andorra* pay lip service to anti-anti-semitism while they actually support the anti-semitic invaders of their country. Acceptance of a cliché role for a Jew leads directly to his torture and execution. Andri, illegitimate son of the Andorran schoolmaster, is "adopted" by him and said to be a Jewish child saved from the anti-semitism of a neighboring country. Though the Andorrans declare all men equal, they force Andri into a Procrustean caricature—money-grasping, country-spurning, incapable of craftsmanship. His schoolteacher father eventually confesses the truth to Andri, but the youth chooses death at the hands of the anti-semitic invaders, having identified himself with his role as Jew.

In Frisch's *Biography: A Play* his Brechtian gambit for obtaining our social judgment gives way to a Pirandellian surface, where appearances are manipulated. In his Afterword to the published play, Frisch warns us against interpreting *Biography* as a conflict of illusion vs. reality; "instead, the theater lights indicate that a variant will now be tried, a variant of reality, which never appears on the stage." And yet his play is composed of such variants of reality—"on the stage," for life, once lived, permits no variants.

The published version of *Biography* is preceded by a quotation from Chekhov's *Three Sisters*, spoken by Battalion Commander Virshinin: "You know, I often wonder what it would be like if we could begin our lives over again—deliberately, I mean, consciously...as if the life we'd already lived were just a kind of rough draft, and we could begin all over again with the final copy. If that happened, I think the thing we'd all want most would be not to repeat ourselves. We'd try at least to create a new environment, say a house like this one, for instance, with flowers and lots of light....I have a wife, as you know, and two little girls; and my wife's not very well, and...Well, if I could begin my life all over again, I wouldn't marry... No, No!" (Robert Corrigan translation). The fleeting wish of a Chekhov character is the basis of Frisch's plot in *Biography*.

As the two-part play opens, Hannes Kürmann, a forty-eight-year-old intellectual, wishes to "begin [his] life over again—deliberately, I mean, consciously...as if the life [he'd] already lived were just a kind of rough draft." He too "wouldn't marry," and he therefore wishes to relive the scene in which he met his wife, so that he might choose not to marry her.

A Recorder, stemming from the Narrator tradition in Epic drama, clarifies the rules of the "play" for Kürmann, and occasionally reminds him of the "rough draft" of the biography, as lived. Kürmann orders three replays of the scene in which he meets his wife—at a party in his own apartment—but in spite of his efforts, each version ends when she spends the night with him. Still seeking to escape his marriage, Kürmann orders a biography that begins years before he met his wife; in overlapping scenes, we witness his blinding a schoolfellow with a snowball, his military service, his cowardly use of his dying mother as a pretext to leave his mulatto mistress in California, his accidental rescue of a Jewish refugee family, his first marriage, and the suicide of his first wife. Accepting these events of his past, Kürmann changes the "rough draft" of his biography by becoming a Communist. In spite of this, he is nominated to a university chair, and he gives a party to celebrate his professorship—the party where he meets his wife, who spends the night in his apartment.

The second part of the play opens on the morning after. In spite of Kürmann's desire for a new biography, he spends the day in the country with his future wife, and he misses the election of a new University Rector. Though he tries, he does not change his adherence to Communism, for which he is fired from the university. When, after two years of marriage, his wife returns from a night out, Kürmann does not bellow and box her ears as in the rough draft of the biography, but he shows his jealousy nonetheless. The Recorder points out that, although he has desired another biography, Kürmann's re-plays have changed only his Communist party membership and the blow to his wife. At this accusation, Kürmann takes a revolver and kills his wife. In prison, however, condemned for life, Kürmann can think only of the unlived life of his wife, so that the murder is expunged, and the scene dissolves to another party at his apartment. Suddenly, that scene shifts to a hospital, where Kürmann has just been operated on—for abdominal cancer. Various characters appear from his past, but Kürmann is too ill to recognize them, and his son (by his first marriage) sends him flowers from America, as he had once sent flowers to his dying mother. His wife visits him faithfully, and as Kürmann sinks into unconsciousness, the Recorder asks her whether she would have changed anything in *her* biography. She replies, "Yes," and the meeting scene is again replayed—for the fifth time. In this variant, however, she leaves Kürmann's apartment after a drink and a cigarette, and the Recorder announces to the unbelieving Kürmann, "You are free—after seven years." But his freedom has come through his wife's decision, of which he was incapable, no matter how many opportunities he had to re-play his biography.

Lengthy as this summary has been, it does not begin to exhaust the re-plays of the man-woman relationship against a background of world events, other people, and humorous nuances. In one of his efforts to avoid their first night together, Kürmann tries to convince his wife-to-be that he is a homosexual awaiting his Sicilian lover "a great-grandson of Pirandello." *Biography* recalls the reluctance of that Sicilian dramatist to commit the fluidity of reality into the rigidity of art. But Frisch's Pirandellian surface suggests that such fluidity, dependent on free choice, is only apparent; that we are imprisoned in our personality, our biography, our role. And yet, Mrs. Kürmann breaks out of that prison with the single word, "Yes."

Superficially similar to Arthur Miller's *After the Fall*, Max Frisch's *Biography* is not a confessional but an ironic re-view. Lacking the art-life dichotomy of Pirandello's Theater Trilogy, *Biography* itself contains the possibility of fluidity, as in life. But the body of Frisch's play seems to support the Aristotelian statement of the rigid Communist in that play: "Ab posse ad esse valet, ab esse ad posse non valet." (From potential to being is possible, from being to potential is not possible.)

More extravagantly than his countryman, Dürrenmatt invents preposterous plots that are obviously play, dependent upon techniques of detective story and farce. Perhaps the most farcical of his plays is also his most serious exploration of the meaning of roles—*The Marriage of Mr. Mississippi*, which focuses less than *Biography* on how marriage fixes roles. The play opens with an execution, whose gravity is immediately undercut when the victim does not crumple to the ground. Instead, Frédéric René St. Claude steps forward to tell the audience that his death does not occur until the end of the play. For the present, the audience can sit back and relax. Three men—their busts descend to the stage —"proceeding by different methods . . . had taken into their heads to change and save the world." (My literal translation differs slightly from that of Gerhard Nellhaus.) Their methods determine their dramatic roles—the intransigent *lex-talionis* justice of Florestan Mississippi, the equally intransigent Marxism of Frédéric René St. Claude, and the all too transigent Christian humanism of Count Bodo von Uberlohe-Zabernsee. Once Dürrenmatt establishes distance through the mock death and ornate names, he permits the complicated plot to unravel. Only in a long monologue by Bodo is there any reference to the play as a play, to himself as a character, and to the playwright as creator: "At this critical point in the action into which a crafty author has drawn you, ladies and gentlemen, as an audience, and us on stage, we must ask ourselves *how* the author became involved in all this. Did he allow himself to be carried along from one free association to another without any preconceived lines, or was he guided by some secret plan?" This direct address to the audience further estranges the caricatured characters from our sympathy. In the preposterous final scene, Mississippi, St. Claude, and the *femme fatale* Anastasia busily poison one another's coffee. Mississippi and Anastasia die of the poisoning, and when three thugs enter to execute St. Claude, we arrive full circle at the opening scene of the play. But again the dead return to life, laboring the obvious and the hilarious: "again and again we return as we have always returned." Thus, Dürrenmatt ridicules historic roles by stereotyping them and estranging them, in order to insist on their cyclical repetition.

In a little-known radio play, *The Double*, Dürrenmatt makes his most direct attempt to probe beneath roles. His radio play is about the making of a radio play whose basic fiction is that a man is told by his double that he will kill that double and be judged for it. After constant interruptions from the director, and revisions by the writer, the murder does occur in the play within the play, through a lovers' triangle. The man fulfills the prediction and is compelled to be his own judge. Somewhat slender for this combination of Conrad, Kafka, and Pirandello, the play nevertheless indicates Dürrenmatt's concern with play-making as a way of understanding the interaction of the role and the real.

Peter Weiss makes the most spectacular use of this play-making technique in his *Marat/Sade*. The long, unwieldy title announces the play within the play: *The Persecution and Assassination of Marat, as Performed by the Inmates of the Asylum of Charenton under the Direction of the Marquis de Sade.* "Performed" is the key-word; this is a *performance* of an imitation, a play within a play. Play itself provides a first degree of illusion, play within the play a second degree, but when the actors are madmen, illusions multiply. Weiss anchors this prism of illusion in a non-historical confrontation of historical characters: the real Marquis de Sade delivered a still extant funeral oration after the real Marat was assassinated by Charlotte Corday in 1793. Under Napoleon, Sade was imprisoned in an asylum at Charenton, perhaps for political reasons, perhaps for sexual deviation, perhaps for his books. There he wrote and produced plays, though not on the assassination of Marat. However, this blend of the historical and imaginary is one of Weiss' themes as well as his method.

The opening lines of Weiss' play introduce the play within the play, and set the ambiguous tone of the whole. M. Coulmier, Director of the Asylum, speaks of the cathartic powers of the theater, but he speaks of them in phrases that recall today's Sunday supplements; through the short rhyming lines, Weiss mocks his sanctimonious Director. Both Coulmier's introduction and that of the Herald might suggest that Weiss is making traditional use of the play within the play—to emphasize the reality of the outer action by the artifice of the inner action. Gradually, however, we see that Weiss is terribly concerned with the reality of the inner action, that the two realities become inseparable, and that both are relevant to the reality in which we live.

The basic situation of Weiss' drama presents the former Marquis de Sade as playwright-director of a play about Marat's assassination, whose presentation as therapy is permitted by M. Coulmier. As continual background of the play within the play, we witness the quivering, spastic, violent movements of the insane, which make an implicit comment upon the violent undercurrents of our own "sane" world. The play within the play contains almost all the dialogue of Weiss' play; it moves from rhyming verse to free verse, from individual arias to crowd scenes, from heroic gesture to slapstick. Inspired by the German Moritat (*mord-tat*—murder) tradition, it focuses on violence, related by satiric and didactic bench singers. The play within the play seems to be performed from a script, for the Herald is a prompter, but there seem also to be departures from the script—perhaps when Sade enters into his own play to expostulate with Marat, probably when the maladies of the actors intrude upon their roles, and certainly when M. Coulmier interrupts the performance over a dozen times.

The sustained conflict of Weiss' play lies in a dialogue between individualist and collectivist, between Sade, who defends individual freedom and passion, and Marat, who defends social commitment and action. Yet rationalist Marat speaks passionately whereas Sade's lines are delivered coolly. It is not clear when Sade's defense is part of his own script, and when, if ever, he interrupts his own play. Sade has himself whipped by the somnambulist who plays Charlotte Corday; describing the cruelties of the French Revolution, he confesses to his disillusion—Corday whipping harder as he more strongly denounces the violence of the Revolution. Marat, in contrast, declares, "I am the Revolution," as Louis XIV declared "I am the state." Marat, the rational collectivist, suffers from a psychosomatic skin disease; he is haunted by memories of his persecutors, whom we see in all their sadism. In only a few scenes do Marat and Sade speak to each other, and yet we hear their lines as a dialogue on familiar positions, but that very familiarity is estranged since the speakers may be madmen.

The Marat-Sade dialogue embodies the main conflict, but a wider conflict exists between the revolutionary action of the play within the play and the "victory in peace" of the frame and, by extension, of our own frame of reference: do revolutions belong to an old barbarous age or to ours? Are mental illnesses anachronistic, or do they intrude on contemporary roles, as those of the Charenton patients intrude upon their roles in the play within the play?

Sade is always himself, having no ostensible role in the play he wrote. Marat, a paranoiac played by a paranoiac, has no identity outside of his role, and yet he occasionally needs prompting in the play within the play, and he speaks after his assassination. Roux, a political rebel played by a political rebel, needs no prompting, and has to be muzzled by the Establishment of the frame play. Unhistorical lovers, Duperret and Charlotte Corday are played by an erotomaniac and a somnambulist, and their illnesses intrude upon their fictional roles. When Duperret meets Corday—"nobility meets grace"—idealism is undercut by the stumbling somnambulism of the one and the compulsive eroticism of the other. Moreover, Duperret, embracing Charlotte Corday, forgets his lines and confuses the various nations involved in the war against France. Thus the might of nations is undercut both by his confusion of countries and by his obsessive eroticism.

We know the patients only by their roles and their illnesses. Farce enters the outer frame, since the nursing sisters are played by athletic men, who sometimes try to subdue violent patients by singing litanies. M. Coulmier is given to Napoleonic attitudes, and the Herald is dressed as a jester. Thus, roles dominate both levels of Weiss' drama.

The drama is structured on the tension between the play within the play and the frame. Coulmier's interruptions are the most obvious signs of such tension, for the Marat story is entirely too relevant to the Napoleonic era, whose enlightenment is belied by Coulmier's repeated references to what has been censored in Sade's script (which is nevertheless spoken on stage). Though Coulmier's wife and daughter do not speak, they simper socially at the real theater audience, utterly oblivious of the passionate action of the play within the play. Sade alone moves from frame play to inner play. He laughs at the heroic tirades he has presumably written, he addresses his own characters, and he seems to triumph over his Marat under the uneasy eyes of Coulmier. And yet, Sade does not have the last word, if the production depicts Marat with sympathy.

Weiss' fiction makes Sade need to write a play about the *persecution* and *assassination* of Marat. This implies that Marat is a hero as well as a victim—perhaps a victim because of heroism, even though Sade declares, "I left heroics to the heroes" (Geoffrey Skelton translation). During the play there are suggestions of a Marat-Christ: a *crown* of non-laurel, the *thirty-three* scenes of Weiss' play, and above all the Herald's ironic: "Marat's heading straight for Calvary/ and crucifixion all good Christians know/ is the most sympathetic way to go." In Scene 26 there is a second-level play within a play, when Marat views the cruel figures of his own past—mother, father, teacher, Voltaire, Lavoisier—all scornful of him. Only the ex-priest Roux speaks in defense of Marat's social commitment, so that Coulmier springs up outraged, and Roux is silenced by asylum attendants, while the Herald assures us that this is only a play, and it is time for the intermission after the long first act. In the second act Marat's imaginary speech to the Chamber of Deputies reveals his dedication to the Revolution, and that speech is addressed directly to us, but the characters on stage mock Marat until Sade signals them to freeze into a tableau.

The somnambulist-actress knows from the beginning that her role is to be climaxed by the murder of Marat. Sade's opening line restrains her: "Not yet, Corday/ You have to come to his door three times." When Corday is awakened for her third visit, "*Herald knocks three times on the floor with his staff while Corday carries out the knocking movement with her hand.*" After elaborate preparation, Corday is poised to strike Marat in an ambiguous act of love-hate, but she is interrupted by the

Herald, who, following Sade's script, reports on fifteen years of war between Marat's death and the date of the Charenton performance. After this semi-documentary interlude, Marat's murder is performed in erotic pantomime, emphasizing the artifice of the climactic event of the play. *"Patients let out one single scream,"* and *"Marat hangs as in David's classical picture."* Even in death, especially in death, Marat assumes his role; one art imitates another in order to reflect upon several aspects of reality.

The murder closes the play within the play, and Coulmier congratulates Sade, but Roux agitates the asylum inmate-extras to renewed rebellion. The patients engage in a dance-march, chanting:

> Charenton Charenton
> Napoleon Napoleon
> Nation Nation
> Revolution Revolution
> Copulation Copulation

In one German version, these were the closing lines of the play— only seeming nonsense, for the rhymes contain a tension stemming from the middle line: the nation can embrace the repressions of the first two lines, or the freedoms of the last two. In the English translation of the play (to which Weiss consented), Roux continues to urge the patients to violence, and Coulmier thereupon "incites the nurses to extreme violence." As civil war rages on stage, Sade laughs triumphantly.

Various actors have affirmed that the chaos on stage has been frightening to them. Ian Richardson, who played Marat in Peter Brook's production of the play, claimed: "We have had actual physical violence of a very serious sort breaking out."[9] Finally, however, order is always restored. The actors freeze into immobility, and the real audience begins its applause. In Peter Brook's production, the actors on stage faced the audience and applauded them, becoming an audience for the audience, and provoking questions. Who is the actor, and who the spectator? How can we know the role from the real?

Marat/Sade appears as a culmination of Germanic reflection on roles, incorporating as it does the romantic irony of Tieck, the role-stressing of Brecht, the cliché-prisons of Frisch, and the scenic inventiveness of Dürrenmatt. Influenced also by Artaud's vision of Total Theater and by a partial commitment to roles as catharsis, Weiss assaults us through the frank artifices of his theater, where characters reveal their roles as roles, but scream with anguish at their reality.

Though French and German drama today exercise reciprocal influences, the response to role-playing has been dissimilar. Writing in German-occupied France, Sartre and Camus are comparable to Brecht in exile, and yet neither French playwright focuses on the theatricality of roles. Concerned rather with social roles, they dramatize this concern in illusionist plays which center on deeds.

Camus' Emperor Caligula has often been compared to Pirandello's Emperor Henry IV in his self-conscious theatricalism, each haunted by his own mirror-image. But Henry, who has no "real" name in Pirandello's play, plays his role in a restricted world, whereas Caligula tries to change the world by playing his role. As Lord of Misrule, Caligula refers self-consciously to his role, but unlike Henry IV, he is a real emperor (within the fiction of the play) who stages a spectacle for a wide audience, explicitly claiming that he is indulging in "dramatic art." Not only impresario, but actor, Caligula plays Venus in a mock ritual. In his private conversation with the *raisonneur* Cherea, who understands him and therefore conspires against him, Caligula inveighs against the "play of sincerity" in which both are indulging. The phrase is apt, for Caligula plays at sincerity, and is in deadly earnest about his role. Yet Caligula is trapped by Diderot's paradox, feeling his role too deeply to play it dispassionately.

Rather, it is Sartre who more exactly dramatizes Camus' view of the Actor as Absurdist hero. His Kean is a living illustration of Camus' description from *The Myth of Sisyphus*: "A mime of the ephemeral, the actor trains and perfects himself only in appearances" (Justin O'Brien translation). In adapting a Dumas play about the English actor, Sartre gives Kean a post-Pirandellian awareness of his commitment to appearance: "Act? Do I know when I am acting? Is there a moment when I stop acting?" In the throes of his jealousy in a romantic triangle, Sartre's Kean exclaims: "Three reflections: each of the three believing in the reality of the other two: that's the theater for you." Laughing at how Shakespeare would have littered the stage with corpses, Sartre's Kean plays his love scene as farce. Kean's real jealousy is expressed as Othello, but his real suffering is viewed as a role, and thus reduced to caricature. Sartre's Kean achieves ironic distance from his own reality through awareness of playing a role in his life.

And yet, as we look back at these roles through later plays, the boundaries seem clear between role and reality: we know quite soon that Henry IV is willfully playing his role, that Caligula has decided never to relinquish his role, and, despite Kean's awareness of acting, we are not confused about what he is feeling when he acts. For Beckett and Genet, on the other hand, boundaries are considerably more fluid. Haunted by the metaphor of the world-stage, man-actor, these two writers are no longer sure of the limits of the stage, even of the world-stage.

Beckett examines roles searchingly in his successive dramas. In his first completed play, *Eleutheria* (written about 1947 but never produced or published), a man of letters brings down the Act I curtain with the appropriate word, "*Rideau.*" Various characters refer to the play in which they play roles. A spectator jumps on stage to criticize and interfere with the action. A glazier behaves like a director during a rehearsal, and there is a Pirandellian allusion to an author named Beckett, pronounced

Bequet. But these are disparate reflections on play in an inchoate play.

In *Waiting for Godot* there are pointed references to the theater as theater: Estragon directs Vladimir to an unnamed lavatory: "End of the corridor, on the left," and Vladimir requests, "Keep my seat." When Estragon seeks to escape backstage, Vladimir cries out, "Imbecile! There's no way out there." Blind Pozzo of Act II asks if they are on the Board, thus distantly recalling a definition of theater as three actors, two boards, and a passion.

The four characters of *Godot* are both actors and audience. As audience, their lines reflect upon the role of the real theater audience. Vladimir complains, "I begin to weary of this motif," and a little later, "This is becoming really insignificant." To Pozzo's question, "You find it tedious?" Vladimir replies, "I've been better entertained." Above all, the following duet emphasizes the reality of theater and the untheatricality of reality:

VLADIMIR: Charming evening we're having.
ESTRAGON: Unforgettable.
VLADIMIR: And it's not over.
ESTRAGON: Apparently not.
VLADIMIR: It's only beginning.
ESTRAGON: It's awful.
VLADIMIR: Worse than the pantomime.
ESTRAGON: The circus.
VLADIMIR: The music-hall.
ESTRAGON: The circus.

All four characters are performing artists; even the long day "is very near the end of its repertory." As actors, Pozzo and Lucky do solo numbers, whereas Estragon and Vladimir engage in duets. In spite of his burdens, Lucky's job is not to carry but to play the buffoon; he is a spectacle for Estragon and Vladimir; he dances and thinks at Pozzo's command, so that thought itself becomes a kind of vaudeville number. Pozzo, a reluctant audience for

Lucky, is himself anxious for acclaim; he sprays his throat before speaking: "Is everybody looking at me?...Is everybody listening? ...I don't like talking in a vacuum." After his discourse on twilight, he asks Vladimir and Estragon, "How did you find me? Good? Fair? Middling? Poor? Positively bad?" And he confesses, "I have such need of encouragement."

Vladimir and Estragon play at exercises, questions, contradictions, insults; they play at being Pozzo and Lucky. Perhaps because he has been a poet, Estragon wants to tell Vladimir his dreams. Although Vladimir refuses to listen to them, he insists upon narrating the story of the two thieves according to St. Luke. He "*minces like a mannequin*" while wearing Lucky's hat. After blind Pozzo's outburst, Vladimir echoes and expands upon his phrases that summarize one metaphysical theme of the "tragicomedy": "Astride of a grave and a difficult birth. Down in the hole, lingeringly, the grave-digger puts on the forceps." Then, looking at the sleeping Estragon, Vladimir gives voice to an awareness of his dual role as actor and spectator: "At me too someone is looking, of me too someone is saying, He is sleeping, he knows nothing, let him sleep on."

Endgame contains more sustained comment on the play as play. Named in terms of chess, called a "play" in Beckett's English translation, *Endgame* thrives on gamesmanship. In a note to his own (Berlin, 1967) production, Beckett wrote: "*Endgame* is only play. Nothing less." The play's dialogue refers to comedy and farce. When Hamm declares that Clov will never leave him, Clov asks, "What is there to keep me here?" Hamm retorts, "The dialogue." Hamm informs Clov that he is uttering an "aside," then that he is "warming up for [his] last soliloquy." When Clov sights a small boy, Hamm hopes that it is "not an underplot." In leaving Hamm, Clov explains, "This is what we call making an exit."

As in *Godot*, the actors are conscious of acting. Early in the play, Hamm despairs, "The thing is impossible." He encourages himself periodically with "We're getting on." He admits, "This is slow work," and "This is not much fun." After Hamm's comment, "This is deadly," Clov enters to announce contradictorily, "Things are livening up." At the end of the endgame, Hamm throws his whistle toward the audience, commenting like an appreciative spectator, "With my compliments." Finally, Hamm sighs, "Since that's the way we're playing it, let's play it that way, and speak no more about it, speak no more."

Less flamboyant actors than the characters of *Godot*, at least two members of *Endgame* are performers. Nagg is a raconteur who remembers nostalgically that Nell used to laugh at his jokes. Hamm is the ham-actor implied by his name: he clears his throat before speaking; blind, he meticulously wipes his glasses; paralyzed from the waist down, he is lavish of gesture. Like Vladimir in *Godot*, he envisions the spectator who may be watching his performance: "Imagine if a rational being came back to earth, wouldn't he be liable to get ideas into his head if he observed us long enough. (*Voice of rational being.*) Ah, good, now I see what it is, yes, now I understand what they're at!"

The "someone" of *Godot* has become the "rational being" of *Endgame*; resonances of divinity have fallen to earth. And on his earth, Hamm is not only an actor, but seems to be the director. However, rather than creation, he has been engaged in destruction of the world outside his shelter: "Outside of here it's death." The shelter has replaced the world. Hamm orders Clov to push his wheel-chair along the walls of the shelter, "Right round the world!"

In translating *Fin de Partie* to *Endgame*, Beckett underlines Hamm's role as director-creator. When Nagg sinks down into his own ash-bin, their son Hamm summarizes the situation, "Finie la rigolade." The English "Our revels now are ended" recalls the similarities between *The Tempest* and *Endgame*. In both plays, the central role is played by the director of the action of the play. Prospero is a deposed duke; Hamm refers to his kingdom, sits on a wheel-chair-throne, and wears a toque-crown. Both Prospero and Hamm direct a play within the play, since Prospero's "Our revels now are ended" refers to a masque.[10]

Hamm's "revels" refer to the major action of *Endgame*; outside the shelter "the insubstantial pageant" has already left "not a rack behind." But in the shelter, Hamm composes his chronicle as Prospero directed his masque. Ironically, Hamm sets his chronicle on Christmas Eve, that time of birth rather than death, of peace and good will, rather than destruction and hatred. Hamm is lord of a lifeless world and sole custodian of its dwindling supplies, and Hamm's narrator-protagonist rules a similar domain. The father of a starving child crawls before him, begging for food. With charity toward none, but crookedly reflecting a divine charity toward a people in exile, Hamm's "I" screams at the groveling father, "But what in God's name do you imagine?... That there's manna in heaven still for imbeciles like you?"

Toward the end of *Endgame*, when Clov says that he sees a little boy through the window, Hamm dismisses Clov, "I don't need you any more." Hamm the performer recites a line of Baudelaire; Hamm the author reviews the situation of the father in his story. In the final tableau, blind Hamm thinks he has been abandoned by Clov, but Clov is still on stage, dressed for all weathers. Will Clov leave the shelter to fetch the little boy who may replace him as Hamm's servant, while Clov goes out to die in a desolate world? Or will Clov, leaving Hamm to die untended, fetch the little boy to play for him the roles of dog, menial, creature, and son? Is there a little boy at all? Was there ever?

In Beckett's work, there is no way of distinguishing "fact" from fiction, from play. The attitude of the begging father is shared by the toy dog that Clov makes for Hamm. The implication of Hamm and Clov that the end of the world has come is echoed in Hamm's reminiscence of "a madman who thought the end of the world had come." Perhaps Hamm invented the madman; perhaps he describes himself. Perhaps Clov invented the small boy in the window, even as Clov may have been the small boy in Hamm's invented chronicle. All may be play, and all is role.

Although no other Beckett play offers so thorough a reflection on the real in the role, different character-creators appear in his dramas, and their creations blur the line between the role and the real. In the radio play *Embers* the protagonist Henry invents stories and sounds to drown out the sea *"audible through-out."* Of his "stories, there was a great one about an old fellow called Bolton, I never finished it." Describing Bolton as "an old man in great trouble," Henry summons "Holloway with his little black bag." But Henry's stories dissolve into tears, drops of the ubiquitous sea.[11]

As the radio play *Embers* draws no distinction between real and imagined voices, so the monodrama *Krapp's Last Tape* draws no distinction between Krapp's works and his memories. An author by his own account, he confines his stage creation to tape-recording, but he spends more stage time in listening to old tapes than in recording his "last tape." Krapp is an active audience for his own tape, reacting explosively to the role that he played in the past; in past tapes, Krapp was already an active audience, reacting to old roles. And we may imagine another Krapp who will react as we do to the tape-role that Krapp records on stage. Instead of the Pirandellian conflict between the flux of experience and the rigidity of art, Beckett suggests a series of Chinese boxes in which experience is inseparable from, unknowable from, art. Like Pirandello's humorist, Beckett shows us a fragmented man, but that man keeps trying to know his reality through his changing roles.

In *Happy Days* Winnie clings fiercely to the reality of her role. Memories and stories float up or down to Winnie, buried in a parched earth, in Act I up to her waist, in Act II up to her neck. Like Hamm in the center of his shelter, Winnie is *"in exact centre of mound,*" from which she engages in and directs the minimal action—the few words and movements of her husband, Willie, and the examination of the objects of her bag. Absorbed in herself, Winnie does not refer to the play as play, but Winnie is acutely aware—more so than any other Beckett character—of her dual role as actor and spectator, and this awareness causes her to doubt her own reality.

As performer, Winnie of Act I prays and sings, and although she abandons prayer by Act II, she closes the play with a song (the Merry Widow waltz). In order to pass the interminable wait for the bell that will end her happy day, Winnie recites fragments of English poetry. She busies herself with the details of her appearance as if she were about to make an entrance before an audience—brushing her teeth, filing her nails, combing her hair, fixing her hat, applying lipstick. Her husband, Willie, is the audience that protects her from the solitude she calls her "wilderness." But beyond Willie, she senses eyes upon her—like Vladimir, like Hamm: "Strange feeling that someone is looking at me." Shortly afterwards she attaches a name to "someone." Perhaps he is called Shower, the one who shows, in the "expanse of scorched grass," perhaps Cooker in the "blaze of hellish light." Mr. Shower or Cooker, an exhibitionistic or sadistic spectator, asks his lady companion crisp questions about Winnie's condition, in the scene perhaps invented by Winnie. Like Hamm's "rational being," he wants to know what Winnie means: "What's the idea? he says—stuck up to her diddies in the bleeding ground—coarse fellow—What does it mean? he says—What's it meant to mean?" And we echo the questions of Hamm's rational being, of fictional Mr. Shower or Cooker, perhaps further roles of Hamm and Winnie.

In Act II, seemingly deserted by Willie, reduced to moving her facial muscles and vocal chords, Winnie creates again: "There is my story of course, when all else fails." A girl named Mildred soon becomes Milly, rhyming with Willie; her Dolly (a slant-rhyme with Willie) has a "white straw hat" like Willie's, and "china blue eyes" like his. Milly wears a "pearl necklet" as Winnie did in Act I. Milly, like Willie, crawls "backward on all fours." Abruptly, Winnie leaves Milly to wonder whether Willie has crawled head first into his hole, so that he is stuck there. She calls to him, but, receiving no answer, turns to "Mr. Shower—or Cooker...No longer young, not yet old." Although Winnie is now buried up to her neck, Mr. Shower or Cooker comments on her bosom, asks pointed questions about her legs. Suddenly, Mr. Shower or Cooker and his lady companion quarrel violently—"Drop dead!"—and Winnie watches them recede in her mind's eye: "Last human kind—to stray this way." Memory or fiction, Winnie has humanized the couple, trying to define her own reality through the roles she gave them.

When Willie fails to answer Winnie, she again resorts to Milly, whom she frightens with a mouse, so that Winnie screams with Milly's terror. After sketchy reminiscences, Winnie prepares to sing to end her happy day, but Willie crawls into view. It is ambiguous as to whether Willie wishes to kiss or kill Winnie, but mutually and explicitly, Winnie and Willie "*look at each other*," each of them actor and spectator, each testifying to the reality of the other—if only temporarily. For this, perhaps, is what they are meant to mean. Man the actor no longer believes in the reality of his play; only a spectator-shower can force the show to dodder on.

In *Play* the experience that was life is belittled as "just play," but that experience seems to be all there is. Three lives are reduced to a cliché lovers' triangle, and eternity to toneless recollection of that triangularity. The drama is built on the fiction that each of the actors is provoked into speech by the spotlight. Though this technique suggests the traditional metaphor of God as light, the theater light is manipulated by a human technician, and in the play the light triggers repetitive dialogue. The play is *da capo* in structure, but the actors do not know this; awareness is reserved for the real theater audience. Similarly, the real theater audience is alone in hearing stage dialogue as communication or mere sound: the three characters speak in separate monologues which are heard as a dialogue.

Structurally, *Play* is very obviously in two parts, since Beckett specifies that the play is to be played through twice. The single playing of the play also falls into two parts, each introduced by the collective (and therefore incomprehensible) voices of the three members of the triangle. The first movement of *Play* consists entirely of recollection of roles in real life, whereas the second movement, played in half-light and at half-volume, takes stock of the stage present. Through both these movements—recollection and reaction—the faces remain impassive, the voices toneless. Despite non sequitur, contradiction, and incomprehensibility, the first part yields a clear picture of the triangle. In the second part, each member of the triangle guesses at what the other two are doing on earth, while each sinks more deeply into his own solitude. Each of the two women insists upon her "I." The man occasionally uses the plural "we" and has a fantasy of the three of them together in a dinghy, and it is he who speaks the final words: "We were not long together—" which comment both upon the brief play in the theater and upon the earthly triangle in which all communication took place. On the purgatorial stage, the three people are reduced to the funereal suggestions of their urns. And to the repetitions of their play, in which they review their roles for all eternity.[12]

Beckett's screen-play *Film* also reflects on play: "All extraneous perception suppressed, animal, human, divine, self-perception maintains in being." The film is a movement from extraneous perception—animal (large cat, small dog, parrot, goldfish), human (elderly couple, old flower-woman), and pictures of human and divine—to E perceiving O, the divided self. In the post-Pirandellian world of ambiguous relationship between person and role, Beckett twists Descartes' "I think, therefore I am" to "I play, but am I?"

Genet's characters refuse this question, assuming a role that asserts, "I am what I play." In contrast to Existentialist heroes who define themselves by deeds, Genet's protagonists choose a role, and then commit the deeds for the role. Through Genet's successive plays, his protagonists are increasingly successful in an assumption of reality through their roles. In *Deathwatch*, Genet's first play, Lefranc attempts to play the role of Green Eyes, but even through murder he fails to realize this goal. In *The Maids* Claire symbolically murders her mistress in her own suicide; through death, she becomes her mistress, and through death she casts her sister as criminal-saint.

In a statement on the purpose of his plays, Genet claims that he has been trying "to crystallize a theatrical, a dramatic emotion." And further, in his 1958 postscript to *The Maids*: "[I hoped] that these characters on the stage would be no more than the metaphor of what they had to portray." In *The Balcony* the Court Envoy enunciates clearly: "Our function will be to support, establish, and justify metaphors" (Bernard Frechtman translation). It is in the nine scenes of *The Balcony* that we find Genet's most insistent dramatization of the relationship between metaphor-roles and social reality.[13]

The dominant metaphor of Genet's *Balcony* is the balcony itself—the raised area of illusion in Madame Irma's brothel. Clients and staff cooperate in the creation of illusion; clients and staff are both actors and spectators, since mirrors figure in seven of the nine scenes. Spectators of balcony pleasures, the real theater audience is cast as a chorus of voyeurs. Herbert Blau has described the intricacy of illusions in his production of *The Balcony*: "So complex is the maze of voyeurs that the spectators become aware of themselves watching too; and if—as in our production—mirrors are actually used on stage, even more wary that they will be able to see themselves watching the actors, who may be watching themselves acting and being watched. And so on."[14]

Role-playing is evident in the opening scene of *The Balcony*.

In *The Maids* we are at first taken in by Claire's role as mistress, but in *The Balcony* we are instantly aware of artifice: a whore in a lace dressing-gown coupled with an Archbishop too fond of the accoutrements of his office. Although we only gradually perceive the cothurni, false shoulder-pads, excessive makeup, and theatrical voices of those who play their roles in Madame Irma's Balcony, we are not deceived about the falsity of each role in that stage house of illusions. Far from confusion of appearance and reality, this is the most flagrant of appearances.

In the opening scene of *The Balcony* a Bishop wheedles a confession from a whore, who complains that sins are not easy to perform. In the second scene a Judge crawls on the floor and licks the feet of a whore, pleading that she confess crimes for which to be judged. In the third scene the most timorous of the three brothel clients has the bloodiest fantasy as General; ironically, his whore-horse is named Dove, the bird of peace. These three opening scenes of *The Balcony* parody Church, Judiciary, and Army ritual. These scenes are as formal as an Aristotelian action, with beginning, middle, and end, reverse order. When the first scene opens, the religious ritual is over; the Bishop is divested of his ecclesiastical garments. The second scene, the Judgment, is the body of the action, a repetitive action that is played full circle to its opening gesture. In the third scene the military action has not yet begun, and the General exults as the props are brought in. Collectively, the three scenes make up society as seen by Jean Genet, who may be suggesting not only the forces upon which society is built, but also the contemporary state of those forces: the waning might of Religion, the full force of legal paraphernalia, and the growing power of War. In these scenes the roles become metaphors for social archetypes, all covertly seeking fulfillment.

In the fourth scene we are presented with an obverse aberration, a kind of satyr play after the three scenes in tragic cothurni. Rather than traditional dreams of glory in Church, Court, or Army, the fourth client in the brothel Balcony seeks wretchedness as a beggar. The function of the whore is to mistreat him and give him pleasure by increasing his abjection. In this scene the entire dialogue is:

> THE MAN: What about the lice?
> THE GIRL *(very coarsely)*: They're there.

In scene 5 Genet labors what was evident—that the Balcony of Madame Irma's brothel is a house of illusion where each client brings his own scenario; Madame Irma's gift is for props and costumes. In his preface to the 1962 edition of the play, Genet specifies that the first four scenes should contain two sharply delineated tones—the exaggeratedly "acted" and the routine business, but from scene 5 on, there must be only one tone "Always equivocal, always overdone." This is the ambiguous tone of the role-real, of a reality approachable only through roles, knowable only in roles.

In scene 5 we are introduced to the Chief of Police George, ex-lover of Madame Irma, now reduced to voyeurism (linking his role to that of the real theater audience). But if his sexual lust is confined to his eyes, his lust for glory seeks a metaphor. Garrulous with immortal longings, George the Police Chief plans to use the Revolution as a stepping-stone to immortality. He will begin by acting; "Afterwards, things'll run themselves. My name will act in my place."

At the end of the fifth scene, pimp Arthur announces that the rebels are in control of the city. Even as he delivers this news, he is shot in the head—that useless part of his anatomy—killed by a stray bullet. Conveniently, since he was to have played a corpse for the necrophilic taste of the Minister of the Interior.

The sixth scene focuses on the rebels, and it has been dissatisfying to Genet, his directors, and his audiences. Omitted in the Paris and New York productions of *The Balcony*, the scene was rewritten in 1960, then brought close to the original version for the 1962 "definitive" version. In the 1956 *Balcony* Roger and Chantal meet in a street before the brothel; in the 1960 version they are moved to a cafe; but in the 1962 version the setting is a vague place from which the façade of the Balcony is visible. At the end of the scene, the dimly lit set disappears into the wings, so that we may believe that the Revolution itself is another Balcony drama. In his preface Genet himself points out: "Do the rebels exist *in* the Balcony or on the outside? The ambiguity must be preserved to the end."

The rebel scene centers on the love of Roger the Revolutionary for Chantal of the Balcony, who is cast in a Joan-of-Arc role. Unlike the Balcony scenes, however, where roles are evident as roles, Genet's "real" love scene rings false, and it is not clear that this is his intention. At the end of the scene Chantal informs Roger that her experience on the Balcony has taught her to portray any role; her lover reacts sharply, "So you know all the parts? Just now, you were answering me on cue?" "And you," she retorts, as the rebels rush her into heroism. Alone on stage, Roger reflects that Chantal will be what each man expects her to be, playing her part as she has been trained to do.

Scene 7 introduces the Court Envoy, surrogate for the necrophilic Minister of the Interior. While the real corpse of Arthur, the Executioner of the Balcony scenes, *"is lying on a kind of fake tomb of fake black marble,"* the Court Envoy announces the probable death of the rulers of the kingdom—Queen, Archbishop, Chief Judge, and General-in-Chief. The Queen must be replaced, and with her the whole governmental structure dependent upon her. Though men are expendable, the Nomenclature is eternal. Only Madame Irma's Balcony of illusion can provide essential metaphors, and the Court Envoy convinces the brothel clients that nothing is more serious, more durable, than playing roles. Swiftly, but with a sentimentality that recalls the farewell of the rebels, Roger and Chantal, George and Irma of the new Establishment say farewell to their reality, in which guise they sometimes loved each other—or played at it.

The eighth scene, like the fourth, is one of near-pantomime.

On the Balcony appear Bishop, Judge, General, Chief of Police as Hero, and, finally, the Queen. All but the Chief of Police are magnifications of social roles, and the populace accepts them in these roles. Even the beggar becomes a metaphor, shouting up to Irma on the Balcony: "Long live the Queen!" When Chantal, the rebel queen, steps on to the Balcony, the false Royal Queen bows to her. A shot is heard, and Chantal falls. The false General and the false Queen carry her off the Balcony, symbolic victim of a more coherent symbolism. As Roger had predicted, when the symbol of the revolution enters the Balcony of illusion, the revolution is over: "If we behave like those on the other side, then we *are* the other side. Instead of changing the world, all we'll achieve is a reflection of the one we want to destroy." The revolution fades away as the private salacious roles of the opening scenes become the public respectable reality of the later ones.

In the long finale (much revised by Genet) photographers emphasize the sham quality of the sham figures, now convinced of their own social reality. The reconstituted government of surrogate Bishop, Judge, and General prepares to carry on business as usual. Only the Chief of Police is frustrated; having no surrogate, no impersonator, he has to continue playing himself. But his search for abstraction is also caricatured, since the aging voyeur wishes to be commemorated as a giant phallus.

Even as the new and newly puritanical heads of state reserve judgment on the Chief's bid for abstraction, the first post-revolutionary client arrives at the brothel Balcony—Roger, the revolutionary leader. In the old pre-revolutionary tradition, he brings his own scenario; his fantasy is that he is Chief of Police on the verge of immortality. As garrulous as the man he imitates, Roger echoes the very words of the Chief of Police, who watches him through a peep-hole, as do the personnel of the brothel and the three old clients, now "really" Bishop, Judge, and General. An obstreperous client, Roger refuses to leave the brothel at the end of his hour of illusion, but insists upon his "right to lead the character I've chosen to the very limit of his destiny...no, of mine...of merging his destiny with mine"—of merging two roles or two realities. Violently, Roger castrates himself, but Queen-Irma undercuts the theatrical shock, exclaiming, "On my rugs! On the new carpet!" The Chief of Police *"very visibly feels his balls, and, reassured, heaves a sigh."*

So violent is Roger's gesture that it seems to symbolize the violence of Revolution in a suicidal act. The Revolution has destroyed itself through accepting myth, and Roger destroys his manhood through accepting the role of his arch-enemy, the Chief of Police. Like Claire in *The Maids*, Roger at once imitates his enemy and destroys that enemy in himself, even though the flesh-and-blood enemy remains unscathed. As Claire is criminal and saint, Roger is rebel and myth-maker, immortalizing the impotence of the Chief.[15]

In the first version of *The Balcony* Roger's action was reported by Carmen, so that the Chief of Police remained at the center of the action. Having attained abstraction through Roger's act, the Chief commanded everyone to kneel (including "dead" Arthur and Chantal), and Irma closed the play reciting the Lord's Prayer. But Genet must have decided that such patent parody would destroy the final ambiguity of reality within roles. In revision, therefore, the Chief of Police retires into his specially prepared tomb. When machine-gun fire is heard again, as in the three opening scenes, the Queen dismisses the metaphors of her state—Bishop, Judge, and General. The Court Envoy is the last to depart, instructed by Irma to call her "Madame Irma." And it is Madame Irma, alone on stage, who delivers the final lines of the play, addressed directly to the real theater audience: "You must go home, where everything—you can be quite sure—will be even falser than here. . . . You must go now. You'll leave by the right, through the alley. . . . It's morning already."

In *The Balcony* we come full circle from appearance to appearance, but the final ambiguity is less preposterous, far more real than that of the opening scenes, and that ambiguity reflects upon our "home" and "morning."[16] In our society "everything . . . will be even falser" than on the Balcony, where false roles are deliberately assumed, even to emasculation.

In *The Blacks* roles have been assigned before the play begins, and the Master of Ceremonies directs the action more flamboyantly and more obtrusively than the Court Envoy does in *The Balcony*. Like most entertainment of our civilization, the stage action demands no emotional involvement: "in order that you be assured that there is no danger of such a drama's worming its way into your precious lives, we shall even have the decency—a decency learned from you—to make communication impossible. We shall increase the distance that separates us—a distance that is basic—by our pomp, our manners, our insolence—for we are also actors" (Bernard Frechtman translation). In the play itself, we know only that the Blacks are actors, and they are the only actors in the play. But despite the insistence on acting, *The Blacks* does worm its way into our precious lives, reflecting the roles in which the white world has cast the Blacks.

Though Genet calls *The Blacks* "*une clownerie*," it is built, like much serious drama, on conflict—between Negoes-as-Negroes on stage and Negoes-as-Whites on a Balcony (always an area of illusion for Genet). That on-stage conflict is a reflection of and a camouflage for an off-stage conflict in which Negro revolutionaries oppose the whole white race.

The Blacks, completed before Genet's final revision of *The Balcony*, contains more economical play of appearance upon appearance. In the first four scenes of *The Balcony* there are two contrasting tones, the patently false and the apparently real; only later are they blended into ambiguity. In *The Blacks*, on the other hand, the only apparent reality is that everyone is admittedly and brazenly false. And yet, Archibald Absalom Wellington, the Master of Ceremonies, declares, "On this stage, we're like guilty prisoners who play at being guilty." He instructs his actors in words that have become prophetic: "Let Negroes negrify themselves." That negrification is the basis of their acting method through which they express their hatred of black for white, their hatred of black for their black situation. This real hatred springs all the more truly from the falsity on Genet's stage; "My anger isn't make-believe," affirms the Master of Ceremonies.

In *Saint Genet, Actor and Martyr,* written before *The Blacks,* Jean-Paul Sartre compares Genet's own career to that of American Negroes: "In the case of Genet as in that of untouchables— Virginia Negroes, for example—we find the same original injustice (the latter are grand-sons of slaves, the former an abandoned child) bolstered by the same magic ideas ('inferior race,' 'evil nature' of Negro or thief) and the same furious impotence which forces them to turn these ideas to their own use, against their oppressors; in short we find the same passive revolt, the same realism masking the same idealism. Genet's *dignity* lies in insisting upon his own evil. . . . This stubbornness in discouraging reciprocity may be called craftiness or treason, but we know that it is *dignity.* The Negro answers those 'generous' whites who claim to drop racial barriers: 'Come on, you can see that I'm black; you keep your place, and I'll keep mine.' "[17] At the end of *The Blacks* the Negro Master of Ceremonies accuses his white audience similarly: "We are what they want us to be. We shall therefore be it to the very end, absurdly."

And from the very beginning. The opening scene is literally black and white. When the curtain is drawn, neon lights shine on a white-draped catafalque. Incongruously, a shoe-shine box stands beside the coffin, and from it the mock-murderer will blacken his face to emphasize and undercut his role. Before the end of the play, a real revolver will be taken from the real shoe-shine box, but no one is "really" shot on stage.

When the curtain is drawn, Negroes in evening clothes *"are dancing a kind of minuet around the catafalque to an air of Mozart which they whistle and hum."* The costumes and conduct breach the decorum of supposedly funereal surroundings. The tan shoes clash with the evening-dress of the Negroes, and the evening-gowns of the Negresses "suggest fake elegance." Such prop clashes point to the central clash between black and white. In the preface to the play Genet writes, "One evening an actor asked me to write a play for an all-black cast. But what exactly is a black? First of all, what's his color?" Genet writes not about Blacks, or for Blacks, but for "an all-black cast," for black *actors*. And though he asks what Blacks are, he has refused to allow white actors to appear in this play, so that he has assumed an answer. His play, however, does not supply an answer, but caricatures the answers that have been given without question—cliché phrases about race relationships.

Though the entire play castigates such clichés, the play within the play clowns savagely around such castigation. While five Negroes play a white court on the Balcony—Queen, Valet, Judge, Missionary, Governor—other Negroes will enact a ritual rape and murder of a white woman by a black buck. But since the play is a clown play, the ritual will be play. Gradually, we see that the white woman will be neither male nor female, and the catafalque will be revealed as a white sheet draped over two chairs stolen from the mock-white court on the Balcony. "There's no crime since there's no corpse, and no culprit since there's no crime." And yet there is judgment.

On the Balcony Negro actors in white masks, resplendent costumes, and the abstract titles of white government play a court of justice. Ridiculous parodies though they are, they inspire fear when they leave the Balcony of illusion for stage reality. On stage the Negro actors pass mock-judgment upon the mock-court, sentencing them to death and damnation—a mock-death, to be sure, but we cannot be sure about the damnation. We, a white audience, are witness to a mock-action on stage, while a real action—also a trial and execution—may be happening off stage.

Though all the Negroes are actors, different degrees of reality penetrate their roles. The dancing Negroes in evening-clothes of *"fake elegance"* seem more authentic than the Negroes in the Balcony, with garish costumes and white masks, and yet the mock-whites may be more authentic than we, a white audience. Newport News, in his woolen sweater and bare feet, seems more authentic than the Negroes in evening-clothes. Shortly after the beginning of the play within the play, the Master of Ceremonies hints at the reality concealed by Newport News, addressing him: "Clear out. Go tell them. Let them know we've started. They're to do their job just as we'll do ours." On stage the job is acting; as a white audience, we can only know the Negroes are acting.

Before the ritual re-enactment of the rape and murder, Village, who will play the rapist and murderer, reveals that he and Mr. Herod Adventure (who never appears on stage) have strangled an old white tramp in order to provide a corpse for the evening's entertainment. Even if his story is true, the corpse in the catafalque is playing a role, as Diouf, the Negro preacher, plays the role of a white woman, in white mask, white gloves, and golden wig. Village speaks the dialogue of both attacker and attacked, the cliché lines of the big black buck and the cliché lines of his white victim who fears and desires him. Before the rape the victim gives birth to a mock-progeny; Diouf-Marie produces five dolls that reflect on the puppetry of the figures of the mock-government on the Balcony. When the play within the play is over, the dolls remain—a second degree caricature of white government.

Rape and murder are performed off stage—"Greek tragedy, my dear, decorum"—to the music of the *Dies Irae*, and Newport News reduces the mock-ritual to stage reality. He reports that Village and Diouf merely chatted behind a screen; when the mock-court descends from the Balcony to search for the white victim, Newport News removes the sheet from the catafalque to disclose two chairs. Newport News is consistently most real in his stage role, and it is he who reports on an off-stage trial and execution of a Negro traitor.

And yet, his report is punctuated by Genet's scenic direction, *"a firecracker explodes off-stage."* A firecracker may be a signal, but it is also harmless display. The white theater audience can never know what, if anything, was happening off stage. When the firecracker explodes, the five Balcony Negroes remove their white masks, and Genet's text designates them more clearly as actors, e.g. "The One Who Played the Valet" instead of "Valet." To these actors, the firecracker is the signal for revelation of authenticity. As Newport News grows lyrical about the Negro Hero who is on his way to replace the traitor, Bobo interrupts, "But . . . at least he's black? (*Briefly, they are puzzled; then they burst out laughing.*)" Nevertheless, the brief silence indicates the Negroes' confusion about the roles they have assumed. Archibald no longer knows whether Diouf is "still acting or is he speaking for himself?" Although the actors seem to have other callings, they insist upon finishing the performance, which no longer has a camouflage purpose. The Negroes-as-Negroes sentence the Negroes-as-Whites to death: "At last they'll know the only dramatic relationship we can have with them." In their white masks, mouthing white clichés, the five Establishment actors fall one by one into a human heap. Then they are escorted off stage "to Hell," leaving Village and Virtue alone.

Village, who played the rapist-murderer, attempts to tell Virtue of his love for her, who played (and may actually be) a prostitute. Searching vainly for a word or gesture that will not imitate love as expressed by the whites, he is comforted by Virtue: "At least there's one sure thing: you won't be able to wind your fingers in my long golden hair." Once clichés are eliminated, we are brought full circle back to Genet's introductory question: "But what exactly is a black? First of all, what's his color?"

In the last scene of Genet's *Blacks* "*All the Negroes—including those who constituted the Court and who are without their masks—are standing about a white-draped catafalque like the one seen at the beginning of the play.*" The Balcony is empty of actors, but just below the Balcony hang the dolls with white masks—

rigid symbols of a rigid white society. As in Frisch's *Chinese Wall* the play is over, but the farce begins again. And yet, as Homer Swander has perceptively noted about the final scene: "[The actors] are further away: the 'distance' (in all of its meanings) between them and us is increased. They are furthermore, behind the point at which the back-drop has defined the stage, which is to say that they are (and this should be a vivid part of the visual image) *backstage*, that mysterious continent to which Newport News traveled: a place where there is not so much as a white mask much less a White. The catafalque, to be sure, is draped in white—a reminder that black is no longer the color of funerals. When Village and Virtue turn their backs on us as if we no longer existed, and the curtain is drawn, the 'distance' has become a total severing."[18] Before that severing, however, the real white audience has been guiltily implicated in all the Negro roles and all the roles of the Negroes, who only now must begin to discover their real identity.

The Screens crystallizes Genet's reflections on roles, combining the intensity of his first two plays with the irony of his next two. *Deathwatch* and *The Maids* dramatize make-believe roles grafted upon a sordid reality, but we are never in doubt that Lefranc and Claire are playing parts so as to escape from their respective selves. In *The Balcony* and *The Blacks*, the real cannot be distinguished from the role, despite the flagrancy of the role. Appearance is revealed as appearance is revealed as appearance—outrageously, paradoxically, sometimes farcically. Never involved except with actors, we are driven to question the very nature and basis of roles, which are the only reality we can know.

In *The Screens*, Genet no longer designates our role as audience; there is no mirror as in *The Balcony*, no direct address as in *The Blacks*. And yet, the titular screens exist mainly for us; upon them, the actors draw for us; behind them, they hide for us and from us; before them, actors perform their roles—individually and archetypically. Literally "to guard against wind" (*parer à vent*), Genet's screens are as pervasive as the actors' breath of speech, counterpointed against that speech and as carefully deployed. Particularly precise are Genet's scenic directions, specifying that real props are always to contrast with those drawn on the screens. In the play, a Lieutenant remarks to a corpse: "Even to knock off an Infidel one has to engage in such theatrical labor that one cannot be both actor and director" (Bernard Frechtman translation). As manipulator of screens and actors, Genet has chosen to be author-director.

Genet specifies that "each actor will be required to play five or six roles, male or female"; into the action, Genet integrates transvestism, multiplicity of personality, role-playing. In each role, Genet calls for a contrast between costumes and either masks or heavy make-up; he contrasts the real objects with those drawn on the screens; in performance, the formalized gestures of the actors contrast with their scatological idiom. The role-playing is both precise and extravagant; Saïd and his mother conjure up the possessions that they do not have, and they create a storm in their desert; Leila and Saïd's mother imitate animals. However many roles each actor may assume, he must play them both intensely and parodically, for Genet seeks to delineate archetypical roles, even as he undercuts the archetypes by emphasizing them as roles. Of the Lieutenant before battle, the scenic direction says, "*in short, he is acting.*"

If one compares Genet's role-playing Legionnaires with Brecht's British soldiers in *Man is Man*, both armies are ridiculed through obedience and obscenity, but even in his pre-Marxist play, Brecht's scenes show that man is expendable cannon-fodder, whereas Genet's soldiers are part of an intricate human structure: "The thing that kills is grease paint on a skeleton of precise gestures." And to combat such grease-paint on skeletons, an arch-actor is required. Saïd is that arch-actor.

Saïd's assumption of a heroic role has been discussed in another context, but it should be stressed that it *is* a a role, consciously assumed. The Cadi assumes the role of Saïd's obverse in the Arab world, since he has learned about justice through watching Saïd determinedly flout it. As Saïd reaches a summit of evil in treason, so does Warda through the prostitution that is reality and ritual. Social symbols are strikingly theatrical—the giant glove that watches over the Arabs in the absence of the European colonialists, the ventriloquist mouth that functions prophetically for the Arabs. Caricatured in 1840 costumes, the ruling Europeans face the Arab populace from a balcony—as in *The Balcony* and *The Blacks*. On stage, the civil war opposes Europeans pinning medals on an eight-foot idol against Arabs swiftly drawing on the screens the weapons and the wounds of the war. But most pervasively theatrical are the titular screens, which conceal the actors, function as settings, and designate different domains of stage action. First, the screens arrive with drawings already on them; then, Leila draws an imitation marble clock to join the useless real objects she has stolen. Other actors draw on the screens; the Arabs draw flames that they fan into a conflagration, and that conflagration becomes the revolution. During the combat, the dying burst through white screens to enter the domain of the dead. The painted Arab grave on the screen of Scene 1 becomes the domain of the dead upon which the drama ends. Real and role are indistinguishable.

In the final complex scene of *The Screens* the action takes place on four scenic levels. "*The actors themselves will set up the screens and utensils described thereafter and will draw what the screen is supposed to represent.*" Finally, then, through playing roles in an action, each actor has not only defined several roles, but has helped define the world in which roles are played—a world of screens that are at the same time props, metaphors, and metaphysical reflectors. By showing us the theatricality of the theater, Genet has shown us the ubiquitous theatricality of what we usually call reality.

Polar opposites stylistically, the dramas of Genet and Beckett are riddled by the problem of play, which they both find profoundly reflective of man's ontological situation. They both dramatize the play of appearance on appearance, of role dissolving into real—Genet with a lavish theatrical imagination and Beckett with one that is spare and precise. No other contemporary writer has probed to such depths, but under their influence younger playwrights search for the real through self-conscious awareness of roles in drama. Jack Gelber's *Connection* (1957) was written too soon after Jean Genet's *Balcony* (first version 1956) to be influenced by it, but there is a similar desire to abandon illusionist theatrical surface. Edward Albee's *Tiny Alice* (1965), on the other hand, shows Genet's influence, as Robert Brustein points out: "The central idea of the play—which treats religious ritual as a form of stagecraft and play-acting—comes from Jean Genet's *The Balcony*."[19] Though Brustein claims that most of the play is "meaningless," even he finds some meaning in *Tiny Alice*. First produced by the Living Theatre company, Gelber's *Connection* was hailed as a milestone of the avant-garde. Produced on Broadway, Albee's *Tiny Alice* was hissed as dull, obscure, or histrionic. But both playwrights have risked boring us in order to penetrate surface appearance if not to truth, at least to the truth of appearance.

In *The Connection* Gelber introduces a playwright and director who claim they have hired real junkies to take false dope while two photographers film the happening. Genet's Negroes play at being Negroes, but Gelber's *actors* play at being addicts. However, the play is not a happening—unique and capricious—since its script is fixed; only the jazz accompaniment is improvised. In the first of the two acts, the actor-junkies wait for dope (a fix), and in Act II they react to dope, though we have been told that it is not real heroin. The connection, the man who brings the heroin (horse), is a Negro named Cowboy, like the mythical American hero. The symbolism of *The Connection* is spelled out by Solly, the junkie-intellectual: "You are fed up with everything for the moment. And like the rest of us you are a little hungry for a little hope. So you wait and worry. A fix of hope. A fix to forget. A fix to remember, to be sad, to be happy, to be, to be. So we wait for the trustworthy Cowboy to gallop in upon a white horse." And illiterate Sam understands the metaphoric connection between the addict world and our own: "the chlorophyll addicts, the aspirin addicts, the vitamin addicts, those people are hooked worse than me."

Among the junkies, there are cowboy-type moral divisions between good guys (Sam, Solly, and the jazz musicians) and bad guys (Leach, Ernie). A conventional rising action is climaxed by Leach's overdose of heroin, and that rising action is interrupted by conventional comic relief—the innocence of the Salvation Army sister, the sickness of the playwright and the second photographer, who try dope for the first time. And there is a facile happy ending: Leach does not die, and everybody has his fix. Though the playwright at first complains about his experiment, even he is ultimately pleased. Learning about art through apparent improvisation, the play's fictional playwright seems to comment on all play when he says, "But one thing I've learned about the theatre. I believe it all fits together."

The Connection fits together very neatly indeed, but Gelber's next play, *The Apple*, leans so heavily upon the effect of improvisation that it does not "all fit together." The basic fiction is random meeting at a coffee-house, and though the published version of the play assigns names to Gelber's characters, he prefers actors to use their real names, as they run through a series of sketches that contain the hostility, charity, and love of Eden after the apple. When the actors disperse, it is implied that everything will be repeated the following night—except for the inevitable variations in each night's Happening. Like Happenings, *The Apple* tries to persuade us that we are viewing unformed reality, and that we affect that reality with our presence. In the tradition of Pirandello's Theater Trilogy, *The Apple* blends actors into the audience, but they are nevertheless actors playing roles—so artlessly that their art has the dullness of much of life.

Though Gelber and Albee both seek to approach the real through actor's roles, Gelber fits his Manichean melodramatic plot into the new form of a Happening in *The Connection*, whereas Albee fits his post-Absurdist plot into the old three-act form in *Tiny Alice*. Post-Absurdist because Albee takes it for granted that "the moral, religious, political and social structures man has erected to 'illusion' himself have collapsed."[20] Albee's plays sometimes dramatize that collapse, and notably *Tiny Alice*.

Brother Julian, the protagonist of *Tiny Alice*, claims to be "dedicated to the reality of things, rather than the appearance," but Julian's name is connected, in Christian tradition, with apostasy. Albee's Julian, who is torn between Truth and Illusion, will be an apostate to Truth rather than to Christianity. The name Alice means Truth, and it is a beautiful woman named Miss Alice, herself a servant to Tiny Alice, who lures Julian from service in his Christian Church, to what appears to him a truer dedication.

Each of the play's three acts contains a lyric monologue by Julian, which dramatizes his tenuous hold upon reality. In Act I Julian describes a perhaps hallucinatory sexual experience with a woman who herself hallucinated as the Virgin Mary. In Act II Julian describes his obsession with martyrdom, shifting roles as he becomes a child, both lion and gladiator, then saint and the hallucinating self of the Act I monologue. In Act III Julian, who claimed that he left the asylum because he was persuaded that hallucination was inevitable and even desirable, plunges into his final hallucination, which leads to his real death.

Immediately after his marriage to Miss Alice, Julian is urged to accept Tiny Alice, but he resists, repeating: "But I have fought against it . . . all my life. . . . I have fought against it . . . all my life." The Cardinal joins the three servants of Tiny Alice in ordering Julian to accept domicile with Tiny Alice, who is real and who is nothing. When Julian persists in refusing, and even threatens to go back to the asylum, the Lawyer shoots him. Alternating in the roles of a frightened child and the hallucinating woman who called for help, Julian is forced to face himself in death. With phrases of the thirteenth psalm, Julian slowly and desperately dissolves Miss Alice into Tiny Alice into the Christian God. Unable to believe "THE ABSTRACT? . . . REAL? THE REST? FALSE," Julian reverts to Christian illusion, to traditional images that protect him from the reality of abstraction. As a "great presence," panting and stamping, engulfs him, Julian takes the crucifixion position, injecting his God into Alice: "God, Alice. . . I accept thy will." Julian dies in imitation of Christ, deaf to Tiny monstrous Alice, who comes to claim him. After Julian has been crucified in and by his illusion, the play ends in the darkness and silence of Alice, the ultimate truth.

On stage Albee uses the model castle as his metaphor for the reality of abstraction, as older playwrights used the stage as a metaphor for the world. More contemporary, as yet minor, American playwrights have used theater roles as a metaphor for reality, rather than reflecting such reality obliquely. James Lineberger's *Song for All Saints* features a road company rehearsing in a warehouse; we learn nothing of their play, but the actors mirror various human relationships; after a sporadic rebellion against the director, during which two actors die, the obviously named Leroy (king) reaffirms his hold on the company. In Elizabeth Johnson's *Bad Play for an Old Lady* a Flowerman controls the action and pointedly comments on the play as play, though his last order to the actress is: "Ad lib it. Go it on your own." In the footsteps of Brecht and Wilder, Norman L. Hartweg uses a Narrator in *The Pit*, a satire of a Congressional investigation. Similarly, a Narrator integrates Jean-Claude van Itallie's *It's Almost Like Being*, a play that takes the form of a "movie being shot by several cameras"; the actors "are 'turned on' for their 'bits,' " and it is these "bits" that dramatize the dehumanization of show business.

In *God Bless Us, Every One* by Charles L. Mee Jr. the world-stage metaphor appears as a world-circus, and the actors are circus-performers who exhibit the oppression, corruption, and bigotry of the world at large. Though circus "acts" are at first differentiated from "interludes" of reality, the boundaries dissolve when the Negro whipping-boy, Jimmy, seizes power. Claiming that he will establish justice and order through his violence, Jimmy shoots through the main tent guy, and the tent collapses in the form of a mushroom cloud, smothering several performers, including Jimmy. In a direct address to the theater audience, the old Ringmaster attempts to restore order in the circus, but murderous hostility punctuates the sanctimonious singing of "God bless us, every one."

Since these plays were published in *The Tulane Drama Review,* one cannot know whether their emphasis on roles is indicative of the editor's taste or of a representative trend. One can, however, know that today's American theater—variously called New, Underground, or Off-Off-Broadway—incorporates acting techniques as never before in written drama. Relevant to the examination of the real through the frankness of role-playing is the "transformation" technique of Chicago's Second City and New York's Open Theatre companies. Two directors offer explanations of transformation:

> Transformation is the term used by Joseph Chaikin to identify an improvisational technique developed at the Open Theatre. I worked there for two years; Miss Terry is still working there. Transformation dramatizes those aspects of personality which in a naturalistic play would be implied by the sub-text. Transformations should not be thought of as dramatizations of fantasies but as exposures of those elements of personality which lie beneath the role which a human being assumes as his identity.[21] (Sidney S. Walter)

> The transformation is adapted from a Second City Workshop device but is not merely an acting stunt. It is an improvisation in which the established realities or "given circumstances" (the Method phrase) of the scene change

several times during the course of the action. What may change are character and/or situation and/or time and/or objectives, etc. Whatever realities are established at the beginning are destroyed after a few minutes and replaced by others. Then these are in turn destroyed and replaced. These changes occur swiftly and *almost without transition,* until the audience's dependence upon any fixed reality is called into question. A member of our audience once said that these continual metamorphoses left him feeling "stationless," which is precisely the point.[22] (Peter Feldman)

The directors made these comments in connection with their respective productions, but transformations have a long history, both theatrical and dramatic; perhaps Dionysius was the first "transformer." What is distinctive about contemporary transformations is that they are at once dramatic and unmotivated. Though "transformation" playwrights tend to snub Absurdism for its intellectual approach, they profit from its disjunctive plots and characters. Absurdist disjunction is framed within thematic coherence, and this tends to be true of transformation plays as well; social or metaphysical reality is revealed through the swift metamorphoses of roles.

At its simplest, transformation operates in *Daddy Violet* by George Birimisa, an unpublished play that depends heavily on improvisation and on actors' mingling with the audience. Three actors—a failure in his forties, a young lead with homosexual tendencies, and a young ingénue with sexual experience—practice Michael Chekhov acting exercises, in which each plays a violet. Through the violet-role, each actor gradually, very gradually, boringly, reveals his psychological background as the violets change their habitat. Suddenly, however, the three violets are growing in the Mekong Delta, and they wither hysterically under a very few phrases of the war. The oldest actor is the first to recover, then weans the other two back to normalcy through insisting upon the geographic reality in which the play is being presented.

More frequently, transformation techniques operate satirically. Thus, the first two plays of Jean-Claude van Itallie's successful *America Hurrah* base much of their effect of a mass-produced society on transformation technique: in *Interview* "*The actors walk straight forward toward the audience and then walk backwards to the rear of the stage. Each time they approach the audience, they do so as a different character.*" Later, "*The rapid movements of the gym class become the vibrations of passengers on a moving subway train.*" In *TV* transformation is the basis of the action: "*After each television segment, the People involved in it will freeze where they are until it is time for them to become another character.*" Both individual and group transformations indicate the mass uniformity of contemporary American society. As in vaudeville, the actors sacrifice individual personality to the satiric comedy of the whole. Only ensemble playing distinguishes these plays from vaudeville.

Even more than Jean-Claude van Itallie, Megan Terry has been associated with the Open Theater, and her plays represent more sustained and coherent efforts to incorporate transformations into the texture of drama. In *Comings and Goings,* which she subtitles a "Theatre Game," some twenty-five "He-She" scenes are played by replaceable actor-actress combinations, the whole suggesting the multiple attitudes in man-woman relationships. In *Keep Tightly Closed in A Cool Dry Place* three actors assume many roles within the tight enclosure designated by the title—itself a reflection of advertising rhetoric, but one which embraces the men's moral situation even more than their imprisonment. In Terry's best-known work *Viet Rock* she combines two kinds of transformation: the group of actors, particularly the women, engage in some dozen transformations of identity; in two scenes individual actors swiftly replace one another, as in *Comings and Goings*. Richard Schechner has written that "*Viet Rock* is significant first, therefore, not because it parodies and satirizes a wide range of attitudes relating to the

war, but because it uses new theatrical techniques."[23] These new
theatrical techniques permit an inclusiveness of attitudes toward
a war that has been widely satirized and parodied, without diminishing its intransigent pace. In none of Terry's three plays does
role-playing reveal a personal reality; in *Viet Rock* a disastrous
social reality is illuminated through the partial roles of which
war is the whole; in *Keep Tightly Closed* the reality is situational,
since the three men are mutually hostile and interdependent; in
Comings and Goings the reality is relational—in the nature of
a Man-Woman relationship, regardless of who the individual
men and women may be.

In two plays written outside the Open Theater radius, transformations are centered in individual actors, though they also
reveal a relationship. In both plays, *Tango Palace* by Irene
Fornés and *The Architect and The Emperor of Assyria* by Fernando Arrabal, the entire cast is a male couple. Both plays contain
remarkable flights of fantasy, and yet both are contained within
an illusionist framework; there are no comments on the actors
as actors, and the actors do not, as in Open Theater productions,
address us directly and mingle with us.

Tango Palace is a three-scene, one-set play, but the single
room of the set is so profusely furnished that it takes a page to
describe, and it shows that Irene Fornés is a painter as well as a
playwright. The many props are so ready at hand that it is difficult
to determine whether they inspire or aid the role-playing of
Isidore, "an androgynous clown," for the education of Leopold,
"an earnest youth." Less systematic and abrupt than transformation exercises, Isidore nevertheless shifts roles swiftly—drawing teacher, worshiper, orange-picker, bull-fighter, beetle-god,
and, after Leopold stabs him, angel. The versatile theatricality
of Isidore explains his dangerous fascination for Leopold. Though
Leopold kills Isidore in an effort to assert his independence,
sadism resides in Isidore. And it does not stop with his death,
for the last scenic direction reads "[*Leopold*] *is ready for the next*

stage of their battle." Their relationship is a battle precisely because Leopold will not lend himself to the sadistic role-playing of Isidore, and yet he is prey to those roles.

In *The Architect and The Emperor of Assyria* by Arrabal, the fantastic nature of the roles is indicated even in the title which introduces the two characters. We never learn what the architect designs, and we doubt whether Emperor is the profession of the sole surviving victim of a plane crash, who arrives on the island of the savage, speechless Architect. After the opening exposition, which exposes little, we witness the civilization created by the Emperor and his Architect-pupil, surely the most brilliant student in all drama. Not only has he grasped language, concepts and outward forms of modern industrial civilization, but he understands the inner loneliness of human relationships in that civilization—mother-son, lovers, doctor-patient. Both the Architect and the Emperor engage in transformations; for the most part, they play symbiotic parts, but each is capable of playing many roles. Thus the Architect carries on both parts of a husband-wife dialogue, but it is the Emperor who is a virtuoso actor; in a single scene he plays Emperor, wife, mistress, and Architect; in another, he plays both a Carmelite nun and her confessor, a woman in labor and her doctor. Though sex is a dominant thread in the transformations of Act I, it does not seem to be centrally thematic. Act II is structured by a trial, in which the Architect is Judge and the Emperor is Defendant. However, various transformations intrude into the trial; after the Emperor's confession that he murdered his mother, the Architect sentences him to death, and then catches himself, "But dying is not another game; it's irreparable." The Emperor then orders the Architect to eat him after his death. This grotesque meal takes place before our eyes, and as it progresses, "*the Architect takes on the voice, tone, characteristics, and expressions of the Emperor.*" By the time the Architect sucks the Emperor's last bone dry, the Architect has become the Emperor, and he celebrates his solitude rhapsodically. But the noise of an airplane interrupts his chant of "Vive moi!" We see flames, hear an explosion, and within a few minutes the Architect enters on stage, looking exactly like the Emperor of the opening scene, and speaking his exact lines. The play will presumably begin again.

Though the plot incorporates a familiar Arrabal obsession—a love-hate relationship between mother and son—the technical brilliance of the transformations intensifies that relationship. In the second act, the many roles suggest a morality of guilt and expiation; more tentatively, they suggest a metaphysical framework as well. While the Architect is the Emperor's pupil, he retains certain powers that the Emperor did not, could not teach him; he commands animals to serve him, mountains to move for him, day and night to appear before him. After the Architect has gorged himself on the Emperor's flesh, he loses these powers, and perhaps this is a meaning of their roles: an Emperor may rule over a human domain whereas an Architect, a master-builder, may command the very forces of nature until he becomes a servant in the human domain. But this is a discursive critical reduction of the most "pan-icky" of Arrabal's "panic" plays, provoking reflection upon relational and metaphysical reality through a dazzling diversity of roles.

Centuries after the introduction of the world-stage metaphor, contemporary playwrights are still preoccupied with the relation of the stage to the world, of the role to the real. Tieck, Pirandello, and Ghelderode variously suggest a tenuous boundary between theater and life; for them the theater imitates life, invades it, and betrays it by imitation and invasion. In contrast to this conception of theater, Brecht, Frisch, and Weiss deliberately emphasize the theater as theater, in order to persuade us of its relevance to our lives. In their plays the familiar is made strange so as to be returned to familiarity, the more convincing for the temporary separation. Influenced by the Pirandellian real-role conflict and by Brechtian insistence on the relevance of roles to contemporary reality, some recent American playwrights use the old device of the play within the play, and others use new acting exercises to satirize American civilization, whose social reality resembles the stereotyped roles of the mass media. But Beckett and Genet are unable to make social or metaphysical divisions between the real and the role, or even to distinguish the role within the role, and the role within *that* role, *ad infinitum*. Far from Diderot's paradox, their actors do not coolly mime emotions they do not feel. Both analytical and emotional, verbal and gestural, their actors know that they are playing roles, and though that may be all they know, it is a great deal. As in the moral admonitions of the Stoic Epictetus, the actor in the plays of Beckett or Genet can tell himself: "Remember that you are an actor in a drama." The Open Theatre playwrights and Arrabal seem to place a question-mark after the word "drama." And none of their actors can apply the final injunction of Epictetus: "For this is your business, to act well the character assigned to you." Characters can no longer be assigned, and serious acting is not a mere business or profession. Today acting and playwriting demand dedication to roles in which are cast passionate reflections on the nature of reality.

Selected Bibliography of Books in English

A. Cross-National Studies

Abel, Lionel, *Metatheatre* (New York, 1963)

Bentley, Eric, *The Playwright as Thinker* (New York, 1955)

Brustein, Robert, *The Theatre of Revolt* (Boston, 1962)

Chiari, Joseph, *Landmarks of Contemporary Drama* (London, 1965)

Esslin, Martin, *The Theatre of the Absurd* (Garden City, N.Y., 1961)

Gascoigne, Bamber, *Twentieth Century Drama* (London, 1962)

Grossvogel, David I., *The Blasphemers: the Theatre of Brecht, Ionesco, Beckett, Genet* (Ithaca, N.Y., 1965)

Lewis, Allan, *The Contemporary Theatre* (New York, 1962)

Lumley, Frederick, *Trends in Twentieth Century Drama* (New York, 1960)

Wellwarth, George, *The Theater of Protest and Paradox* (New York, 1964)

B. National Studies

Bigsby, C. W. E., *Confrontation and Commitment: A Study of Contemporary American Drama 1959–1966* (London, 1967)

Chiari, Joseph, *The Contemporary French Theatre: The Flight from Naturalism* (New York, 1959)

Downer, Alan S. (ed.), *American Drama and Its Critics* (Chicago, 1965)

Fowlie, Wallace, *Dionysus in Paris: A Guide to Contemporary French Theatre* (New York, 1960)

Garten, H. F., *Modern German Drama* (New York, 1962)

Gould, Jean, *Modern American Playwrights* (New York, 1966)

Guicharnaud, Jacques, *Modern French Theatre from Giraudoux to Genet* (New Haven, 1967)

Pronko, Leonard, *Avant-Garde: The Experimental Theater in France* (Berkeley, Calif., 1962)

Taylor, John Russell, *The Angry Theatre: New British Drama* (New York, 1962)

Weales, Gerald, *American Drama Since World War II* (New York, 1962)

C. INDIVIDUAL STUDIES

Albee:

Debusscher, Gilbert, *Edward Albee: Tradition and Renewal* (Brussels, 1967)

Anouilh:

Bishop, Thomas, *Pirandello and the French Theatre* (New York, 1960)

Harvey, John, *Anouilh: A Study in Theatrics* (New Haven, 1964)

Pronko, Leonard, *The World of Jean Anouilh* (Berkeley, 1961)

Beckett:

Coe, Richard, *Samel Beckett* (New York, 1964)

Cohn, Ruby, *Samuel Beckett: The Comic Gamut* (New Brunswick, N.J., 1962)

Esslin, Martin (ed.), *Samuel Beckett* (Englewood Cliffs, N.J., 1965)

Fletcher, John, *Samuel Beckett's Art* (London, 1967)

Jacobsen, Josephine and William R. Mueller, *The Testament of Samuel Beckett* (New York, 1964)

Kenner, Hugh, *Samuel Beckett: A Critical Study* (New York, 1961)

Scott, Nathan A., *Samuel Beckett* (New York, 1965)

December, 1966 issue of *Modern Drama*

Brecht:

Demetz, Peter (ed.), *Brecht* (Englewood Cliffs, N.J., 1962)

Esslin, Martin, *Brecht: The Man and His Work* (New York, 1960)

Ewen, Frederic, *Bertolt Brecht: His Life, His Art and His Times* (New York, 1967)

Gray, Ronald, *Bertolt Brecht* (New York, 1961)

Kenney, W., *The Major Plays of Bertolt Brecht* (New York, 1964)

Spalter, Max, *Brecht's Tradition* (Baltimore, 1967)

Weideli, Walter, *The Art of Bertolt Brecht* (New York, 1963)

Willett, John, *The Theatre of Bertolt Brecht* (London, 1964)

The Drama Review, Issues #37 and #38

Camus:

Brée, Germaine, *Camus* (New York, 1964)

Brée, Germaine (ed.), *Camus* (Englewood Cliffs, N.J., 1962)

Parker, Emmett A., *Camus, the Artist in the Arena* (Madison, Wisc., 1965)

Thody, Philip, *Albert Camus, a Study of His Work* (London, 1957)

Claudel:

Beaumont, Ernest, *The Theme of Beatrice in the Plays of Claudel* (London, 1954)

Chiari, Joseph, *The Poetic Drama of Paul Claudel* (New York, 1954)

Fowlie, Wallace, *Paul Claudel* (New York, 1957)

Eliot:

Donoghue, Denis, *The Third Voice* (Princeton, N.J., 1957)

Frye, Northrop, *T. S. Eliot* (New York, 1963)

Gardner, Helen, *The Art of T. S. Eliot* (New York, 1959)

Jones, D. E., *The Plays of T. S. Eliot* (London, 1960)

Smith, Carol H., *T. S. Eliot's Dramatic Theory and Practice* (Princeton, N.J., 1963)

Smith, Grover, *T. S. Eliot's Poetry and Plays* (Chicago, 1956)

Spanos, William V., *The Christian Tradition in Modern British Verse Drama* (New Brunswick, 1967)

Frisch:

Weisstein, Ulrich, *Max Frisch* (New York, 1967)

Wilbert-Collins, Elly, *A Bibliography of Four Contemporary German-Swiss Authors: Friedrich Dürrenmatt, Max Frisch, Robert Walser, Albin Zollinger* (Bern, 1967)

Fry:

Stanford, Derek, *Christopher Fry: An Appreciation* (London, 1951)

Genet:

Coe, Richard, *The Vision of Jean Genet* (London, 1968)

Knapp, Bettina, *Jean Genet* (New York, 1968)

Jacobsen, Josephine and William R. Mueller, *Ionesco and Genet* (New York, 1968)

McMahon, Joseph H., *The Imagination of Jean Genet* (New Haven, 1963)

Sartre, Jean-Paul, *Saint Genet: Actor and Martyr* (New York, 1964)

Thody, Philip, *Jean Genet: A Study of his Novels and Plays* (London, 1968)

Ghelderode:
Tulane Drama Review, Issue #21

Ionesco:
Coe, Richard, *Eugene Ionesco* (New York, 1961)
Tulane Drama Review, Issue #19 (with Genet)

Miller:
Huftel, Sheila, *Arthur Miller: The Burning Glass* (New York, 1965)
Moss, Leonard, *Arthur Miller* (New York, 1967)
Welland, Dennis, *Arthur Miller* (New York, 1961)

Pinter:
Hinchliffe, Arnold P., *Harold Pinter* (New York, 1967)

Sartre:
Champigny, Robert, *Stages on Sartre's Way* (Bloomington, Ind., 1959)
Cranston, Maurice, *Jean-Paul Sartre* (New York, 1962)
Kern, Edith (ed.), *Sartre* (Englewood Cliffs, N.J., 1962)

Williams:
Donahue, Francis, *The Dramatic World of Tennessee Williams*, (New York, 1964)
Falk, Signi, *Tennessee Williams* (New York, 1962)
Jackson, Esther, *The Broken World of Tennessee Williams* (Madison, Wisc., 1965)
Nelson, Benjamin, *Tennessee Williams: The Man and His Work* (New York, 1961)
Tischler, Nancy, *Tennessee Williams: Rebellious Puritan* (New York, 1961)

Notes

1. CONTEMPORARY DRAMA

1. Quoted in J. C. Trewin, *Drama in Britain* (London, 1965), p. 8.

2. Reprinted in *American Playwrights on Drama*, ed. Horst Frenz (New York, 1965), pp. 152–3.

3. Program of Buffalo, New York, Studio Arena Theater production of *Box-Mao-Box*.

4. *Newsweek* (October 29, 1962), p. 52.

5. "The American Drama, 1944–1954" in *American Drama and Its Critics*, ed. Alan S. Downer (Chicago, 1965), p. 188.

6. *On Poetry and Poets* (London, 1957), p. 260.

7. "For Other Voices" in *T. S. Eliot* (Englewood Cliffs, N.J., 1962), p. 189.

8. *Selected Essays* (London, 1932), p. 189.

9. *Tynan on Theatre* (London, 1964), p. 42.

10. *Anger and After* (London, 1963), p. 38.

11. "Writing for Myself," *Twentieth Century* (February, 1961), p. 173.

12. Ibid., p. 174.

13. *Writers at Work: The Paris Review Interviews* (New York, 1967), p. 362.

14. Unless otherwise noted, translations are mine. Translator is named in parenthesis after first quotation from a particular play.

15. *The Theatre and Its Double*, tr. Mary Caroline Richards (New York, 1958), p. 99.

16. *Drama Survey* (Winter, 1964), p. 448.

17. *American Playwrights on Drama*, p. 170.

18. Helen Hellman, "The Fool-Hero of Michel de Ghelderode," *Drama Survey* (Winter, 1965), pp. 264–271.

19. *Tulane Drama Review* (Spring, 1963), p. 124.

20. "Forgers of Myth," in *Playwrights on Playwriting*, ed. Toby Cole (New York, 1961), pp. 123–124.

21. *Camus* (New York, 1964), p. 165.

22. *The Theatre of the Absurd* (New York, 1961), p. xx.

23. Program of the Théâtre Montparnasse production of *L'Architect et l'Empereur d'Assyrie*.

24. Ibid.

25. "The Inner and the Outer Reality," *Tulane Drama Review* (Spring, 1963), pp. 187–217.

26. "Being without Time" in *Samuel Beckett*, ed. Martin Esslin (Englewood Cliffs, N.J., 1965), p. 140.

27. Ibid., p. 151.

28. Sartre's analysis, prefaced to the Grove Press edition of *The Maids* and *Deathwatch*, p. 16, was excerpted from *Saint Genet, Actor and Martyr*, tr. Bernard Frechtman.

29. Ibid., p. 8.

30. "Jean Genet's *Les Paravents*," *L'Esprit Créateur* (Winter, 1962), p. 183.

31. See Walter Sokel's excellent introduction to his *Anthology of German Expressionist Drama* (New York, 1963).

32. I prefer the translation *estrangement* to *alienation*, which carries Absurdist overtones that Brecht would surely have rejected.

33. *Bertolt Brecht: die Struktur seines Werkes* (Nürnberg, 1962).

34. *Theater Problems*, tr. Gerhard Nellhaus, in *Four Plays* (London, 1964), p. 33.

35. Gordon Rogoff, "Mr. Dürrenmatt Buys New Shoes," *Tulane Drama Review* (September, 1958), pp. 27–34.

36. *Plays and Players* (February, 1963), p. 15.

2. Dialogue of Cruelty

1. Focusing on the setting, Lawrence Kitchen views Strindberg as the father of a particularly virulent form of modern drama, which he names Compressionism: "A compressionist play is one in which the characters are insulated from society in such a way as to encourage the maximum conflict of attitudes. . . . The course of Compressionism could be summed up as history falling into line with Strindberg's tortured vision." "The Cage and the Scream," *The Listener* (January 24, 1963), pp. 157–159.

2. *The Theater and Its Double*, tr. Mary Caroline Richards (New York, 1958), p. 79.

3. Ibid., p. 99.

4. In *The Playwright as Thinker* Eric Bentley points this out. Bentley also claims that Sartre is influenced by Ibsen's delayed exposition, with crucial information withheld until the climax. However, all information is "crucial" in *No Exit,* and the play's impact depends on accumulation rather than climax.

5. In spite of the inaccurate American title, *No Exit,* there *is* a possiblity of exit when the door opens, and part of the meaning of Sartre's Inferno lies in the fact that the characters *choose* not to make an exit.

6. In an earlier version, Green Eyes leaves the stage to receive a last visit from his girl, but this was revised before translation into English.

7. Introduction to the Grove Press edition of *The Maids* (p. 25), excerpted and translated by Bernard Frechtman from Sartre's *Saint Genet, Actor and Martyr.*

8. "Jouvet version" only. On the differences between French and English versions, Bernard Frechtman wrote me in 1964: "About the different text of *Les Bonnes:* There are two texts, both of which were written at the same time, one of which represents the changes Genet made at the request of Jouvet, who directed the original production. When I translated *Les Bonnes* . . . Genet preferred the original version. He has since come to prefer—rightly in my opinion—the 'Jouvet version,' and it is the latter which you have in the Arbalète edition. However, I have recently brought the English translation into line with the 'Jouvet version.' " I do not know what happened to Frechtman's revision, since Grove continues to publish the non-Jouvet version.

9. "The Inner and the Outer Reality," *Tulane Drama Review* (Spring, 1963), pp. 187–217.

10. *The Impossible Theater* (New York, 1964), p. 251.

11. "Ionesco and the Comedy of Absurdity," *Yale French Studies* #23, p. 8.

12. "The Homecoming," *Tulane Drama Review* (Winter, 1966), p. 186.

3. THE HERO AND HIS PEOPLE

1. Joseph Campbell, *The Hero with a Thousand Faces* (New York, 1949), pp. 245–246.

2. *The Third Voice* (Princeton, 1959), pp. 105, 108.

3. *On Poetry and Poets* (London, 1957), p. 84.

4. For these suggestions (and others) I am indebted to Käte Hamburger, *Von Sophokles zu Sartre* (Stuttgart, 1962).

5. The Suhrkamp edition of Brecht's *Antigone* contains "Materialien zur *Antigone*," in which Anouilh's play is not mentioned. On the other hand, Andrzej Wirth, who worked with Brecht in the 1950's, informs me that Anouilh's play was discussed at rehearsals of Brecht's play.

6. Reported by Joseph Wood Krutch in his "Introduction" to O'Neill's *Nine Plays* (New York, n.d.), p. xvii.

7. "Brecht's Shavian Saint," *The Quarterly Journal of Speech* (April, 1964), p. 139.

8. *Le Drame de Paul Claudel* (Paris, 1947), p. 382.

9. East German critics claim there are only two versions, but see Peter Demetz, "Die kritische Brechtforschung beginnt," *Die Zeit* (Hamburg, October 11, 1963), p. 12. The Vesey translation in the British Methuen edition may be contrasted with the Laughton version, published by Grove in this country. My discussion is based mainly on the Suhrkamp German text.

10. Cf. Walter H. Sokel, "Brecht's Split Characters and His Sense of the Tragic" in *Brecht* (Englewood Cliffs, N.J., 1962), pp. 127–137.

11. "Brechtian Europe," *The Drama Review* (Fall, 1967), pp. 156–157.

12. *Playwrights on Playwriting*, ed. Toby Cole (New York, 1961), p. 117.

13. It is difficult to date the versions of *Caligula*. See I. H. Walker, "The Composition of *Caligula*," *Symposium* (Fall, 1966), pp. 263–275, and Germaine Brée, "Camus' *Caligula*: Evolution of a Play," *Symposium* (Spring-Fall, 1958), pp. 43–51. Conceived in 1936 or 1937, a first version of *Caligula* may have been completed by 1941. A revised version was published and produced in 1944, and this in turn was revised in 1958.

14. "The Theatre of Albert Camus," *Modern Drama* (May, 1961), p. 53.

15. *L'Existentialisme est un humanisme* (Paris, 1946), pp. 62–63.

16. Oreste F. Pucciani, "An Interview with Jean-Paul Sartre," *Tulane Drama Review* (March, 1961), pp. 12–18.

17. *L'Existentialisme est un humanisme*, p. 27.

18. *Modern French Theatre* (New Haven, 1967), p. 139.

19. *Our Theatres in the Nineties* (London, 1954), Vol. II, p. 19.

4. THE MIXED MOOD

1. Marvin T. Herrick, *Tragicomedy* (Urbana, 1962) examines tragicomic terminology, theory, and works in Latin, Italian, French, and English. Karl S. Guthke, *Modern Tragicomedy* (New York, 1966) examines criticism and works since the Enlightenment. I have learned from both scholars, but my approach is freer.

2. *Modern Tragicomedy*, p. 58.

3. *The Life of the Drama* (New York, 1964), Section 10.

4. Michel de Ghelderode, *Seven Plays*, tr. George Hauger (New York, 1960), Vol. I, pp. 146–147.

5. *Notes and Counter Notes* (New York, 1964), p. 27 (Donald Watson translation).

6. *Eugene Ionesco* (New York, 1961), p. 30.

7. "Ionesco and the Comedy of Absurdity," *Yale French Studies* #23, p. 10.

8. *Notes and Counter Notes*, p. 180.

9. Cf. Jacques Dubois, "Beckett and Ionesco: The Tragic Awareness of Pascal and the Ironic Awareness of Flaubert," *Modern Drama* (December, 1966), pp. 283–291.

10. "Parodie und Grotesque bei Dürrenmatt," *Der unbequeme Dürrenmatt* (Stuttgart, 1963).

11. Cf. Bruce Morrissette, "Narrative 'you' in Contemporary Literature," *Comparative Literature Studies* (1965, Vol. II, i), pp. 1–24.

12. In *Elements of Drama* (Cambridge, 1963) J. L. Styan analyzes the inadequate tragicomic effect of Eliot's *Cocktail Party*.

13. *Anger and After* (Baltimore, 1962), p. 312.

14. Cf. Martin Esslin, *Pinter* (Hanover, 1967), p. 27.

15. *On Poetry and Poets* (London, 1957), p. 82.

16. In the movie *All About Eve* Marilyn Monroe murmurs something about how funny it would be if a butler were named Butler.

17. Ruby Cohn, ed., *Casebook on Waiting for Godot* (New York), pp. 171–172.

18. Cf. Jacques Guicharnaud, *Modern French Theatre* (New Haven, 1967), Chapter 9, for a fine discussion of Beckett's tramp as "concrete universal."

19. "The Theatre of Samuel Beckett," *Perspective* (Autumn, 1959), p. 149.

20. "Being without Time," in *Samuel Beckett* (Englewood Cliffs, N.J., 1965).

21. "The Beckett Hero," in *Samuel Beckett* (Englewood Cliffs, N.J., 1965), p. 46.

22. This old German ballad appears in a 1937 letter from Beckett, now in the University of Texas library. Beckett translated the song for *Godot*, first into French, then into English.

23. Lawrence Harvey, "Art and the Existential in *En attendant Godot, Publications of the Modern Language Association* (March, 1960), pp. 137–146.

5. THE ROLE AND THE REAL

1. Ernst Robert Curtius, *European Literature and the Latin Middle Ages* (New York, 1953), pp. 153–154.

2. Cf. Anne Righter, *Shakespeare and the Idea of Play* (London, 1962), Part Two.

3. *Tulane Drama Review* (Spring, 1966), p. 59.

4. Cf. Robert Brustein, *The Theatre of Revolt* (Boston, 1964), Chapter VII.

5. Cf. Eric Bentley, "Father's Day," *The Drama Review* (Fall, 1968), pp. 57–72, for the full complexity of this opposition.

6. Thomas Bishop, *Pirandello and the French Theatre* (New York, 1960); John Harvey, *Anouilh: A Study in Theatrics* (New Haven, 1964); Leonard Pronko, *The World of Jean Anouilh* (Berkeley, 1961).

7. "An Un-American Chalk Circle?" *Tulane Drama Review* (Summer, 1966), p. 75.

8. Cf. Martin Esslin, "Brecht and the English Theatre," *Tulane Drama Review* (Winter, 1966), pp. 63–70.

9. "Marat/Sade Forum," *Tulane Drama Review* (Summer, 1966), p. 222.

10. Cf. Ruby Cohn, "Tempest in an *Endgame*," *Symposium* (Winter, 1965), pp. 328–334.

11. Cf. Louise O. Cleveland, "Trials in the Soundscape: The Radio Plays of Samuel Beckett," *Modern Drama* (December, 1968), pp. 267–282.

12. Cf. Bernard F. Dukore, "Beckett's Play, *Play*," *Educational Theater Journal* (March, 1965), pp. 19–23.

13. In revision, Genet reduced the number of scenes in *The Balcony* from fifteen to nine. There are three versions of the play—1956, 1960, and 1962. I discuss mainly the last version, though Frechtman translated the 1960 version into English.

14. *The Impossible Theater* (New York, 1964), p. 269.

15. Cf. David K. Jeffrey, "Genet and Gelber: Studies in Addiction," *Modern Drama* (September, 1968), pp. 151–156.

16. Cf. Robert Brustein, *The Theatre of Revolt* (Boston, 1964), pp. 388–389.

17. *Saint Genet, Actor and Martyr*, tr. Bernard Frechtman (New York, 1963), p. 234.

18. "Shakespeare and the Harlem Clowns: Illusion and Comic Form in Genet's *The Blacks*," *Yale Review* (Winter, 1966), p. 225.

19. *Seasons of Discontent* (New York, 1967), p. 307.

20. "Which Theatre Is the Absurd One?" in *American Playwrights on Drama*, p. 170.

21. Megan Terry, *Viet Rock and Other Plays* (New York, 1967), pp. 206–207.

22. Ibid., pp. 200–201.

23. Ibid., p. 16.

Index